Not in a
Million
Years

BOOKS BY SOPHIE RANALD

Out with the Ex, In with the New

Sorry Not Sorry

It's Not You, It's Him

No, We Can't Be Friends

Just Saying

Thank You, Next

He's Cancelled

P.S. I Hate You

Santa, Please Bring Me a Boyfriend

It Would be Wrong to Steal My Sister's Boyfriend (Wouldn't it?)

A Groom with a View

Who Wants to Marry a Millionaire?

You Can't Fall in Love with Your Ex (Can You?)

Not in a Million Years

SOPHIE RANALD

bookouture

Published by Bookouture in 2023

An imprint of Storyfire Ltd.
Carmelite House
50 Victoria Embankment
London EC4Y 0DZ

www.bookouture.com

ISBN: 978-1-83790-186-9
eBook ISBN: 978-1-83790-185-2

For my darling sister Vicky, with all my love.

ONE

THEN

2007

We'd been in the pub for over an hour when the boys finally arrived, and to be honest by that point we didn't particularly care whether they showed up at all. There'd been no official arrangement after all – just a group of five of us, who'd dutifully turned up on a blustery autumn night to watch our other halves play football, and realised before half-time that standing on the sidelines in the rain watching them take an absolute pasting was about as much fun as a root canal.

Decamping to the nearest pub was my suggestion, but the others had agreed without hesitation, and in just a few minutes, we found ourselves in the warm, sitting round a small wooden table getting acquainted (and increasingly sloshed on cheap red wine). At the time, they were just four random women of about my own age: Abbie, Naomi, Rowan and Zara. The most I'd hoped for was that, if my boyfriend Ryan ever persuaded me to come along to a game with him again, these girls would be there and the experience would be made a bit less tedious. Although in the back of my mind, I was aware that Ryan and I were on borrowed time, which was sad in a way, of course, but likely meant no more Wednesday evenings pretending to be interested in five-a-side football – proof, if it were needed, that every cloud has a silver lining.

I didn't know – I couldn't have known – the significance that night would have in my life. I'd realised pretty quickly that these women – Abbie, with her laser-sharp sense of humour; Rowan, whose beautiful smile made you feel like you were the only person in the world; Naomi, radiating kindness as warm as her brilliant red hair; and Zara, who had a way of delivering cuttingly bitchy observations in a way you couldn't help dissolving in laughter at – would all become my friends.

But I hadn't guessed that, fifteen years later, they'd have become my *best* friends in all the world. Not Zara, of course. Which was no great loss, really, Zara being the absolute piece of work that she was.

Anyway, there we were, two bottles of Shiraz down and a substantial dent made in the third, our table littered with empty crisp packets, mobile phones, Zara's fags and lighter, and some make-up samples Rowan had picked up at a product launch earlier that day, which she'd kindly shared out with the group, when our menfolk arrived at the pub.

'Well, fancy finding you lot here!' Ryan laughed.

'How did the game go?' I asked, not particularly interested but wanting to show willing.

'Not great.' He pulled over a chair and sat down, wincing performatively. 'I got subbed off in the second half. I think I've pulled something in my groin...'

Which would mean even less bedroom action for me than there'd been in the past few weeks, I thought uncharitably. Ryan and I had only been dating for a few months and, nice as he was, I was becoming more certain every time I saw him that this relationship was nearing its sell-by date. It was just a question of which of us was going to call time on it, and I suspected it was going to have to be me – a prospect I didn't particularly relish, given that he was a lovely guy. Just not the lovely guy for me.

'Can I get you a drink?' I asked him, my guilty thoughts spurring me to be kind, which would probably be unhelpful in the long term.

He brightened. 'Thanks, Kate. Pint of Stella, if you don't mind.'

'Sure.' I collected orders from the other guys – pints all round for Matt, who was Ryan's brother and Abbie's boyfriend; Paul, Rowan's other half; Naomi's bloke, whose name I didn't catch and never learned, as they split up soon after; and impossibly ripped Patch, who apparently belonged to Zara.

I went to the bar, placed our order and waited while the pints were poured, another bottle of wine opened and packets of crisps piled on the counter in front of me.

'Need a hand with those?' a voice at my elbow asked. I turned and saw a man – possibly the most handsome man I'd ever seen in my life. His hair was shining blonde in the lights over the bar. His eyes were clear denim-blue. He wasn't wearing a hastily pulled-on tracksuit over football kit like the other guys but a long plum overcoat that looked like cashmere. His smile was movie-star magnetic.

And I knew straight away that, while gazing at him would afford hours of pleasure, gazing was all I'd ever do, because he couldn't have been more obviously gay if he'd been wrapped in a rainbow Pride flag instead of that expensive coat.

'Thanks.' I smiled. 'What can I get for you, since I'm ordering?'

'Double vodka and tonic, please, nurse. Grey Goose if they have it, which they won't.'

I scanned the row of bottles, knowing he was right. We'd picked the pub on the basis of its proximity to the football pitch, not the quality of its food and beverage offerings.

'You'd be lucky,' I said. 'Looks like it's Smirnoff or nothing.'

'I'll take the Smirnoff then, obviously. But better make it a triple – if I can't have quality, I'll go for quantity.' He flipped a credit card onto the bar. 'And I'll get this. You don't want to get in the habit of subbing that bunch of freeloaders.'

I laughed. 'It was just one round, but thanks. I'm Kate.'

'Andy. And which of these reprobates are you here with?'

'Ryan.' Already, my mind was adding, *But not for long.*

It was like Andy had read my thoughts. 'Seriously? Fond as I am of Little Ryan – I've known him for donkey's years; Tall Matt and I were at school together – I wouldn't have thought he was your type.'

'Really? What is my type then?'

He looked at me, his bright eyes narrowed. 'I can see you with a banker. One of those flash fuckers who drives a Porsche and wears Gucci slippers of an evening. He'd take you out to Michelin-starred restaurants and support you in the style to which you want to become accustomed.'

'Actually, I'm kind of hoping to support *myself* in the style to which I want to become accustomed.'

'Oooh,' he said. 'Ambitious. Driven. Although not in the passenger seat of a banker's Porsche.'

'I mean, it's not like I'd say no. I'm not too sure about the Gucci slippers though. They sound kind of naff. And who wears slippers, anyway, if they're under sixty?'

Andy looked wounded. 'I do, as it happens. Nothing I like better, after a hard day selling bad art to people who don't realise it's bad, than getting home, slipping into something comfortable and mixing myself a perfect dry Martini.'

'You don't play footie with this lot then?' I asked, although I already knew the answer – it was as impossible to imagine Andy wearing shin pads and covered in mud as it was to imagine Ryan drinking a cocktail in designer loungewear.

'Heaven forbid! I'm just here for the craic, although it seems to be in short supply. You're the most interesting person here by far.'

I smiled, flattered but immediately feeling the pressure to do – or say – something that was actually interesting. I could quote Shakespeare, except I didn't know any. I could buy a round of flaming sambucas, except I'd probably singe my own eyebrows off. I could rip my kit off and dance on the bar, except in a place this dodgy they'd probably think I was paid entertainment provided by the management.

I settled on, 'So. Tea or coffee?'

Andy shouted with laughter. 'Oh, so we're playing that game. Coffee, of course. You?'

'Coffee.'

'Cats or dogs?' he asked.

'Cats, I guess. I don't really have time or space for either right now – certainly not a dog. But we had a cat when I was growing up. It was cute.'

'What was its name?'

'Wanda. She was all-over black.'

'No fucking way! I had a cat called Wanda growing up, too. After the John Cleese film?'

I nodded, feeling a massive smile spreading over my face.

Andy said, 'And you wear an analogue watch, I see, not digital. That's good. I could never be true friends with a tea-drinking, digital-wearing dog-lover.'

I racked my brains for my next question. 'White bread or brown?'

Andy frowned. 'I oughtn't to eat bread at all, really. It's so bloating. But oh my God, the joy of a plastic white sandwich on a hangover, with—'

'Fish fingers?'

'Yes! Or sausages. The really cheap lips-and-arseholes ones that are so, so wrong but also *so* right.'

'Red sauce or brown?' It was a trick question – I hoped it

wouldn't trip him up.

And it didn't.

'Red or brown sauce? What kind of heathen do you take me for? Mustard. The very hot English kind, to—'

'Disguise the taste of the lips and arseholes?'

'Precisely. Ideally eaten in bed, alone, so no one you want to impress sees you dripping butter on the sheets. Correct?'

'It's like you've got CCTV installed in my flat or something. So, next question. Do you—'

'Oi!' Ryan's voice penetrated the increasing volume of the busy pub. 'Why don't you two bring over our drinks, instead of standing there yakking away? We're all dying of thirst here.'

'*Sorreeeee.*' Andy gave me a theatrical roll of his eyes and I giggled conspiratorially.

Together, we ferried over the drinks and snacks.

The dynamic of the group had changed now that the men had turned up.

Ryan was expounding about the severity of his groin injury, debating whether heat or cold would be more effective on the strained muscle – or tendon, or ligament, whatever he thought it was – and Matt and (mostly) Abbie were cooing sympathetically over him.

Rowan and Paul were sitting close together, their knees pressed against each other's, leaning in and talking as softly as the background noise allowed, occasionally throwing back their heads in laughter or leaning them in for a kiss.

And Zara was focused entirely on Patch, flicking her curtain of almost-black hair back over first one shoulder then the other, holding his attention with her violet eyes, her French-manicured fingers moving in front of their faces like those of a magician weaving a spell as she talked.

Naomi was watching them, transfixed, all the happy animation wiped off her face. In the seat next to her, the boyfriend whose name I'd forgotten was watching the proper, professional football on the big screen, seemingly oblivious to her presence or the strangely rapt way she was gazing at the couple next to her.

I would have gone to speak to her, to attempt to find out what it was that was troubling her and cheer her up, but the only two remaining seats were at the opposite end of the table and Andy led me straight to them.

'So, now that you're single, Kate...' he began, taking a deep swallow of his lethally strong drink.

'I'm not single,' I protested. 'I'm dating Ryan, remember?'

'Pfft. I give that five days. Or, more likely, five minutes.'

(As it happened, he was wrong. It took all of five hours before, later that night, Ryan accused me of being callous, cold-hearted, overly focused on my career and not enough on his pulled tensor fasciae latae, and dumped me. My only real regret about our break-up – apart from worrying that it would cause awkwardness between Abbie and me, which it didn't – was that he waited to deliver the killer blow until the last Tube had departed, and I had to get the dreaded night bus home.)

'Okay, so assuming I was single, which I'm not,' I replied, 'you were going to say?'

'I was going to say, you'd be the perfect match for my friend Daniel. Only thing is, I can never introduce you.'

'Why not?'

'Because I want to keep you all to myself.'

And I basked in the warm glow of his admiration, which felt both entirely undeserved and entirely unthreatening. I was delighted with myself, with these new friends, with the way an unpromising night had turned into one of the most fun ones I'd had that month.

Back then, twenty-two-year-old me gave hardly a thought to the unknown Daniel, or the complex web of relationships I'd found myself a part of, or indeed anything much, apart from how many more rounds we could squeeze in before last orders.

TWO

NOW

In the fifteen years Andy and I had been friends, we'd discovered loads more things we had in common. We were both Scorpios. We both thought *The Rocky Horror Picture Show* was the best film ever made. When we talked about our favourite colours, we both said purple. We both liked olive, caper and anchovy pizza best. We'd even both lost our virginity to a man named Dave.

Not the same Dave, obviously. That would've been seriously weird.

So it kind of made sense that on the day Andy had a near-death experience, I had one too.

Although that's not really fair. Andy's was a proper brush with mortality – one that would have real, far-reaching implications. Mine just *felt* that way.

It all started when my former colleague Claude (who I'd fancied rotten for the six months we'd worked together, though I'd resisted doing more than mildly flirting with him in the office on the basis that it would be unprofessional and, as a freelance contractor, I had my reputation in the wider industry to consider) slid into my DMs on LinkedIn the day after my contract ended and asked me out.

I'm not going to lie, I literally punched the air and went, 'Yesss!'

Because Claude was properly hot. Originally from Cameroon, he'd moved to France with his mum as a child and had the sexiest accent ever to show for it. He was six foot two of pure muscle, with glossy dark skin I could barely resist reaching out to stroke, longing to discover whether it was as silky smooth as it looked. He wore bespoke tailored suits and a vintage Longines watch. When he smiled at me, I could practically feel my ovaries twang.

And besides, I didn't exactly have a rich and fulfilling love life. It felt as if, over the past decade, I'd messaged and dated every last no-hoper Tinder, Bumble and Hinge had to offer, practically working my way through the *Kama Sutra* with as many of them as I could bear to, on the basis that they just might turn out to be The One. It had started to feel, as I'd lamented to Andy over a Bloody Mary (me) and a Virgin Mary (him) just a few weeks before, like there were literally no blokes left on online dating – possibly even in the world – who I hadn't assessed as a potential boyfriend.

I was running out of men. And, at thirty-seven, I was running out of time too. I wasn't sure whether I wanted marriage and kids, but I wanted the opportunity to have them, and that chance seemed to be slipping remorselessly through my fingers with every day, month and year that passed. I'd seen Naomi and Patch get together after – or perhaps it was during, or even before; I'd never been quite sure – Patch and Zara's split, and have their twin babies, a boy and a girl. I'd been a bridesmaid at Matt and Abbie's wedding. Even Rowan, whose romantic life had been as bleak as my own for ages, was now happily loved-up with Alex, who was not only gorgeous but a successful tech entrepreneur to boot.

Sure, I was having all the sex I could shake a stick at. But that didn't alter the fact that I was chronically, habitually single and had been for as long as I could remember. There was no one for me to go on romantic holidays with, no one for me to stroll hand in hand through the park with on summer days, no one for me to take to events as a plus-one, unless I practically abducted some random off the street.

So Claude's message – formal yet friendly, confident yet not cocky – seemed like a gift sent straight from heaven. Maybe, finally, Mr Right (or possibly Monsieur Whatever-Right-Is-In-French) had arrived in my life. Maybe, at last, I'd found someone I could not only find attractive enough to date but also not dump (or be dumped by) in short order because he wasn't— well, just because.

When I'd finished doing a gleeful little dance around my flat, I returned to my laptop and read Claude's message for the hundredth time.

Then I set about composing a reply – although I had no intention of sending it straight away. I mean, I had about five weeks off until my next contract began and very little to fill it (tidying my knicker drawer was the highlight of my to-do list for that day), but I didn't want Claude knowing that. I wanted him to picture me at a luxury spa having scented oil rubbed into every inch of my body, or waiting to board a flight for a far-flung destination in the sun (as if – there was about as much chance of that as there was of me turning up in the office in my bikini – not least because I had absolutely no idea where in my wardrobe it was), or possibly strolling round an art gallery. Rather than the reality, which was me checking my emails in the frenzy of anxiety that always gripped me when I was between jobs.

Two hours later, after spending too much time staring into my wardrobe assessing my clothes for Claude-date-worthiness and none sorting out my underwear (a highly short-sighted omission, given I couldn't wait for Claude to see me in it), I eventually hit send on my message, and then waited in nervous anticipation for him to answer, which he did with surprising speed. A few rapid-fire back-and-forth exchanges followed, and by lunchtime, we'd arranged to meet that Saturday.

Saturday: excellent. A Saturday for a first date showed that he was taking this seriously.

Saturday at eight a.m.? Not so good. What was this, some kind of 1990s-style power breakfast?

Still, a date with a handsome man was a date with a handsome man, and a significant improvement on the big fat zero there had been in my diary until that morning.

Buoyed, I returned to my bedroom and stared into my wardrobe some more, this time pulling open the drawer where I kept my pants and wondering if any of them were of a high-enough quality for Claude to see. He'd be a white boxers man, I was willing to bet, allowing myself to imagine his naked torso rising from a pair of tight shorts, his hard-muscled buttocks and sculpted abs inviting my hands to caress them.

But that was enough. We'd arranged an early-morning first date, not a steamy session between the sheets. For all I knew, we'd discover that we had absolutely nothing to say to each other outside of work and the date would be a total disaster.

But I could never have imagined just how bad it would actually turn out to be.

My elation lasted into Friday night, which I spent painting my nails, putting a deep-moisturising mask on my face and giving my hair an industrial-strength blow-dry that used so much hairspray I half-expected Friends of the Earth to come knocking at my door, but which I hoped would buy me an extra half hour in bed in the morning. It had faded somewhat when my alarm clock went off at five, but I still jumped enthusiastically out of bed, dressed and headed to get the train to our appointed meeting place, a station in rural Surrey I'd never heard of, let alone visited. It rose again in a bubble of happy excitement when I saw Claude waiting for me, leaning against the door of his sleek midnight-blue Bugatti, and almost lifted me off my feet when he kissed me on both cheeks.

That soaring feeling should have been a warning of what was to come, but when I asked Claude what he'd planned for our morning, he only smiled mysteriously and said it was a surprise. So I climbed into the sumptuous leather passenger seat of his car and allowed myself to enjoy the anticipation as he drove quickly and skilfully through the countryside.

And then, with a sickening thud that I feared was very much a warning of what was to come, my excitement turned to horror.

'And here we are.' Claude expertly swung the car off the road and into a small parking area. Ahead of us was an open field, a line of trees at its end. Above us soared an infinite dome of blue sky. But I had no eyes for the glorious spring morning, or even for Claude himself as he swung out of the car and stood, hands on his hips, surveying the scene. In the field was a hot-air balloon, its canopy half-inflated, rainbow segments bright against the sky. I could hear the roar of the burner expanding it with hot air, terrifying as a dragon.

My only thought was, *How the hell do I get through this without him finding out I'm terrified of heights?*

By two o'clock that afternoon, I was home. My legs still felt like wet spaghetti as I stepped out of the lift and walked the short distance to the front door of my flat, and my hands were trembling as I fitted the key into the lock. But I'd made it. Never had my apartment felt so safe; never had I been so glad to pour a hefty gin and tonic from my own fridge and sit down on my own bed.

I was overcome by a wave of tiredness; the adrenaline that

had coursed through my body was all depleted now, and I was limp with exhaustion.

But before I could have the long nap I so desperately needed, I knew I had to update my friends. Over the past four days, the Girlfriends' Club WhatsApp had been abuzz with excitement about my forthcoming date, and I'd overshared liberally: everything from the trainers I was planning to wear to the Hollywood wax I'd endured as part of my preparations.

The news I had for my friends wouldn't be what they were hoping for, but I'd have to tell them anyway.

Lying on my back on the blissfully solid bed, I tapped through to the group on my phone.

Abbie: So I wonder how Kate's date is going? Any news?

Naomi: She's probably shagging him as we speak, the lucky thing.

Rowan: Or having lunch in some swanky restaurant.

Abbie: Maybe he took her to Paris on the Eurostar or something.

Kate: None of the above. I'm home.

Rowan: Already? Playing it cool? How did it go?

Kate: It was awful. I had a near-death experience.

Naomi: Why? What happened? Where did you go?

Kate: Up in a hot bloody air balloon.

Rowan: No way! That's so cool! How could you not shag him after that?

Abbie: Oh my God! Oh no, you poor thing.

Rowan: What? What did I say?

Kate: You've forgotten that I'm shit-scared of heights.

Rowan: Oh man! Of course – I knew that. Sorry, Kate – I remember telling you about taking Clara to Go Ape and you made me stop because you said you might faint just thinking about it. Not the ideal choice by him, then.

Naomi: Did you say something to him?

Kate: I couldn't, could I? I mean, come on. This man I've had a crush on for months, finally asking me out and planning something so amazing. I wasn't going to tell him I'm the world's biggest wimp and want to cry when I'm standing at the top of the escalator at Angel Tube station.

Abbie: So... what did you do?

Kate: I went through with it. What else could I do?

In my mind, I replayed the scene. How we'd stepped into the basket, the roar of the burner above us, the billowing rainbow silk of the balloon – so fragile; how could anyone possibly imagine it could support any weight at all? – gradually filling up with hot air, eclipsing the blue sky above us. The moment the basket had left the ground and the solidity of earth had been replaced by the swaying sensation of – well, nothing.

The way Claude had looked over at me, grinning broadly

like this was the best idea ever, and I'd realised I had no choice but to style it out.

The first five minutes hadn't been too bad, I remembered. The balloon had ascended gently, to about the height of the treetops. If this was as high as it went, I thought, I could bear it. If it fell from this height, I might survive; escape with a few broken bones but alive.

But then the burner had roared again, and the craft had climbed higher and higher into the sky, the fields of Surrey spreading out below it in a patchwork of green, the Thames coming into view like a narrow silver ribbon in the distance, snaking through the landscape.

I couldn't bear to look – I longed to turn around, but that would mean releasing my death grip on the edge of the basket. And there was no way I could do that. My knuckles were white, my fingers already cramping with the intensity of my grasp.

'Cool, huh?' Claude smiled again, but not even the delicious curve of his lips and the crinkles I could see at the corners of his eyes behind his Saint Laurent shades could lessen my terror.

The only thing I felt more intensely than my fear was the need to not let him see I was absolutely bricking it.

'Really cool,' I squeaked. My voice sounded almost normal, although it didn't feel like it was coming from me but more like I'd left my own body and been replaced by a ventriloquist's dummy with a killer blow-dry.

'Look over there,' Claude went on, leaning casually over the rim of the basket, actually letting go with both hands and pointing with one. 'That's Windsor Castle, I reckon.'

'Sure is,' the pilot confirmed, abandoning the burner (*What? Don't do that, you wannabe kamikaze fuckwit!* my mind screamed) to come and join us. 'Ascot Racecourse is over there, and over in the distance you can see Heathrow Airport.'

Great. So any second a massive jumbo jet was going to take off and collide with this tiny craft, and that'd be it. Game over.

All done, except for the screaming as we plummeted to earth in a ball of flame.

And then I realised that that wasn't what was going to happen. I glanced down at my feet, my trainers planted firmly against the wicker base of the basket, my knees above them visibly trembling. Where the base of the basket met its sides, I could see a strand of wicker that had unfurled. It wasn't long; it was barely moving in the breeze that passed through the open weave. But it was definitely, unquestionably, separated from the cane strut that rose up to form the corner of the tiny, fragile box that contained us.

It was going to work loose, then looser still, I realised. After a bit, the entire base of the basket would fall away, and then the only thing that would lie between me and that final, fatal, howling fall to the earth hundreds of metres below would be the strength of my hands and forearms as I clung to the rim of the basket.

I did not have strong hands or forearms. When my personal trainer had suggested abandoning my workout gloves to improve my grip strength, I'd declined on the basis that I didn't want calluses on my hands. If only I'd known that she was – literally – trying to save my life.

'You all right there, madam?' the pilot asked.

I realised I was sweating, in spite of the chilly air that surrounded us. There was no wind – or at least there was, but it was carrying the balloon on its course, so the air on my face felt still.

'Fine!' I croaked. 'Great! This is so fun!'

'Are you sure?' Claude reached out a hand and brushed my fingers, which were still rigidly clamped to the rim of the basket.

It was the first time he'd touched me. Under different circumstances, I'd have relished the warm contact; now, all I could think was: *If you try and make me let go of this basket, I'll scream.*

'Of course.' My voice definitely wasn't sounding so normal any more – more like the same ventriloquist's dummy had been hitting the nitrous oxide hard.

I just want this fear to end, my brain screamed. *I just want this to be over so I can never, ever go through it again.*

I forced myself to lower my eyes from the horizon on which they'd been fixed and look down. Good God, the ground was far away – the clouds above had looked way closer. But – surely it wasn't just my imagination? – it seemed to be growing slowly, ever so slightly closer.

Either the bastard thing had sprung a leak, or we were finally coming in to land.

'We'll be coming in to land now,' the pilot called.

Yes! Thank you, God! Now we just had to return to terra firma in one piece – an outcome I devoutly hoped for but in which I didn't feel even slightly confident.

Behind me, the pilot was tinkering with ropes and pulleys. The roar of the burner, I realised, had been silent for a while now. Claude moved from me to the pilot, and I heard him asking various technical questions, which – together with the answers – I willed myself not to hear. In this situation, knowledge would be the opposite of power; there was literally nothing the guy could say about thermodynamics or parachute valves that would reassure me even a tiny bit.

I forced air through my dry lips and made myself watch as the ground edged closer and closer. I could make out sheep in the fields now (one of those would probably make a reasonably soft landing, I thought) and the individual branches and even leaves on the trees. The balloon drifted across a four-lane motorway, which gave me a fresh surge of dread – we'd land there, and just when I thought we were safe, we'd be crushed by a passing pantechnicon. But we reached the far side, gradually descending further and further.

Then the burner roared again behind me, and the balloon rose again.

Fuck! Nonono! Just when I thought it was over.

'Just clearing that line of trees.' I made out the pilot's voice over the sound of burning gas. 'Then we'll complete our descent.'

Assuming we don't crash into the trees first, I thought darkly.

But we didn't. The basket just cleared the topmost branches before the craft dropped once more, steadily but still making my stomach feel as if it was trying to push my heart out of my chest. At last, we were low enough for me to know that even if the base of the basket dropped out, the ropes snapped or I decided I couldn't bear another moment of this and jumped out, I'd survive.

And then the basket touched the ground with a gentle bump, bounced once and came to a stop.

'Stay there while I secure it,' ordered the pilot.

I couldn't have moved if I wanted to.

Naomi: My God, you poor thing. You must've been terrified.

Abbie: Although technically it wasn't actually a near-death experience. I mean, I get that it felt that way, but...

Rowan: What happened next?

Kate: I spewed my guts up all over the side of the basket.

I felt a bit sick just remembering it.

It had been totally unexpected – one minute, I'd been limp with relief, suddenly aware of the pain in my hands and wrists where I'd been gripping the rim of the basket, but mostly just elated that it was over. The next, I'd been overcome with violent nausea.

'Oh my God, Kate, are you okay?' Claude had asked, his hand resting gently on my back while I heaved and gasped.

'It's not motion sickness, is it?' the pilot asked. 'No one gets air sick in a balloon.'

It wasn't motion sickness, obviously. It was almost like all the terror I'd felt had to leave my body somehow, and that was the only way it could come up with to do it.

Claude passed me his water bottle and I washed my mouth out and spat, all thoughts of dignity forgotten. My carefully applied lipstick was history now, my blow-dry blown to pieces, my Hollywood wax half an hour of wasted pain, because there was no way I'd be shagging anyone any time soon. I waited a few seconds, wondering if I was going to be sick again, then realising I wasn't.

'We normally lay on a full English breakfast, with mimosas,' the pilot said. 'But I'm guessing...'

A fresh wave of nausea hit me, but I managed to keep it down. 'I don't think that would be the best idea,' I said. 'You go ahead though, if you want?'

'*Certainement pas.*' Claude extended his arm and I placed a hand on the leather sleeve of his jacket, noticing the hard muscle beneath it, and stepped carefully out of the basket. 'Main thing is to get you home safely.'

'Thanks,' I quavered. Then I lied, 'I was out for dinner last night. Must have had a dodgy mussel. I'm so sorry – it's been the most wonderful morning and now I've ruined it.'

'Not at all.' Claude pushed his sunglasses up onto his head and looked at me, smiling, his eyes full of concern. 'You know what, you're tough like nails. You didn't look like you were feeling too good up there, but you managed it.'

'It didn't really hit me until we landed,' I replied, truthfully this time.

Thinking about it, my unscheduled vom was a blessing in disguise. Not only would I be able to cut short the date, which I'd have struggled to even pretend to enjoy in my state of nervous exhaustion, but I'd actually managed to come out of it looking reasonably okay, if not actually good. So long as Claude didn't mind women puking up inches from his limited-edition cream Comme des Garçons high-tops.

Rowan: So you're going to see him again?

Kate: He said so. He drove me to the station and saw me right onto my train, and bought me water and mints. He didn't kiss me, but I guess that wouldn't have been on the cards.

Abbie: Well, it'll be quite the story to tell at your wedding, right?

Kate: Steady on, we're definitely not there yet. But I can't wait to tell Andy. He'll piss himself laughing.

But when I sent Andy a message to say I'd had the date from hell, and couldn't wait to reveal all the details, there was no response at all.

THREE

By the following Wednesday, when the Girlfriends' Club met for drinks as usual, there'd still been no response from Andy and I was starting to worry.

Back in the day, when he'd had a drug (and indeed any other substance he could get his hands on) habit that would make Pete Doherty look like a clean-living influencer, it hadn't been unusual for Andy to go AWOL for days or even weeks at a stretch. I'd worried then too, of course – but equally, I'd realised that there was very little I could do to steer him off his path of self-destruction, apart from be there to pick up the pieces when the inevitable crash occurred.

But Andy had been clean for almost two years now. And not only that, he'd recently been dropping hints that he'd met someone, and that it might be getting serious. Perhaps, I thought, that was it – he was just too loved-up with this Ash fellow to pay any of us any mind.

But that wasn't like Andy. Not at all. Certainly not like the new, reformed Andy, who was more surgically attached to his phone than he'd ever been and was constantly texting us, his

Narcotics Anonymous sponsor, his family and presumably also Ash. Whoever Ash was.

'Have you tried calling him?' Abbie asked, once she'd assured us that Matt was well and that Shrimp, their cat, was adorable, and tipped Viognier into our four glasses. 'Matt has, a few times, but it just went straight to voicemail.'

'Same,' I said. 'Except I couldn't even leave a message, because it said his mailbox was full.'

'Really?' Naomi tore open a packet of crisps and took one. 'I didn't know that was even a thing any more. How many messages do you have to have before it shuts down? Literally no one leaves me voice messages except the twins' nursery and obviously I respond to those right away.'

'Search me,' said Rowan, her hazel eyes concerned. 'At work, Kimberley hits the roof if we don't return calls within about five minutes so mine never gets anywhere near full.'

'Maybe like thirty? Forty? Something like that.' I gulped my wine, anxiety fizzing in my stomach. 'But Andy's got loads of friends. He'd only have to be away from his phone for a day or two for that to add up. I've tried WhatsApping him as well, and leaving voice notes, but he hasn't seen any of them.'

'He's still up in Manchester, right?' Naomi asked.

I nodded. 'Still doing that sales job. He was loving it, and acing it, apparently. And now this thing with Ash has been happening, for about four months now, and it seemed like things were really coming good for him finally.'

'Has he posted on Insta at all?' Rowan asked.

'Not for ages,' I said. 'He came off it in a strop because it kept serving him videos of people making cocktails and he said it was too triggering.'

'Mine's wall-to-wall ads for plumbing equipment,' Abbie said. 'Ever since Matt and I put our new bathroom in. It's relentless. I mean, how many loo seats does a girl need? And what's a flange when it's at home, anyway?'

'God knows. Sounds anatomical to me. I think my social media feed's been infected by LinkedIn, because all I get is dead-eyed corporate types spouting motivational nonsense about their five a.m. "power hour" and how they answer emails on their Pelotons.'

'Cute babies here,' Naomi said. 'I mean, come on, I like an adorable kid as much as the next person, but there's a limit to how much time I can spend scrolling through videos of them gurning away and blowing raspberries.'

'But anyway,' I said, catching the eye of our waiter and gesturing towards the almost empty bottle. 'Andy. None of us have even met this Ash guy, have we?'

Around the table, my friends shook their heads in unison.

'How about Daniel?' Abbie asked. 'He's always been really close to Andy, ever since they were at uni. Closer than Matt, even.'

'Search me,' I said. 'Daniel might be close to Andy, but he certainly isn't close to me.'

'I've never understood what went on between you two,' Naomi said.

'That's because it's a highly complex dynamic,' I replied seriously.

Naomi raised an eyebrow. 'Complex how?'

'Daniel doesn't like me, and therefore I don't like him back.'

'But you *used* to.' Rowan leaned across the table and topped up our glasses. 'You and Andy and Daniel – you were really close, for ages. What happened?'

'Long story,' I muttered. 'Water under the bridge. Took me a while to realise what he's really like.'

Abbie raised her eyebrows. 'Okay, you don't want to talk about it, that's fine. But someone needs to call him and ask if he knows what's going on with Andy.'

'I would,' Rowan said, 'but it would be kind of weird. I

haven't seen Daniel since that night out we had together before Christmas, and that was months ago.'

'I'll message him,' Abbie said, pulling her phone out of her bag and tapping at the screen for a few seconds.

Reflexively, I fished for my own phone and glanced at it. There was a message from Claude, which brought a smile to my face – a view of the Thames winding through London, taken from high up, presumably the top floor of some office block where he was attending a meeting.

Saw this and thought of you, he'd written, adding a winking emoji.

I replied with a green vomiting face, then regretted it almost immediately. Whatever happened between me and Claude – and I still wasn't even slightly confident that anything was going to – I wasn't ready to reveal what had led to my fit of the colly-wobbles on our date. Not appearing weak had been a corner-stone of my relationships with men (almost all men) my whole life, and revealing vulnerability could lead to revealing all sorts of other things that I'd prefer to keep to myself.

'Hot Claude?' Abbie asked.

'More like Chaud Claude,' said Rowan, who'd worked in Paris when she was younger and spoke fluent-ish French. Maybe I could ask her how to say Mr Right, just in case.

'Haha.' I rolled my eyes, smiling nonetheless. 'He's talking about seeing each other again. Wonder what he'll come up with this time.'

'Parachute jump?' Naomi suggested. 'Patch and I did one of them on the fifth anniversary of us getting together. It was epic. Oh, sorry, Kate...'

The very idea of jumping out of an aeroplane made me feel instantly weird – my stomach lurched, and I could feel sweat breaking out on the soles of my feet.

'Parkour adventure?' Abbie volunteered. 'One of those

hardcore things where you scale the sides of vertical buildings and hang off bridges?'

'And then he'll suggest that you join him training to climb Everest,' Rowan said. 'And by then you'll be so invested you'll say yes, and all your fears will be conquered.'

'I don't want my fears conquering,' I said. 'I'm a risk manager, remember? Knowing what stuff can hurt an organisation – or a person, for that matter – is literally what I do for a living. Fear is good. It breeds survival. And I'll keep mine just as it is, thanks all the same.'

After that, the conversation moved on from me and my hang-ups to other things: Naomi's twins' refusal to eat anything other than chicken nuggets, and whether scurvy was still a thing, and if so whether tomato ketchup would prevent them getting it; the new marketing campaign Abbie was working on; how happy and loved-up Rowan still was with her not-so-new-any-more boyfriend Alex.

As everyone except me had work the next day, we called it a night at about eleven. The evening was still warm and I was wearing trainers, so I decided to walk home to my flat along the river. I hugged my friends goodnight outside the Tube station and set off across Waterloo Bridge, wondering if I'd ever get tired of the glorious view of London that spread out in either direction: the Houses of Parliament to one side, St Paul's Cathedral to the other, Tower Bridge glimmering in the distance.

I was lucky, I thought. Beyond lucky. I had a home I loved, the most amazing friends in the world and a career that, while mind-numbingly boring a lot of the time, meant I could buy all the shoes I wanted.

With all that going for me, did having a boyfriend really matter all that much? If things didn't work out with Claude, there were other fish in the sea; I could revisit online dating, and even though I'd long abandoned hope of finding a soulmate in that particular shark-infested water, I'd meet people who'd give me interesting stories to tell my friends.

Being alone wasn't so bad really, I reflected, descending the stairs on the far side of the bridge and turning east, weaving through the crowds of tourists and theatregoers emerging from the South Bank's bars and restaurants.

The vibration of my phone in my bag tugged me away from my thoughts. It could be Claude, ringing for a late-night chat. It could be Sam, the guy I'd dated briefly a few months back, until I realised his skinny jeans gave me the ick so badly there was no coming back from it, but who still occasionally rang in the hope I'd be up for a booty call. It could, I realised with a lurch of hope, be Andy.

But the name on my screen below the green and red buttons was Daniel.

'What the fuck?' I muttered.

Daniel literally never called me. We only had each other's numbers because we'd been in various WhatsApp chats over the years to organise flowers when Naomi's babies were born, a surprise party for Abbie's husband Matt's thirtieth birthday, a pre-Christmas night out when Rowan had been going through a tough time the previous year – stuff like that.

He hadn't had a reason to contact me directly for years – until now.

There must be news about Andy. And for him to call at this time of night, it wasn't likely to be good.

I pressed the green button. 'Daniel? What's up?'

'Hi, Kate. Sorry to call so late. I reckoned you'd have been out on the lash with the girls, since it's the second Wednesday of the month.'

'Since when were you my social secretary?' I snapped. 'And actually, I'm just on my way home.'

'I'm calling about Andy.'

'Yeah, I thought so.' I felt a similar sensation to the one I'd felt when Naomi had talked about skydiving. 'Have you heard from him? Is he okay?'

'No and I don't know,' Daniel said. His voice was matter-of-fact and emotionless – flat, almost. But there was no reason why he'd share any emotion with me of all people – other than concern about our friend, which he'd know I shared.

But if he hadn't heard from Andy and didn't know anything more than I did, why on earth was he calling me?

'Kate? Are you still there?'

'I'm still here. I was just wondering...'

'Why the hell I'm calling you?'

'Well... Yes, if I'm honest.'

'I spoke to Matt earlier, after I got Abs's text. Andy hasn't been in touch with him, either. He's worried, and I'm worried.'

'I'm worried too. But I'm not sure what we're meant to actually do. I mean, Andy's a big boy. He's allowed to do stuff without telling us, if that's what he wants. We're not his parents. If he's gone on holiday or something with this Ash, he's probably too busy having fun to answer his phone.'

'Come on, Kate. Have you actually ever met Andy?'

This silenced me. Daniel knew Andy as well as I did – or almost as well – and we both knew that if he was having a fabulous time with a new love interest, he'd have been providing his friends with a constant running commentary about how great it was, how happy he was, how much off-the-scale sex he was having.

'Yeah,' I admitted, 'that's kind of why I've been concerned. I was thinking, if things had gone wrong between them and Andy was... well, you know. Upset about it. Then he might have gone silent on us while he got over it.'

'But you've never seen Ash, have you?' Daniel asked, his tone almost accusatory.

'Nope.'

'None of us have. That's weird, too, isn't it?'

It was weird, I had to acknowledge. Again, with a (presumably) desirable new man in his life, it would have been typical of Andy to want to show him off, to arrange nights out, to ask us endlessly what we thought of him.

'It makes me think...' I began, then hesitated.

'That maybe Ash isn't totally on board with the sober lifestyle?'

'*Exactly.*'

Now that Daniel had expressed the thought that had been on my mind, as annoying and persistent as a fly buzzing against a half-open window, unable to find a way out, it seemed more likely and more worrying. If Andy had fallen in love with someone who was a drug user, what were the chances of him being able to stay sober himself? And if Andy relapsed... Well, we both knew how complex and dangerous the consequences of that would be.

I'd reached my apartment block now, and I tapped my key fob against the door panel, which emitted its usual high-pitched beep.

'You home?' Daniel asked.

'Just got here,' I confirmed, stepping into the cool, marble-floored lobby. 'I'm about to get in the lift. The signal will probably cut out in a minute.'

'Look, there's no point talking about this any more now,' Daniel said. 'You free to meet for a coffee tomorrow?'

'I...' Normally, I'd have had the cast-iron excuse of work. As a freelance contractor, I couldn't just swan off to meet friends – or not friends – in the middle of the day. But I didn't have work tomorrow, nor for the next few weeks. And besides, this wasn't about me, or Daniel, or our instinctive antipathy towards each other. It was about Andy, and Andy might be in trouble.

'Okay,' I said. 'Text me where and when.'

Then I ended the call and stepped into the lift, immediately regretting my moment of weakness. Coffee with Daniel had about as much appeal as another hot-air balloon trip, only without the incentive of Claude's company.

But if it would help us find Andy, I was just going to have to suck it up.

FOUR

As soon as I got into the flat, I undressed, took off my make-up, brushed my teeth and got into bed. Our girls' night out, while not as aggressively cocktail-fuelled as they sometimes were, had left me feeling pleasantly light-headed, and although my conversation with Daniel had been somewhat sobering, I was still confident that I'd be able to sleep well and wake up in the morning feeling refreshed, if slightly hungover.

But my body (or more likely my brain) had other ideas. As soon as my head hit my lavender-misted pillow and my eyes closed, my mind shot into overdrive.

I pictured Andy lying in some dark alleyway, a needle in his arm. I imagined him having been robbed by a dealer, beaten up, his phone stolen, left for dead. I imagined him getting into his car intoxicated and wrapping it round a lamppost.

I groped for my phone on the bedside table and found Andy's number, right near the top of my recent calls log, tapped it and listened yet again to the message telling me I couldn't leave a message of my own.

'Shit.' I turned over, pulling the duvet more tightly around myself against the cooling breeze coming through the open window.

I forced myself to think of Claude, his smiling, handsome face, his strong hands, the concern he'd shown me. I tried to conjure up an image of our next date – cocktails in a glamorous bar or perhaps even dinner. Me in my new Sandro dress. Claude putting his hands on my shoulders and leaning towards me for a kiss.

But my mental picture of his features refused to come into focus. Instead, I saw Daniel's face, the last time we'd seen each other alone, nearly seven years before. And that image was clear – his grey eyes almost silver-bright with anger, his hand impatiently pushing his too-long, dark blonde hair off his forehead as he told me a bunch of stuff I categorically hadn't wanted to hear at the time and certainly didn't want to remember now.

But his voice was as vivid in my mind as if he was standing next to me in my bedroom, his words as clear as if I'd recorded them.

It was no good. This was going to be another one of those nights.

Reluctantly, I got out of bed and pulled on tracksuit bottoms and a T-shirt.

Rule one of sleep hygiene: keep your bedroom cool. Rule something – I couldn't remember which; there were so many of them and I followed them all to the letter – your bed is for sleeping. If you can't sleep, get up.

I walked through to the living area and switched on the lights. My kitchen wasn't large – just a run of units along one wall and a small island – but it did the job. I pulled a cookbook from the shelf and flicked through the pages: cherry and almond loaf cake, lemon drizzle cake, fudge brownies. All of them were good friends that had seen me through more than their share of sleepless nights.

But I knew the recipes too well – if my mind was to be

distracted from the unwelcome thoughts and memories, I needed a challenge.

Rainbow layer cake – that would do. Lots of weighing and dividing of batter, lots of careful adding of food colouring to frosting, multiple tins to be lined with baking parchment.

By four a.m., it was done. A magnificent – if I say so myself – structure eight inches tall, smoothly frosted in white butter-cream, rainbow sprinkles scattered evenly over its top. And I was done too – my eyes were scratchy with fatigue, my feet aching from standing on the tiled floor, my mind finally empty. I left the cake on its stand and went to bed, calculating that I'd be able to get a tolerable four hours of sleep before getting ready to meet Daniel at ten thirty.

But I found myself setting my alarm for half past seven, because it felt important to wash my hair and put on make-up before heading out. Why I cared whether Daniel saw me looking like a raddled hag or a well-rested goddess, my sleep-deprived brain couldn't quite articulate.

The next morning, I took the cake with me when I left the flat, balancing it carefully on one hand as I pressed the button to summon the lift with the other. By the time I arrived at St Mungo's, just ten minutes' walk but also a world away, my arms were trembling with the effort of holding it upright. Next time, I promised myself, as I had all too often before, I'd make biscuits – light, portable and relatively robust.

As usual, Mona was in the church hall, bustling about laying cups and saucers, napkins and teaspoons out on a long trestle table, the stainless-steel urn steaming gently behind her. When she saw me, she beamed a welcome but at the same time tutted disapprovingly.

'Oh, Kate.' She set down the stack of paper napkins she was holding and folded her arms across her ample chest. 'The insomnia playing up again? You know how much our guests welcome your offerings, but I do sometimes think we'd all rather you got a good night's rest.'

'I think so too, believe me.' I set the cake stand down on the table and stretched my weary biceps. 'But you know what? Discovering that this group existed has been a bloody godsend. Where would I be without you? Ruining my professional credibility by taking cake to work once a week or not being able to get into my clothes because I've scoffed the lot myself, that's where.'

Mona laughed. 'I always tell our guests, come for the social interaction and chat with others who are feeling a spot isolated, stay for the quality baked goods. I'll just give you back your tin from last time. Those salted caramel blondie things went down a treat. But something must be troubling you, if you've been up all night. Fancy a sit-down and a cuppa?'

'Thanks,' I said, thinking I'd far rather be having a chinwag with Mona about her grandson's violin lessons and her spaniel's mysterious diarrhoea than seeing Daniel, 'but I'm on my way to meet someone for coffee. I'll pick the tin up next time I come, if that's okay?'

'Another of your dates?'

'Sadly not. This is someone I've known for years, and we don't really get on.'

She eyed me shrewdly, taking in my blow-dried hair, no-make-up-make-up, wide-legged linen culottes and cropped cream blouse. 'You've put some effort in, just the same.'

I sighed. 'You know me, Mona. Putting effort in is what I do.'

She shook her head. 'Putting effort in for someone you don't even like seems like a mug's game to me. Although I can't say I'm not grateful for the effort you put in baking for a load of lonely old people you've never even met.'

'It's no effort at all. It's literally a sanity saver. But I must dash, or I'll be late.'

She pulled me into a brief hug, and I breathed in the smell of her almond hair oil and the fragrance of stewing tea, enjoying the comfort of her strong arms, imagining some of that strength passing from her to me.

Then I said goodbye, waving away her thanks, and headed off to meet Daniel.

FIVE

It was my own fault, I realised, sweating on a bus inching its way across South London next to a woman who apparently wanted the entire top deck to hear, see and smell her chomping her way through a bargain box of chicken wings. I'd asked Daniel to suggest a place to meet, and he had. I could hardly blame him for opting for somewhere near his own home – and half an hour's journey from mine.

But I blamed him anyway.

But what was wrong with meeting in Central London? Why did I have to mission all the way to bloody Peckham just for his convenience?

As the bus grew hotter and hotter and the woman next to me chewed louder and louder, I felt my simmering annoyance nearing boiling point.

Calm down, Kate, I told myself. *You're just irritable because you didn't sleep last night. No point getting this meeting off on the wrong foot. This isn't about you, anyway – it's about Andy. Focus on what matters.*

But what mattered to me most at that point was a group of teenagers making their way to the back of the bus, ska music playing loudly and tinnily through the speaker on one of their mobile phones.

Enough. I edged past the chicken-wing woman and made my way downstairs, then got off at the next stop. It was only a kilometre or so to my destination, according to Google Maps – I'd walk, and if I was a few minutes late, Daniel would just have to deal with it.

In the event, I was more than twenty minutes late. It took me ages to find the coffee shop, which turned out to be hidden away in an arcade shared with a fishmonger, a dodgy-looking phone-repair place and two rival vape shops. The café was tiny – two small tables at the front and a long, shared table down the centre, lined with uncomfortable-looking tall wooden stools.

Daniel was seated at the far one, an empty espresso cup in front of him. He was wearing camo shorts and a white T-shirt worn almost transparent with age and washing, and I felt foolish in my own carefully chosen outfit, my linen trousers already creased to buggery from the long bus ride. He looked like he'd been spending time outdoors recently – his arms were tanned and his jaw-length hair bleached almost golden. His smile when he saw me was guarded, but still a deep dimple showed in his right cheek beneath what looked like a couple of days' worth of stubble.

'Sorry I'm late,' I muttered.

'Have to admit I'd just about given up on you. Are you okay, Kate? You don't look well.'

Cheers for that – way to make a girl feel special. And so much for the light-diffusing, radiance-boosting claims of my forty-quid face powder. 'I'm fine. I just didn't sleep well last night.'

'Then you need a coffee. Sorry to make you schlep all the way across South London – this place just recently opened. It's a community initiative helping kids leaving care into careers in hospitality, so I try to support them whenever I can. What can I get you?'

'Double espresso please.'

I eased onto the stool next to Daniel's and watched as he approached the counter, saying a few words to the timid-looking young girl in charge of the espresso machine, making her smile shyly and then laugh. He'd always been like that, I recalled – gifted with the sort of easy charm that made people like him instantly. Shame it had never worked on me.

Moments later, he returned with our coffees and two pastries. 'Chocolate or almond?'

I realised I was hungry – the chips I'd eaten in the pub last night were a distant memory, and this morning I'd prioritised extra sleep (okay, and an enzymatic peeling face mask) over breakfast.

'Don't mind,' I said. 'You pick.'

Daniel carefully cut both pastries in half and bit into the chocolate one. I hesitated a second, then took my half of the almond.

'So, how's work going?' he asked.

'Look,' I said, 'this is all very nice and everything, but you didn't get me here to eat croissants and make polite chit-chat. Work's fine. I presume the furniture restoration gig is going strong too. My mum and dad are well. Lovely weather we're having; it's unusually warm for May. Now, what are we going to do about Andy?'

The corner of Daniel's mouth twitched, but he didn't smile. 'Fair enough,' he said. 'Let's cut to the chase. No one's heard from Andy or knows where he is. Only intel I have is that Ash had accepted a job abroad and Andy was thinking of going for a bit to see if he liked it. If he did, maybe he would spend a few months out there every year.'

'Wow. Okay. I never knew about all that. Abroad where exactly?'

'He didn't say. He left me a voice note on WhatsApp a week or so back. That was the last I heard from him. You know Andy's voice notes – always a bit stream of consciousness.'

I nodded, remembering fondly the last one I'd received.

Hi, Katie babe (no one, but no one else in the world got to call me Katie, never mind babe). *You're not going to believe this, right, but I'm just leaving a place in Salford that does posh jelly shots. Like, chocolate bourbon ones. They looked fucking epic. Obviously yours truly didn't indulge – my body being a temple these days – but I was thinking, next time you come up here to visit – if you ever do; I know you get the shits if you leave the inside of the M25 – we should go there. I can have a healthy, vitamin C-packed virgin margarita and you, my darling, can have a boozy chocolate shot and describe it to me in the most minute detail, and it'll be almost like having it myself. I might even ask you to breathe on me afterwards. Do we have a deal? Yes we do. Love you, bye.*

I'd listened to it, smiling, and then forgotten all about it. If anything had happened to Andy, I'd feel terrible for not having responded, for not having been up to Manchester to visit him, for being a crap friend.

I'd treasure that message, and the others he'd sent over the years, and listen to them over and over just to hear his voice. The prospect was horrifying. I felt a lump come into my throat and my eyes sting with the threat of tears, but swallowed determinedly and turned to face Daniel.

'Okay. But did he give you a clue? Like, snow-capped mountain ranges, herds of wildebeest, parrots shrieking in the rainforest canopy? Anything like that?'

'He said something about sea and sand and fabulous food. Could be anywhere, really.'

'Except Skegness.'

Again, Daniel did that not-laughing thing with his mouth. 'That's not abroad.'

'True. Did he say when he was planning to go?'

'Kate, he didn't even say *whether* he was planning to go. I've listened to that message again and again and none of it's clear. You know what he's like.'

'And there's nothing on his Facebook or Instagram.'

'Twitter?'

'He's not on there.'

'And he hasn't updated his LinkedIn since he got his new job,' Daniel said. 'I even tried calling his work to ask if they knew where he was, or if they were concerned because he hadn't been in or whatever, but they wouldn't tell me anything because I'm not his emergency contact.'

'Right. Who do you suppose is? His mum or dad?'

'I guess so. In spite of the fact they don't exactly get on, not since they had that massive falling-out over money when his parents had to sell their investment property that he was living in.'

I remembered that episode in Andy's life well. He'd been immersed in the party lifestyle that had eventually spiralled into full-blown addiction at that point and had seen the implosion of his father's business during the financial crash as a personal affront, and the sale of the property as a betrayal by his parents.

Basically, he'd been enjoying the ultimate cushy number and didn't like it ending. It definitely hadn't been his finest hour, but his feelings of hurt had been genuine. Looking back, I could see it had been more of a crisis and less of a man-child tantrum than we'd all realised at the time.

'So, do you think we should call them?' I asked. 'I mean, if something has happened to Andy – he's their only son, after all. Even if they aren't on good terms at the moment, they'd want to know.'

'He mentioned his mum's been ill,' Daniel said. 'I got the impression things between them had kind of thawed a bit. But we shouldn't worry them if it turns out he's just gone on holiday and run out of credit on his phone, or something daft like that.'

'Yeah, I can see Andy going on holiday and running out of credit on his phone.'

'Exactly.'

'But then he'd top it up right away, wouldn't he? Or connect to Wi-Fi. I mean, if he was somewhere fabulous with a gorgeous guy, there's no way he'd not be telling us about it, like, non-stop.'

Daniel nodded. 'Exactly,' he said again.

I finished my coffee and the glass of water that had come with it, and started on my half of the pain au chocolat. We'd been in the café for half an hour, and it already felt as if we were running out of road.

Then Daniel said, 'I wonder if he's on TikTok.'

'On TikTok? What? Is he fourteen?'

Daniel rolled his eyes. 'Thirty-eight going on fourteen.'

It was my turn to not-quite laugh. 'I haven't got TikTok. On account of not being fourteen.'

'I have. I post videos on it for work, and they get loads of views. I've got ten thousand followers on there.'

'Seriously?'

'Sure.' Daniel tapped the screen of his phone and passed it to me.

There was a video playing of a brush smoothing varnish over a tabletop, in a wood that I guessed might be teak – not that I knew anything about wood. It was kind of mesmerising, and I could see why people might want to watch it, if they had absolutely nothing better to do. Then the picture cut to Daniel standing at a workbench, smiling and gesturing as he explained something to the camera, and his huge following didn't seem quite so mysterious after all. Not that I was going to say that to him.

'Lots of woodworkers and metalworkers have accounts on

there,' he went on. 'It's a thing. And the way the algorithm works, the more you watch, the more you get served.'

'So it helps you sell loads of tables that cost north of five grand?'

'Why? You thinking of buying one?'

I flushed. The truth was I had longingly stalked several of the beautiful mid-century modern pieces Daniel had restored over the years, but felt that relations between us were too strained for me to ask if I could buy one at mates' rates.

'Nope,' I said. 'I'm all good on the table front, but thanks all the same.'

'Anyway,' Daniel said. 'Like I said, I get new followers all the time. I don't follow them back, mostly, only other wood-workers. It's too much of a time suck. But let's see if Andy's one of them.'

Daniel scrolled rapidly through a list of accounts that seemed to go on forever.

'Can't you search for him?' I asked.

'It depends on whether he uses his own name. He might not. If he's even on here, which I doubt.'

'This isn't going to work, is it? It's like looking for a needle in a haystack. A haystack made of fourteen-year-olds doing dance videos.'

'Hold on. There's a thing where you can search for people you're connected to on other apps. I've never bothered because none of my real-life friends are on here, but let's see. Andy didn't delete his Facebook account, as far as I know – he just doesn't really use it.'

Frowning with concentration, he tapped the screen a couple more times. I watched, curious but not confident.

'Any luck?' I asked after a few seconds.

'Give me a second.' Daniel tapped again. There was a scar on the pad of his finger, I noticed – presumably he'd slashed himself with a chisel or something. 'Bingo.'

'You've found him?'

'Sure have.'

Daniel handed me his phone. On the screen, I could see Andy, shirtless, wearing board shorts and sunglasses, beaming at the camera. Madonna's 'La Isla Bonita' played through the speaker before I hastily muted it – Andy had always loved an '80s classic. I watched as he turned slowly, the camera panning over the beach where he stood, the sea behind him dotted with small boats and one vast yacht. On the other side of the beach, green-clad mountains rose up to meet a cloudless blue sky.

Relief flooded me. 'Well, that's that then. He's on holiday with Ash. He's fine.'

'I'm not so sure.' Daniel took the phone from me and tapped the screen again, his brow furrowed with concentration. 'Andy started his account three weeks ago. He posted videos every day, until that one. It was six days ago, and he hasn't posted since.'

'He probably got bored of it. It looks like a bit of a mission, making those videos and editing them and putting soundtracks to them. Maybe he wasn't getting as many likes and follows as he hoped, so he gave up.'

'I'd buy that if he hadn't dropped off the radar completely in other ways,' Daniel said. 'Look, call it superstition or paranoia or gut instinct or whatever you like, but I'm worried.'

'Yeah, I kind of do call it paranoia.' Although, even as I spoke, I could feel Daniel's worry infecting me, a knot of anxiety tightening in my stomach. 'He's most likely just busy. He'll be having a great time. I bet he's cracked an invite to a party on that yacht.'

'The yacht!' Daniel turned his attention back to his phone, tapping the screen rapidly. After a few seconds he said, 'Alsaya. That's where he is. At least, that's where that boat, the *Rhapsody*, is moored. Some Kazakh oligarch owns it.'

'Al-what? How do you know that?'

'There's a website that tracks the location of all the superyachts in the world,' Daniel explained smugly. 'I worked on one a while back, fitting panelling in the staterooms – that's how I knew. And Alsaya is in Turkey, on the Mediterranean coast.'

'So it looks like Andy's having a great time on the Mediterranean coast of Turkey, then.'

'Maybe he is. But if I don't hear from him in the next twenty-four hours, I'm going to go out there and look for him.'

'What? He's a grown man, not a toddler who's run off in Tesco.'

Daniel shrugged, palms raised so he looked just like that annoying emoji. 'He's my friend and I'm concerned about him. So if there's still radio silence this time tomorrow, I'm booking a flight. You can come with me if you want.'

'But that's bonkers.'

'Maybe it is. But it's what I'm going to do.'

I gawped at him. Not only was he suggesting going abroad to try and track down our friend, but – assuming I'd heard him right and wasn't having some sort of aural hallucination – he'd suggested that I join in on this mad mission to rescue someone who, as far as I could tell, didn't need rescuing. At least I really, really hoped he didn't.

'Knock yourself out,' I said. 'Sounds like you need a holiday. I'll download TikTok and follow you both and look out for videos of you on yachts. Now I'd better be off – thanks so much for the coffee.'

But despite my bravado, my feet and my heart felt heavy as I stalked out of the coffee shop. Reluctant as I was to reveal it to Daniel, I wasn't that reassured by the evidence that, just a few days ago, Andy had been safe and well. That didn't mean he still was – it didn't really mean anything. Anything could have happened in the intervening days and nights.

I didn't want to admit it – not even to myself – but I had a growing sense that Daniel might be right.

SIX

I emerged from the dimly lit arcade into dazzling sunlight. The street was busy, and a series of smells assaulted me: the weird herbal, bready aroma of a Subway; a blast of washing powder from a laundromat; a waft of dope smoke from somewhere.

The smell of weed reminded me inevitably of Andy. Unlike Daniel, I hadn't really partaken of the party lifestyle he'd embraced so fervently in his twenties and been unable to escape until just a couple of years ago. But I'd seen the aftermath: those endless, dragging Sundays when Andy had hung out at my flat, rattling with come-down, devouring the sausage baps I made him, then lighting spliff after spliff and smoking them on my balcony 'to take the edge off'.

Eventually, the neighbours' complaints had gone from 'Could you maybe do that inside?' to 'We're going to call the cops if this doesn't stop', and Andy and I'd had to decamp to the park instead, so he could take the edge off there. Sometimes, Daniel had joined us. It was around then I'd started to realise that Andy's lifestyle was segueing from 'party' to 'problem' – a fact universally acknowledged, except by Daniel.

Because Daniel, I'd quickly realised, was *part* of the problem. He'd begun popping up when Andy and I had arranged to meet for drinks or a meal or to see a movie or whatever, just tagging along, uninvited by me but presumably welcomed by Andy – in spite of his protestations about not wanting to share me. Often, when I left to go home early because I had work the next day, the two of them would head off somewhere unspecified to make a night of it. But one time, when I'd known Andy for just over a year, it had ended up being just Daniel and me, because Andy had texted fifteen minutes after we'd been due to meet saying he was legit dying of man flu and had taken to his bed. So it had seemed like a golden opportunity to share my concern with his mate.

'Listen,' I'd said, once we were installed on bar stools with mojitos and a little bowl of rice crackers, 'I don't know about you, but I'm worried.'

'What's up, Kate?' Daniel had looked at me steadily. His eyes were no colour at all, I noticed – a flat silvery grey, like five-pence pieces dropped on a pavement in the rain.

'It's Andy,' I said. 'He came round to mine last night – well, at about three this morning actually – and he was absolutely wasted.'

Daniel shrugged. 'That's our Andy. Always fond of a mind-altering substance.'

'But it was Tuesday night. He'd lost his keys and locked himself out. He couldn't get up to go to work this morning, and he's already on a written warning.'

'Might be a good wake-up call if he gets sacked.'

'It's not his career I'm bothered about, Daniel,' I said. 'Come on, he works for that art gallery practically for free – it's not like he needs the money. But he's taking coke, like, every night. It's getting out of hand.'

'It's no big deal, Kate. Come on. Loads of people use it. It's just recreational.'

'I'm sure it is just recreational for loads of people. Maybe it even is for you. But I don't think it is for Andy.'

'Oh, give over,' he said. 'Look at you, caning the cocktails. Should I stage an intervention?'

Things would have escalated after that, and I didn't want them to escalate, so I left it there – but I was seething with frustration at Daniel's wilful blindness as well as becoming increasingly concerned about Andy. That night may have been the first time I'd tried to talk to Daniel about Andy's issues, but it wasn't the last. And the fact that I was right didn't leave me feeling even a bit of satisfaction.

Now, though, our roles were reversed. Daniel was the one worrying about Andy, and I was insisting that everything was fine.

What if, this time, he was right and I was wrong? What if I was trying to convince myself rather than him?

While I mused, the bus had been making its tortuously slow way through South London, and at last it reached my stop. I disembarked, thinking of the long afternoon ahead of me. I could head to Tate Modern and give myself a good dose of cultural enrichment. I could walk across the river and do some shopping in Covent Garden. I could visit Naomi and go to the park with her and the twins.

But, somehow, I didn't feel like doing any of those things. Instead, I popped past St Mungo's, where Mona was clearing up the last of the cups and saucers from the coffee morning.

'That cake went down a treat, Kate,' she told me, handing over the carefully washed cake stand. 'Absolutely all gone. Did you have a nice time with your friend?'

'He's not exactly a friend. And he wants me to go with him to Turkey.'

Mona tilted her head quizzically, and I gave her a brief rundown of the state of play.

'In these situations,' she said, pulling the white cloth off the table and bundling it up to take home and wash, 'I always ask myself: would I regret doing something or would I regret not doing it?'

I thought about this. Did Daniel regret his inaction over Andy all those years ago? He'd never said so – at least not to me. And if I stood by my decision not to go to Turkey with him, would I end up regretting that?

'I get that,' I said. 'It's good advice. But it seems like such a massive overreaction. And besides, Daniel and I don't get on. I don't want to go to Turkey with him – or anywhere else, for that matter. If I'm honest, I'd rather stick pins in my eyes.'

'Now don't be melodramatic,' she scolded. 'It's a lovely country. Delicious food. When George was alive, we went all-inclusive there a couple of summers and we ate like kings. And you could do with a rest.'

I wasn't sure how spending time with Daniel could be described as restful, delicious food or no delicious food. His infuriating smile-that-wasn't-a-smile, his annoying hair, his insufferable air of having made up his mind and being right – it would be enough to put anyone off their izgara kofte. And besides, there was the small matter of actually getting there, if I did decide to go. Which I hadn't.

'What would you do without me and my cake, though?' I asked. 'Your guests would riot.'

'They'd do no such thing. They'd be perfectly happy with custard creams. Maybe not *as* happy, but they'd make do.'

I laughed, gathered up the cake stand and tin, and headed for home.

The flat was cool; I'd closed the blinds that morning to keep out the sun. But now I opened them and stepped out onto my balcony, feeling a sense of wonder as I always did at the view of the river sparkling below in the spring sunshine.

And then I thought: *Imagine waking up in the morning and looking at the sea.* I hadn't seen the sea for years – one of the downsides of my friends being in couples while I was single was that the rowdy holidays we'd had together in our twenties were a thing of the past. And I hadn't exactly been up for expensive trips abroad. My fear of flying was part of that, but another part was that, once I'd managed to save enough money for the deposit on my first, frankly grotty flat, I'd felt the need to save more, to upgrade to a slightly nicer apartment and then to the lovely one where I lived now. That need for security, for independence, to prove that I was managing perfectly well without a man in my life, had outweighed any desire I might have had to lie on beaches sipping cocktails.

Of course, Mona had a point: I could do with a rest. But how could Daniel's company ever possibly be restful? And while lying on a beach sipping a cocktail definitely had its appeal, the idea of Daniel by my side while I was doing it was enough to bring me out in hives.

I fetched my laptop from my desk and perched at the little café table that was all I could squeeze onto the balcony, then googled Alsaya.

This small yet glamorous town offers something for all discerning travellers, I read. *From tranquil eco resorts to five-star luxury; vibrant night-life to quirky shopping; relaxed days on the beach to adrenaline-fuelled watersports.*

Not to mention the twenty-four-seven company of a man you can't stand, I thought.

And then I told myself not to be ridiculous. This wasn't a *holiday* holiday. It wasn't like I'd be spending hours lying on the beach with Daniel showing off his naked chest – ridiculously buff from lugging heavy furniture around – on a sunlounger next to me.

Daniel and I would be there for a purpose. We'd be there to find Andy. And once we'd reassured ourselves that he was safe and well, I could come home again and pick up my plans for my weeks off work. Which, admittedly, didn't amount to a whole lot more than working through the latest season of *Married at First Sight Australia*, attempting to grow some basil in my window boxes and hopefully going on a few more dates with Claude.

Married at First Sight Australia versus travelling across Europe with Daniel? A clear win for trashy reality telly. Basil versus Daniel? Maybe a nil–nil draw. Claude versus Daniel? Total wipeout.

But still. *Andy.*

I picked up my phone and dialled his number. Just as it had done the past dozen times – just as it had last night, when my mind had fought sleep and insisted on fretting about Andy – it rang through to voicemail and the automated message told me his mailbox was full. Daniel was right: this was odd. It was out of character. And it was concerning.

I tapped through to WhatsApp and my chat with Daniel, but I didn't text him – instead, I started a voice call.

His phone rang and rang too, and I thought there'd be no answer from him either. But at last he picked up.

'Kate? Sorry about that, the circular saw was going and I didn't hear my phone. Have you heard from him?'

'Nope. Just tried calling again and no answer.'

'Right. I had a look at flights and I reckon I'll leave the day after tomorrow. I'll keep you posted.'

'You won't have to. I'll come.' My words took me by surprise – it was like the decision had been made somewhere between my heart or my instinct and my mouth, and none of them had given my brain a heads-up about what I was going to say.

'Seriously?'

'Seriously. Let me know what flight you'll be on, and I'll buy my ticket.'

'Great. I'll text you the details.'

Without a goodbye, he hung up.

I looked at my phone in my hand and noticed I was trembling. What the hell had I let myself in for? An undetermined stretch of time in a foreign country with a man I totally despised, that was what. And it got worse. I looked down from my balcony to the street far below and felt my stomach give a familiar lurch of fear.

I certainly wouldn't be walking there or catching a bus. This was going to mean getting on an actual aeroplane.

SEVEN

The day of our departure, although our flight was only due to leave at midday, I was awake at five.

Actually, I hadn't been conscious of sleeping at all. All night, as soon as I felt myself nodding off, I'd drifted straight into weird dreams, in which the plane disappeared around us and there was only Daniel and me, flailing our arms in the air like swimmers to stay aloft; finding Daniel in a bar, only he morphed into Claude and kissed me passionately; and the old favourite, arriving at the airport to discover I'd forgotten not only my luggage but also my clothes.

Each time, I jerked awake again and lay staring into the darkness, unable to get back to sleep. There wasn't even any point getting up and baking, as I was leaving too early to drop anything off at St Mungo's, and I still didn't know how long we'd be away for.

So at last, scratchy-eyed and cross, I got up and started packing.

Back in the day, I used to travel often for work, and I'd become expert at rapid and space-efficient packing. But work travel was different. This was more like a holiday and I hadn't been on an actual holiday for the best part of ten years – not abroad anyway. Not anywhere that involved flying at least. I'd need bikinis – and diazepam.

Too anxious to eat, I gulped two black coffees in rapid succession – knowing full well they'd make me even more jittery than I was becoming anyway – washed my mug, glanced around the flat for the last time, checked yet again that I hadn't forgotten my passport and that my boarding pass was saved on my phone, and departed, wheeling my case behind me, making sure that I'd double-locked the door and then getting the lift back up to make doubly and triply sure.

In spite of all my dithering, I arrived at the airport three hours early. But that was okay – I'd learned over the years that even the slightest threat of being late would send me into a frenzy of anxiety. As calmly as I could, I dropped off my bag, navigated passport control and made my way to the branch of Pret where I'd arranged to meet Daniel. By the time he arrived half an hour later, I'd managed to eat a smoked salmon sandwich and drink yet another coffee, and was sipping water and flicking through the *Financial Times*, presenting what I hoped was a picture of poise.

'Morning, Kate.' He approached me, grinning, a shabby leather jacket slung over his shoulders, sunglasses holding his hair back from his face. 'Made it on time?'

'No, I'm just an avatar,' I said. 'The real Kate's still in bed.'

I instantly regretted my sarcasm, but Daniel laughed.

'Got your passport?' he asked. 'I must've checked about ten times for mine. Funny how paranoid you get, isn't it?'

His words sparked a reflexive twinge of paranoia in me, but I said, 'Of course I have,' and waited until he'd gone to get a coffee before making sure it was actually in my handbag. Then, after glancing over my shoulder again and confirming that Daniel was still waiting in the queue, I quickly unzipped my make-up bag and checked that too.

My lip balm was there. My hand cream was there. The sachet of wet wipes I'd packed in case I needed to clean my eye make-up off and reapply it was there.

But not the most important thing: the precious tablets I'd managed to persuade my GP to prescribe a few years back, first explaining my extreme fear of flying, then bursting into tears, then practically promising her the blood of my first-born child and swearing that no, I would never, ever exceed the recommended dose and yes, I was aware of the highly addictive nature of the medication.

And I'd kept my promise. I'd only ever used the pills on flights, and even then, only when I was feeling particularly nervous. I'd husbanded them carefully, and I remembered seeing them in the bathroom cabinet that morning, two little tablets left, securely in their blister pack, a promise that if things got bad, I'd have something to take the edge off.

Except I didn't.

I'd somehow managed to forget them.

'You all right, Kate?' Daniel sat down opposite me and took a gulp of coffee. 'You look kind of stressed.'

Kind of? I'm so stressed I'm practically levitating.

'I'm fine. Just thinking we should go and board in a few minutes.'

'Sure. But there's no rush – they always call business class first.'

'Exactly, that's why we— Hold on, did you not book a business-class seat?'

'For a four-hour flight? Of course not. That's madness. Massive waste of money, not to mention carbon emissions. Oh, I take it you did?'

I opened my mouth to tell him that of course I had; I hadn't flown economy for years and I'd rather eat my own hair than do so now.

But instead, I heard myself replying, almost apologetically,

'Yes, well, I had loads of frequent flyer miles and I thought I might as well use them.'

Daniel gave a rather humourless laugh. 'Good for you. In that case, I guess you'll turn left and I'll turn right and we'll see each other there.'

I felt a twinge of guilt. I could offer to upgrade him, I supposed – but then I'd be faced with spending the entire four-hour flight in proximity to him, and while not as close as in economy class, it was still too close for comfort.

Especially without my wonderful, panic-easing drugs.

'Yeah,' I said. 'We'll see each other there.'

I zipped up my bag, trying unsuccessfully to conceal the very obvious tremor in my hands, and left the café. I topped up my aluminium bottle at a water fountain. I went to the ladies' and spritzed my skin with soothing lavender face mist. I focused on my breathing, trying to relax the knot of sick tension I could already feel under my ribs.

I wished I had time for an enormous gin, but the fear of somehow being delayed and missing the flight altogether was even worse than the fear of getting on it.

So, alone, I made my way to the boarding gate.

Twenty minutes later, I was in my seat, the seatbelt possibly too securely fastened around my waist, one hand gripping my complimentary glass of Moët (which I knew wasn't even going to make a dent in my fear) and the other clamped around the armrest of my seat.

Breathe, Kate, breathe.

The safety announcement began, and I resolutely ignored it. I'd heard it often enough and I knew that if the worst happened, no amount of removing high-heeled shoes or inflating life jackets would save me.

I thought of Daniel, towards the back of the plane, no doubt looking forward to the journey with pleasurable anticipation, and my heart hardened.

What the hell had possessed me to agree to this?

But it was too late to back out now. The cabin crew were taking their seats, and the aircraft was taxiing gently towards the runway.

And then it began. The roar of the engines, the sudden acceleration that pressed me against my seatback, the backwards tilt and upwards lift that left my stomach behind then sent it surging into my throat.

I. Must. Not. Puke.

I flicked on the in-flight entertainment and found the flight tracker, knowing that for the next four hours I wouldn't be able to focus on a movie or a book, only on the little white aircraft icon making its way across the English Channel and then onwards, slowly and inexorably, towards our destination.

So long as the pilot didn't take it into his head to crash it into a mountain. So long as the engine didn't fail. So long as a passenger – quite possibly me – didn't cause a disturbance that would require it to be rerouted.

I sipped my water, my ears straining to hear the welcome rattle of the drinks trolley. I wasn't hungry and I knew that alcohol on flights was a Bad Idea, but I didn't care. Anything at all that would make this time pass more quickly was fair game as far as I was concerned.

I drank a gin and tonic and ate my chicken, rice and salad without enthusiasm, my throat almost too dry to swallow. I watched the aircraft icon on the screen crawling across Belgium like a fly walking over a windowpane, seeking a route out to freedom.

And then the fasten-seat-belt sign flashed red, with an accompanying bong.

The pilot's voice crackled over the tannoy – something about clear-air turbulence and asking passengers to return to their seats.

I was already in my seat. I couldn't have moved for anything.

The aircraft lurched and swayed, dropping through the air then steadying, one wing and then the other dipping then rising. I gripped the armrests, knowing perfectly well that when the pilot lost control and the entire craft dropped from the sky to land in a field of cabbages somewhere far, far below, before bursting into flames with everyone trapped inside, the armrests would be no help to me whatsoever.

Another lurch. Another stomach-churning drop. More swaying. Then things steadied a bit and I tried to force myself to breathe. And then the aircraft plummeted again. I had no idea how far it fell – probably only a matter of a few feet. But it felt terrifying – like dropping off a cliff. My breath rasped in my throat – I needed water, but I couldn't let go of the armrest to reach for my bottle.

I could only wait and endure.

Somewhere behind me, I could hear a frightened toddler screaming, 'Mummy! Mummy!' and it was literally all I could do not to join in.

Eventually, after some fifteen minutes that felt like an eternity, the plane steadied again and then the seat-belt sign flicked off. Slowly, I released my grip and drank some water. The little icon on my screen showed that we had crossed the Alps – the worst must, surely, now be over.

It was and it wasn't. Even if there was no more turbulence, there was still two hours to endure – two hours of fearing that it would all start again: the rocking, the plummeting, the trying not to scream. I couldn't do this – not alone, anyway.

Unsteadily, I got to my feet and walked towards the back of the aircraft, brushing aside the curtain that separated business class from economy. Daniel was near the front, behind a woman with a baby on her lap, with an empty seat next to him. He was lounging back in his chair, his eyes half closed, headphones in his ears, a relaxed half-smile on his face. When he noticed me, his eyes snapped open.

'Ah, come to slum it with the plebs?' he asked mockingly.

'Something like that. Is this seat taken?'

He shook his head and I slipped in, fastening the seat belt immediately.

He looked at me more seriously now. 'Kate, are you okay? You look a bit weird.'

I forced a smile. 'I don't love flying, if I'm honest.'

'It got a bit bumpy back there, didn't it?'

'Bumpy? The fucking thing was going to fall out of the sky.'

'Kate, it really, really wasn't. You know when an aircraft last crashed as a result of turbulence?'

I shook my head. 'Week ago? Two?'

'More than fifty years ago. Airline safety has improved massively since then. You were in more danger in your cab on the way to the airport than you are now.'

'I got the train, but that's not the point. It might be safe in theory, but if something happens you're still... well, high. Until you aren't, obviously.'

'Right,' he said. 'I see I'm going to have to stage an intervention here.'

'What do you mean?'

'I'll start. Oxford Circus.'

'What?'

He sighed. 'Oxford. Circus.'

And then I got it. He was challenging me to Mornington Crescent, the silly and arcane sort-of-game in which players have to make their way around the London Underground, with random rules made up as they go along, which he, Andy and I used to play for hours back in the day.

'Are we playing under the expanded ultra-low-emission-zone rules of 2021?'

'No, let's follow the 2004 Livingstone Protocol.'

'Gotcha. And are Elizabeth Line interchanges permitted at Bond Street?'

'Only for westward travel, with a transfer onto the Reading branch at Paddington.'

'In that case...' I conjured up the Tube map in my head. It didn't really matter what route I took – that wasn't the point. The only aim of the game was to spin it out as long as possible, while accusing your opponent of the most absurd infringements of the non-existent rules. 'I'll go to Earl's Court.'

'Oooh, an impressive start. Although I'm not convinced it's permitted following the 2008 Hounslow decision, I'll let it go. Clapham South.'

'Clapham South? Sneaky. Looks like you're aiming for the Seven Sisters manoeuvre, which relies on my taking the former Circle Line, before trains terminated at Edgware Road. So I'll foil your cunning plan by going to Mile End.'

'A transverse diagonal?' he said. 'Nice one. I fear I'm going to have to invoke the Overground exception and travel to Dalston Junction.'

My hand wasn't gripping the armrest so hard any more. And not only that, it felt oddly warm. I glanced down and saw that Daniel had placed his hand over mine, just resting there, natural and – quite amazingly – comforting. Part of me wanted to swat it away like an annoying fly, but a much bigger part simply felt relieved that it was there.

But I didn't say anything about it – I just returned to the game. 'Damn it. That forces me to Dalston Kingsland, and I miss a turn.'

'Correct. Which leaves me free to perform the Plumstead Bus Garage change – which you might remember was the decisive move in the Willis versus Cummings 1974 World Cup – and go to Shepherd's Bush via Walthamstow Central.'

'Walthamstow Central, you say?' I sucked my teeth. 'A bold

move. But the 1974 World Cup was played under Three-Day Week rules, you might remember. Which leaves me with...'

I'd barely noticed it, but the seat-belt sign had been illuminated again while we were talking, and the plane was descending, smoothly and benignly, before touching down on the runway as lightly as a cat. Relief flooded me – along with a startling surge of gratitude for Daniel's steadfast presence. He gave my hand the smallest, almost imperceptible squeeze, then moved his away.

My skin felt cold without it there.

'Mornington Crescent,' I said.

EIGHT

THEN

2008

Hands on hips, I turned in a slow circle, surveying my domain. Mine. It had been mine officially (although, even more officially, most of it still belonged to the bank, but I didn't allow myself to think about that too much) for three weeks, and I'd moved past the stage of kissing the walls every time I got home from work.

But the sense of pride, of ownership, was still intoxicating. All the weekends working in pubs and at supermarket check-outs while I was at university, saving every penny I possibly could, never going abroad on holiday, deliberately choosing the pokiest, cheapest bedroom in every houseshare, had paid off. I'd scraped together enough of a deposit to buy a home of my own. Even my heady excitement couldn't blind me to the fact that, objectively, it was a bit of a dump. The estate was undeniably sketchy, the bedroom was so small I had to keep one side of the bed firmly pressed against the wall and anyone who slept with me would have to climb over me to get out. The bathroom was dated and shabby, and there was nowhere to put the ironing board.

But still, it was mine, and tonight I'd be sharing it with my friends for the first time.

I'd taken the previous day off work and prepped mountains of fancy canapés, imagining I was Nigella Lawson having one of her glamorous soirées. Handmade blinis were in the freezer, ready to be warmed up and topped with smoked salmon and snipped chives. Cocktail sausages were wrapped in bacon ready to be roasted. Sticks of carrot, cucumber and pepper were in the fridge waiting to be artfully arranged around a bowl of bagna cauda, a dip so fancy and sophisticated I hadn't known it existed until a week before.

Admittedly, my chive and gruyere choux buns had collapsed in a manner worthy of the 'Nailed it' meme, but I'd hidden the evidence in the bin and done an emergency dash to Iceland for pre-made vol-au-vents instead.

My ill-matched assortment of IKEA wine and champagne glasses were arrayed on the kitchen counter, flanked by paper plates and napkins. Fairy lights were strung over the door to the balcony. Tall white candles stood in the fireplace, and white towels were neatly folded in the bathroom next to a fresh cake of soap.

And the fridge, obviously, was groaning with booze.

I was ready, too. My hair was freshly blow-dried, my make-up carefully applied, my white sequinned Primark dress elevated to fashionista status by the silver Steve Madden heels I'd found in TK Maxx.

I was ready. My flat was ready. All that remained was for my guests to arrive.

Abbie and Matt, typically punctual, were first, Matt carrying a bottle of champagne and Abbie a huge bunch of lilies. I didn't own a vase so I fished the lemon slices out of the jug of water I'd prepared and shoved the flowers in there – it wasn't like anyone was going to be drinking water, anyway.

'Oh my God,' Abbie breathed. 'It's amazing, Kate. Your very own flat! You're like someone out of *Sex and the City*.'

'Show us round,' Matt urged. 'Come on, we need a proper grand tour.'

'Explain absolutely everything,' Abbie urged. 'We won't care how long it takes.'

So I led them through all forty square metres of my home, glowing with pleasure as they exclaimed over the view (admittedly of a rank of wheelie bins and a half-dead laurel bush), the laminate floor (tactfully ignoring the fact that one corner was peeling away), the proximity of the fridge to the sink and the fitted wardrobes in the bedroom. They even found nice things to say about the bathroom, which was frankly grotty, with a shower that went randomly from scalding to arctic, and a stain in the toilet that looked like something had fallen in there and died, and was destined to be ripped out as soon as I could afford to replace it.

Matt opened the bottle of champagne, and I was pouring drinks for us all when the doorbell buzzed again.

Rowan and Paul had brought tiny Clara, in a sling on her father's chest, but insisted that there was no need for quiet – she could sleep through Armageddon. They got the full tour too and did just as much exclaiming over things. Naomi arrived with an African violet in a pot, which I thanked her profusely for despite knowing that, with the best will in the world, I'd kill it within a week. Zara and Patch (who were still an item at that point) brought a box of posh champagne flutes that actually matched and another bottle of fizz.

Friends from my work arrived too, and old friends from school and university. Everyone brought gifts, everyone enthused and admired. The drink was flowing, I started to bring out the food and I was basically feeling like the hostess with the mostest.

Except Andy wasn't there yet. I tried not to mind – it was

only nine o'clock. He hadn't said what time he'd be there, only that he would be.

But all the same, I couldn't help feeling hurt. He knew how much I'd scrimped and saved to buy the place, how stressful it had all been, how much it mattered to me. Of course, he didn't know that at every stage of the process, from looking in estate agents' windows to picking out my cream sofa, I'd imagined his opinion.

God, you don't want to live near Elephant and Castle, he'd sneered in my head when I viewed a flat that had been perfect in every other respect. *It's all right, but it's miles from a Tube station*, my internal Andy had commented on another. *You don't want to have to get the bus with a bunch of povvos eating fried chicken every afternoon. Do not paint the walls magnolia, Kate*, he'd insisted, *or you'll be dead to me forever.*

He didn't know that, because obviously I hadn't told him. But he surely knew how much his opinion mattered to me. Over the past year, we'd become close friends. He'd been shopping with me and helped me pick out clothes that looked like they cost ten times as much as they did – my Primark dress being a case in point. He'd advised me on my love life, and it was thanks to him that I'd jettisoned my latest boyfriend, Stevie, after three months.

'He's no good for you, Katie babe. He's a no-hoper. He'll drag you down when you need to fly.'

He'd even rehearsed interview questions with me when I'd applied for my current job, although he was currently unemployed and had never been through an interview process in his life.

He *knew*. And now he wasn't here.

I didn't let anyone see that I minded, and I still went all out to enjoy my party, my housewarming, the pleasure of welcoming so many friends to the home I'd strived for. But without him there, it all felt less special – less real, even.

Ten o'clock came and went. Rowan and Paul took Clara home. Patch and Zara went on to another party. I cleared away the empty plates, worried that I'd under-catered. People were out on the balcony now, leaning over the balustrade, looking down at the water and chatting. I collected up empty glasses and washed them up in the sink, longing for the day when I could afford a dishwasher.

Abbie appeared at my elbow, holding a drying-up cloth. 'Honestly, even your tea towels are amazing. This is all so cool, Kate. I'm so happy for you.'

I looked into her smiling face, and she pulled me close and hugged me.

And then, abruptly, I started to cry.

'Oh my God, Kate. What's wrong? Are you okay?' She steered me to the sofa and sat me down, rummaging in her bag for tissues.

'I'm fine,' I muttered between sobs. 'Just a bit... you know.'

'Tired and emotional?' she suggested. 'Literally. You worked your socks off making all that amazing food. You should've let me help.'

'Thanks. I know. But I didn't want—'

'Anyone to see the place before your big reveal? I get it. And besides, you know what a crap cook I am. I'd have given everyone listeria or something.'

I managed a laugh, remembering my ruined gougères, but it turned into a sob.

'Is it because Andy hasn't turned up?' she asked gently.

A tissue pressed to my eyes, I shook my head, then nodded.

'Oh, love. That's rubbish. You wanted everyone to be here, and now he's not. But you know...'

'I know what?'

Abbie took my hands. 'You love Andy. Of course you do – we all do. But I've known him longer than anyone – anyone except Matt, of course; they were mates at school before I turned up on the scene. And the thing about Andy is this.'

She paused again, and I waited for her to collect her thoughts and turn them into words, as she was so good at doing.

'Andy's a complicated person, Kate. He's got issues. He always has done. I don't think his parents were that great, if I'm honest. He's always wanted to be adored, but he's not always very good at adoring back.'

'I don't need him to adore me,' I protested. 'I just need him to—'

'Do what the hell he says he'll do? I'm afraid that's always likely to be a problem.'

I didn't want to admit it, not even to myself. But deep down I knew she was right. I hugged her again and dried my eyes, opened another bottle and returned to the dwindling crowd of my guests.

Then, just before midnight, the doorbell buzzed for the last time that night.

Of course, it was Andy, always one to make an entrance. He was wearing a peacock-blue silk shirt, open almost to the waist, over black leather trousers. His golden-blonde hair was flattened a bit, duller than usual, as if he'd been sweating heavily. His eyes were unnaturally bright, sparkling in the waxen pallor of his face. He was carrying a bottle of champagne, but the cork had been pulled and half of it drunk.

And he wasn't alone.

With him was another man, taller than Andy and just as lean and angular. His hair was longer than Andy's and a darker blonde, almost honey-coloured. I couldn't see his eyes, because he was wearing lilac-lensed shades. A battered suede jacket that might once have been black but was now a faded charcoal was slung over his shoulders. There were rips in the thighs and knees of his low-slung jeans. He exuded glamour and a kind of power, a lion alongside Andy's leopard.

'Katie babe.' Andy dropped to his knees in front of me. 'There's fashionably late, and then there's indefensibly late. Will you forgive us? I brought you a consolation prize.'

I'd seen Andy drunk before, often – and been drunk with him. I'd seen him slip off to the bathroom on nights out and known he was doing coke, and declined when he offered to share. But I'd never seen him like this before. Still, nothing could suppress the flash of pleasure I felt at his presence – he'd come. He'd come after all. He hadn't forgotten me.

I reached out a hand to help him to his feet. 'Don't be daft. You're here now.'

He didn't take my hand; he stood up by himself, stumbling into the door frame and thrusting the bottle into my hand. 'Not this. Him. He's the reason why I'm late.'

'I'm Daniel,' said the man in the shades. He did take my hand, sandwiching it between both of his and giving me a smile so warm and natural I couldn't help smiling back. 'And I really, really need a slash. Excuse me.'

I stood aside, gesturing towards the bathroom, but he shimmied past me, ricocheted off both walls of the hallway and disappeared into my bedroom.

If he pisses on my bed, I'll wring his neck, I thought. But I heard Abbie's voice behind me telling him the right way to go.

'He's an appalling influence, you know.' Andy peered at me owlishly. 'If you ever go on a night out with our Daniel, you'll know all about it the next day.'

'Come in,' I said. 'Come and see the flat.'

But Andy wasn't interested in seeing the flat. He weaved over to the sofa and sat down, taking a deep swig from an abandoned champagne glass on the coffee table. Then he pulled out a pack of fags and lit one.

No one will ever smoke in here, I'd promised myself. And so far that night, no one had – they'd used the ashtray I'd left out on the balcony. But Andy was, and I did nothing to stop him.

A few moments later, Daniel joined us. He sank down onto the floor, leaned his head back against the sofa and appeared to fall asleep.

'Oh my God, that was such a mad night,' Andy said. 'Well, afternoon really. We started at midday at a bar in Soho. Actually we didn't. We started after he finished work yesterday afternoon. We might have had a couple of hours' kip at some point – I can't quite recall. Any chance of a canapé, Katie babe? You mentioned something about blinis.'

'The food's all gone,' I said. 'Sorry. Let me see if I've got some crisps.'

The last of my work and university friends trickled in from outside and said they really ought to be going. Naomi and Matt began clearing up, while Abbie sat next to Andy, listening to him talk. After a few minutes, I heard a long, sonorous snore come from Daniel. His head was tilted sideways, his mouth half-open, his too-long hair flopping down over his absurd tinted glasses, and yet he still managed to look handsome. Not handsome enough for me to forgive him, mind, but undeniably hot all the same.

I sat on a hard dining chair, suddenly exhausted. Around me was my perfect new home, not exactly trashed but clearly feeling the impact of its first party. The lilies Abbie had brought were shedding pollen on my table. Someone had spilled red wine on the dove-grey rug. The air smelled of smoke, and Andy's cigarette butt was upended on the coffee table, a precarious tower of ash waiting to fall from it.

I'd wanted it all to be perfect, and now it wasn't.

I looked at Daniel's face, serene and almost smug in sleep, and thought, *I hate you.*

NINE

NOW

As soon as the plane touched down, my fear melted away. It always happened that way – it wasn't as if I suddenly realised how irrational my phobia was; intellectually, I knew that all the time, but that did nothing to lessen the screaming awareness that pulsed through my entire body and mind that here I was, kilometres up in the sky, and how could that not be insanely perilous?

But once back on land, the relief was so enormous that there was no space left in me for fear. Even the gratitude I'd felt when Daniel had held my hand and distracted me felt irrelevant now – he hadn't needed to do it. I was fine. I'd always been going to be fine. But I'd made myself look a fool in front of him, and I didn't like that one bit.

I felt a sense of deep weariness, and with it came profound annoyance. I just wanted to be on my own, have a shower, unpack my stuff, settle in – restore some sense of routine and normality.

We disembarked and collected our luggage, and I followed Daniel to the car-hire desk.

'Got your driving licence?' His tone was curt, as if he'd picked up some of my narkiness.

'No,' I replied.

'What? Why not?'

'I don't have one.'

'You mean you...?'

'I don't drive.'

'Jesus, Kate. It's a basic life skill.'

I shrugged. 'Not for a Londoner it's not. We have public transport, and taxis, and feet. And besides, think of the environmental impact of private cars.'

That silenced him briefly. Then he said, 'But you're perfectly happy for the planet to take the hit of *me* driving us.'

'Not necessarily. I'd be equally happy with a cab. But if being behind the wheel of a car is central to your sense of your own masculinity, then please don't let me stand in your way.'

He rolled his eyes. 'It's central to my sense of being able to get us where we're going and being able to find Andy once we're there.'

It was my turn to be silenced. The trauma of the flight had almost pushed my concern about Andy from my mind, but now it came rushing back. I was safe and in one piece, but what if he wasn't? Why was I sniping at Daniel when we were here with a shared purpose, on a mission that might have a tragic end?

You need to grow up, Kate, I told myself firmly. *Don't let him get to you. Eyes on the prize.*

I waited while Daniel completed the paperwork and picked up the keys, then followed him to the car, a basic red sedan, and watched him load our bags into the boot. His was a battered blue-and-grey backpack that looked like the veteran of many festivals and camping trips; my own wheeled lilac case looked somehow prissy and impractical by comparison.

He opened the passenger door and held it while I got in, and I automatically thanked him.

While he fiddled with the satnav and air conditioning, I peered out through the windscreen. The sky was a clear, deep blue, the sun about to set. Even with evening drawing in, it was still roasting hot. Beyond the anonymous stretch of car park and the concrete bulk of the airport building, I could see a fringe of palm trees – the first sign that we were actually abroad, rather than just in any airport anywhere.

'You've got the booking confirmation for the hotel?' he asked.

'No, I thought we could just sleep on the beach, Daniel.'

He turned towards me, his eyes hidden behind his sunglasses. 'Fine with me. I just didn't picture you as the wild-camping type.'

'Of course I have it. Two adjoining rooms, with sea views. Although you're welcome to sleep on the beach if you prefer.'

Unbidden, an image came into my mind of Daniel with sand in his hair, stretching his arms up to the morning sky, walking naked into the sea. I pushed it away – I'd often muttered, 'Oh, get in the sea,' to myself in annoyance at him, but that was definitely not what I'd meant.

The mental image lingered for an infuriatingly long time while Daniel started the engine, reversed out of the parking space and swung out of the car park onto an access road and then a motorway. And then it vanished, abruptly replaced by another picture in my mind – that of Daniel and me lying dead in a pile of crumpled metal.

'Daniel! Jesus Christ, you're driving on the wrong side of the road!'

The steady hum of the tyres wavered for a second, and I saw Daniel's knuckles whiten on the steering wheel.

Then he said, 'Kate. This is Turkey. They drive on the right. Didn't you wonder why you were on the far side of the oncoming traffic?'

My thudding heart stilled, the prospect of imminent death

receded and I felt a flood of mortification. 'Oh. God, of course. I'd forgotten. It was just kind of...'

'Disorientating? Yeah, maybe. But, Kate...'

'What?'

'Please don't *ever* do that to me again.'

'Do what?'

'Scare the living crap out of me when I'm driving. Because even though I knew I was right, you made me doubt myself for a second, and a second is quite enough, in motorway conditions, to cause a serious accident. Okay?'

I looked sideways at his face. It might just have been my imagination, but I could swear he'd paled a bit. The line of his jaw was tight, and his hands were still gripping the steering wheel harder than they needed to.

Who knew – Mr Cool could be rattled after all.

'Sorry,' I said. 'Best behaviour from me from now on, I promise.'

His mouth softened into that almost-smile. 'Bloody better be, or you can get out and walk.'

'If your driving's not up to scratch, I might well volunteer to.'

But Daniel drove skilfully, navigating the unfamiliar motorway, then following a sign to Alsaya and turning off onto a minor road. Darkness fell rapidly, and I could see little of our surroundings bar a few twinkling lights. The motion of the car lulled me, and I closed my eyes, feeling the deep fatigue of the sleepless night, early start and long journey wash over me.

I was woken by the car coming to a stop and Daniel announcing unnecessarily, 'We're here.'

My eyes snapped open and I released my seat belt, climbing stiffly out into the hot night. Ahead of me, I could see a brightly lit, stone-floored lobby, low buildings stretching out on either side of it. More palm trees bordered smooth pathways leading out in various directions, and in the distance I could see the darkness of water. For the first time, I caught the smell of the sea.

'Get settled in then meet downstairs for dinner in half an hour?' Daniel suggested.

Dinner. As if we were a couple on a romantic holiday together. I mean, obviously I'd known we would have to eat, but it hadn't quite occurred to me that we'd do so together, or that we'd be spending pretty much all our time for the next... the next however long it took, in each other's company. Daniel was right, I supposed – we were here for a reason, and we needed a plan.

We needed, however unwelcome it might be, to co-operate with each other on at least one level.

Just not yet. And certainly not over a candlelit table and a bottle of wine like we were on a fricking honeymoon or something.

'Tempting as that offer is,' I said, 'I'm knackered. I think I'm going to order room service and get an early night.'

'Suit yourself. Breakfast at eight?'

'Sure.' Breakfast was safe – there'd be no romantic vibes there. It would be like a business meeting. I might even bring a notepad and pen.

Daniel moved to heft our bags from the boot of the car, but a porter got there first. I followed them both into the lobby to check in.

Half an hour later, I was alone in my room, unpacked and showered, wrapped in a soft cotton bathrobe as I'd longed to be. I'd opened a bottle of pink wine from the minibar and was sitting on the balcony, looking out over a turquoise swimming pool. Lanterns sunk into the ground at regular intervals illuminated green lawns studded with olive and lemon trees. I could hear the rhythmic sigh of the sea and see the pinprick lights of boats out on the water.

And I could hear Daniel breathing. Not loudly – he wasn't

snoring like a walrus or anything like that. He was just sitting on his balcony, same as me. Only his balcony was just a few inches from mine, which of course meant he was just a few inches from me. Occasionally I could hear the clink of a glass as he set it down on the table, as I was doing. The head of my white muslin-draped four-poster bed was against the wall adjoining his, so we'd be as close as lovers, even in sleep.

I heard a discreet tap on my door and started, hurrying back through the cool, stone-floored room to answer, my heart hammering nervously even though I knew there was no way he could have teleported from his balcony to the corridor outside and come knocking on my door to... To what?

But it wasn't Daniel – it was only the meal I'd ordered. I thanked and tipped the waiter, then carried the tray of cheese, fruit, olives and bread back out to the balcony. I'd chew quietly, I told myself, and if I didn't, Daniel would just have to deal with it. But I could tell straight away that he was no longer there. The sense I'd had of his presence was gone; there was no more soft breathing and no more sounds of liquid glugging into a glass.

Presumably he'd gone out for food. Fair play to him. Hopefully he wouldn't meet some tourist on the pull and keep me up all night shagging on the other side of the wall.

Ugh. The thought made me far more uncomfortable than it ought to have done. He was entitled to shag if he wanted to – it wasn't like we were colleagues away on business together, and even if we had been – well, my own business trips hadn't been entirely shag-free zones.

I ate quickly, moved the tray back indoors, and fetched my phone and headphones. I quickly updated the Girlfriends' Club with the news that we'd arrived safely, but there had been no sign of Andy yet. Then I flicked through to TikTok and watched Andy's video again, the Madonna soundtrack loud in my ears.

The beach where my friend had stood to record it could be the very same one I could barely make out in the darkness beyond the hotel gardens. Tomorrow, I might feel the same sand between my toes he had felt. For all I knew, he might have slept in the very same room where I was sleeping.

Or he might not. The town wasn't large, but when I'd researched our accommodation, I'd seen dozens of hotels. Andy could have been – or could still be – in any one of them. Or he could be somewhere else entirely – the website where Daniel had found the location of the yacht could have been inaccurate or out of date. And, of course, there were the other possibilities, the ones I didn't want to think about...

'Where the hell are you, Andy?' I asked the room aloud. 'And where – and who – the hell is Ash?'

A flash of movement below caught my eye, and I almost dropped my phone off the balcony. In the pool beneath me, a figure was slicing through the bright water, swimming strongly. I could see the muscles in his back and arms moving smoothly with each stroke, the fabric of his shorts billowing around his legs, his water-dark hair slick as an otter's over his head.

Daniel.

All at once, I felt exhausted by the prospect of the days that lay ahead. I gulped the rest of my wine, cleaned my teeth and went to bed. But when I closed my eyes, I could still see Daniel's body in the pool, the length and strength of his limbs, the stream of bubbles coming from his lips, his back covered only by a thin skin of water. And the gentle pressure of the sheet on my hand reminded me of his palm resting over it on the plane, warm and comforting when I'd been afraid.

TEN

To my amazement, I slept brilliantly that night. I woke beneath the meringue-like softness of the white duvet to dazzling sunshine and the sound of birdsong drifting through my open window, and for a second I wondered if I'd actually died and – by some miracle – ended up in heaven.

But I quickly remembered where I was, who was there with me and why we were here.

Quickly, I got up and showered, pulling on shorts and a T-shirt. I peered anxiously at my hair in the mirror and saw that although my roots were beginning to show, they hadn't yet entered disaster territory. I debated going make-up free but couldn't quite face that prospect, so slapped on a bit of CC cream and some mascara. I spent a frustrating few minutes figuring out the unfamiliar coffee machine, which eventually obliged with a double espresso.

And then I opened my balcony door – silently, almost stealthily – and stepped out into the morning sunshine.

At last, I could properly see the sea, stretching away beyond the pool and the gardens, impossibly blue. Dozens of boats were moored near the shoreline and, in the distance, I could see the huge white bulk of a yacht. I wondered if it was *Rhapsody*, the one Daniel had found online that had led us here. I wondered whether Andy was looking out over the same view, somewhere close by. I wondered how on earth we were going to go about finding him.

And then I jumped out of my skin, sending a tidal wave of coffee down my top, as I heard Daniel's voice, so close I could almost have touched him, if it weren't for the whitewashed wall between us.

'Morning, Kate. Sleep well?'

How the hell did he know I was out here? My stealth door-opening clearly hadn't gone according to plan – just as well I wasn't planning a career pivot to the Secret Service any time soon.

'Coffee smells good,' Daniel went on. 'I couldn't manage to figure out the machine.'

Smugly, glad he couldn't see that I was not so much drinking it as wearing it, I said, 'It's easy. You just put the pod in, then press the button and hold it. It's so simple it's practically counter-intuitive.'

'Right. I'll give that a go. Clearly I need caffeine in order to make coffee.'

I rolled my eyes at his feeble joke, then realised he couldn't see me.

I propped my elbows on the warm stone of the balustrade, thinking about taking a photo of the view to send to Claude. But then I saw that Daniel was leaning on his balcony wall too, gazing towards the sea.

'Did you enjoy your swim last night?' Might as well let him know he wasn't the only one doing a bit of spying.

'Sure did. The water's lovely. See you in fifteen minutes?'

'Right.' I caught myself remembering seeing him swimming the previous night – how his body had glided through the water as if it was his natural element – and forced down a surge of resentment – as well as forcing the image of his wet, naked torso firmly to the back of my mind.

Don't be ridiculous, Kate, I scolded myself. *The man's allowed to swim, right? Do you expect him to do it in full evening dress or something?*

I decided not to bother waiting for him. I might as well head down for breakfast on my own, check out the lie of the land and find a table – as soon as I'd changed into a top that wasn't covered in coffee.

I slipped my feet into flip-flops, perched my sunglasses on top of my head and tucked my key card into the pocket of my shorts, then made my way downstairs to the main building, where we'd been told breakfast was served. By the time Daniel arrived, I was seated at a table overlooking the swimming pool, a plate of fresh cherries and watermelon in front of me.

Daniel was evidently straight out of the shower. He smelled of the same citrussy shower gel I'd found in my own bathroom, and his hair curled damply over the neckline of his T-shirt. (*Why don't you go to a bloody barber?* I thought. *Instead of slobbing around like some 1990s raver way past his sell-by date?*) And he clearly hadn't bothered to shave – the designer stubble I'd noticed when we'd met for coffee a couple of days before was now looking more like an attempted beard.

'There you are.' He flashed a smile at me, and I felt myself smiling back, against my will and better judgement. 'Food first, then a plan? Is that all you're having?'

I ate my last cherry, placing the pit on the plate along with the others, their stalks and a small heap of watermelon seeds. Fleetingly, I remembered the rhyme my granny had taught me for counting cherry stones to predict your future husband's occupation: *Tinker, tailor, soldier, sailor, rich man, poor man, beggar man, thief.*

Any ideas I might have had about the desirability of

marrying a rich man would have been kiboshed by the impossibility of stopping after five cherries.

'This was just the warm-up round,' I said. 'You should see the buffet – it's incredible.'

'Right then, lead me to it.'

He followed me indoors and we both loaded plates with charcuterie, pastries, bread, cheese and more kinds of olives than I'd ever seen in my life, then returned to our table and began to eat. It was a table for two, as were almost all the others, and all the other people there seemed to be couples. Several were reaching over to hold hands. One woman held her partner's gaze and whispered something to him, and they both giggled. Another man was literally peeling grapes and popping them into his girlfriend's mouth with his fingers, one at a time.

I was willing to bet that none of them were looking at me and Daniel and thinking: *Oooh, couple goals!*

'So,' Daniel said, tearing off a chunk of bread and dipping it in olive oil, 'I reckon we start by ringing round the hotels here and asking if Andy's staying there.'

'What, in your fluent Turkish?'

Daniel looked taken aback. 'True. I mean, I'm sure most people speak some English, but—'

'From "I'd like a large glass of rosé" to "We're trying to locate our friend, who travelled here about a month ago, and might or might not be staying at your fine establishment" is quite the stretch.'

'I guess it is,' Daniel admitted with a grimace. 'So I guess we're going to have to—'

'Go round in person?' I suggested. I'd already reached this conclusion, but I knew Daniel was more likely to buy into it if he reached it himself, independently of me.

'There's still going to be a language issue, though, isn't there?'

'No there's not. Look.' I passed him my phone. On it was a

photo of Andy, taken from my Facebook feed and cropped to show his face as distinctly as possible. Typed underneath were a few words in Turkish.

'What does that say?'

'It says, "Our friend Andy Sinclair has gone missing in the area. Have you seen him?"'

'So you do speak the language?'

'Of course not. But Google Translate does.'

Gratifyingly, Daniel looked quite impressed. 'Nice work. You could go far.'

'I already have. Almost two thousand miles, I believe.'

'I meant...'

I took pity on him. 'I know what you meant. Now, are we done stuffing our faces, because it's half nine and if we're going to track down Andy, we might as well get started.'

'Whatever you say, boss.' Daniel stood up with a mock-deferential salute.

I hope he's not going to keep that up, I thought. *It could get very old, very quickly.*

'We may as well start here,' I said.

I led the way to the reception desk and showed the smiling woman my phone. She looked bewildered for a second, then said in perfect English, 'No, Mr Sinclair hasn't been a guest here. Perhaps you might like to try other hotels in Alsaya? I can provide a list.'

Behind me, I swore I could hear a faint snigger come from Daniel. I resisted the urge to step backwards, faux-accidentally, and lean my full weight on his smug toes.

The receptionist turned to her computer and seconds later handed me a sheet of A4 paper. There were around fifty names on it, together with addresses and telephone numbers.

Daunted by the scale of the task, I thanked her, and Daniel and I trooped out of the front door, where we stood in the sunshine looking down at the printout.

'It's a big ask,' he said uncertainly.

I shrugged. 'You got a better idea?'

He hesitated, then shook his head. He was close enough for me to feel his hair brush against my cheek; close enough for a whisper of a different, more lemony fragrance to reach me.

'It's pretty warm. Sure you don't need a hat?'

As if I was going to trot off to my room and fetch one on his instructions, like a compliant child. 'I'll be fine. It's not exactly the middle of summer.'

'Even so. There's a heatwave, apparently. My weather app said it's going to be unseasonably hot – pushing thirty degrees. I guess that's global warming for you.'

'Global warming or not, I still don't need a hat.'

He shrugged. 'Right. I'll get the map up on my phone and we'll get cracking.'

But we couldn't get cracking right away, because the list of hotels was in alphabetical order, not in order of their proximity to our own hotel. After much frowning and tapping at his screen, Daniel disappeared inside again and came out with a pencil. He took the list from me and placed ticks alongside a dozen or so of the names.

'Those ones are closest,' he said.

'Turquoise Villas looks like it's right round the corner.'

'We may as well walk – it hardly seems worth taking the car.'

'Good shout. I could do without being terrified by your driving again.'

'What the hell's wrong with my driving?'

I looked up at his furious scowl, trying not to let the smile that was threatening to crack my face open show. I'd definitely found a vulnerability there, and I was going to have fun exploiting it.

'Evidently you think something is,' I said, 'or you wouldn't be so defensive about it.'

'Just as well you're so keen on walking,' he countered, 'because you're going to be doing a *lot* of it.'

He led the way down the stairs into the street. The day was hot already – I could feel the heat of the pavement coming through the thin soles of my shoes and the sun prickling the back of my neck.

But by midday, it was even hotter. We'd visited fourteen hotels and drawn fourteen blanks. Fourteen smiling faces had dropped into seriousness when they heard our request; fourteen heads had shaken sadly. One guy had gone off to find his colleague, and my heart had leaped with hope, but then it was the colleague who did the face-falling and head-shaking.

I couldn't help noticing that when it was Daniel holding out his phone with the message and picture on it, rather than me, there was a lot more smiling and the head-shaking looked genuinely regretful. I remembered Daniel's easy charm from back in the day, before it had well and truly stopped working on me, and it was disconcerting to see it in action again. It made me feel – not resentful, exactly, but... well, resentful. Although I couldn't quite explain to myself why that might be.

We'd seen rustic hotels and luxurious ones, large ones and small. We'd walked through paved side streets and along the main waterfront promenade. We'd passed shops selling yacht paraphernalia and shops selling groceries and shops selling Turkish delight.

And we'd passed more cats than I'd ever seen in my life: tabby ones, black ones, ginger ones, white ones and ones that were a mixture of all those colours. Short-haired ones and fluffy ones. Timid ones and friendly ones. And every time Daniel saw one, he insisted on stopping, talking to it, making clicking noises with his tongue to encourage it to approach him and fussing it if it did.

If it hadn't been for the cats, I reckoned we'd have got through at least half a dozen more hotels.

'Do you have to?' I asked as Daniel squatted down, holding out a hand towards a scrawny ginger cat he'd spotted reclining in the shade of a parked car.

He looked up at me in surprise. 'What's wrong?'

'The cats. Every single one, every single time.'

The ginger cat stood up, stretching languorously, and strolled towards him, taking its time.

'Do you not like cats?' he asked, letting it sniff his fingers before he embarked on an extensive ear-scratching session.

'I mean, I don't mind cats. I'm not an animal hater.'

The cat flopped onto its side, then rolled over on its back, and Daniel stroked its belly, talking nonsense to it.

'We should buy some treats for them,' he said. 'They're all pretty thin, but they're clearly well looked after.'

'Really? What's wrong with that one's ear then?'

'When charities trap feral cats and neuter them so they can be released and not cause a cat population boom, they clip the tip off one of their ears,' he explained.

'Why? Isn't that cruel?'

He looked up at me, his eyes hidden behind his sunglasses. 'I don't suppose they love it. But it's for the best long-term. Otherwise there'd be loads more of them, and they'd be starving and sick. That would be a whole lot crueller.'

'Oh.' I squatted next to him and extended my hand as I'd seen him do.

He made the clicking noise again. 'Come on then, say hello to Auntie Kate.'

I attempted the noise, but what came out sounded more like I was trying to suck in a strand of spaghetti. 'It doesn't understand English, anyway,' I pointed out.

'True. We should try Google Translating, "Who's a good cat then?" into Turkish.'

In spite of myself, I laughed, startling the cat, who squirmed back onto all fours and regarded me suspiciously, then turned and stalked off, its tail at half-mast.

'It didn't like me,' I said, feeling absurdly offended.

'More like it knew you didn't like it,' Daniel replied, then added under his breath, 'Kind of know how that feels.'

'What did you say?'

'You heard me.'

'Oh, for God's sake! Look, Daniel, we're here for a reason. We're here to find Andy. Or to try and find him. We don't have to be best mates, right? We just have to get the fuck on with it.'

Still squatting, I eased the strap of my flip-flop away from my skin. The plastic had rubbed blisters on the tops of my feet, and then the blisters had burst and left raw patches, so that every step, for the past half hour or so, had hurt. The base of my neck between my hair and my T-shirt felt hot and angry, and I knew I had sunburn. I thought longingly of the pool and my dimly lit, air-conditioned room where there were no cats and no Daniel.

'So let's get the fuck on with it then,' he said, rising effort-lessly off his heels like someone had fixed a string to the top of his head and setting off in the direction of the next hotel, leaving me limping and sweating in his wake.

ELEVEN

We stopped for a bite of lunch shortly after that, but it was too hot to eat much. Daniel had a chicken kebab and a beer; I picked at some salad then had an ice cream. Again, I thought longingly of my cool bedroom and the turquoise water of the hotel pool. Even the sea looked inviting, but I dreaded to think how badly the salt water would sting my poor shredded feet.

Daniel noticed me limping and asked if I was okay, but I kept my game face on and insisted I was fine.

'Sure? You don't want to head back for a break? And maybe pick up a hat? It's hot as hell out here.'

Of course I need a break – and a damn hat. But we needed to find Andy, who for all I knew could have far worse problems than sunburn and blisters.

'Nope, let's push on.'

And so on we pushed. Gradually, we were checking off the places on the map that were nearest to our home base; Daniel was having to zoom out on his phone to make out our next destination, and the one after that was even further, inland a bit, towards the forested mountains that reared up behind the town.

'Who even stays there?' I asked. 'Why would you want to be so far from the beach?'

'Not everyone comes here for the beach,' Daniel pointed out. 'There's other stuff too. Adventure sports, archaeology. People like different things.'

I thought of Claude and wondered if adventure sports were his thing when he went on holiday. I suspected they would be.

'We can go and get the car if you'd rather?' Daniel said. 'Picking holes in my driving skills might cheer you up a bit.'

'Look, I'm fine,' I snapped. 'I'm not some pampered princess who can't even walk on her own two feet, you know. And you're not my chauffeur – and if you were, I'd sack you.'

Daniel's face said quite clearly that a pampered princess was exactly what he thought I was, but he replied, 'All right. Sorry I asked.'

At the next hotel, the only person we could find was a chambermaid pushing a cart laden with sheets, towels and cleaning products along a cobbled walkway between rustic-looking chalets. I showed her my phone and she smiled sweetly but shook her head and raised her hands in helpless incomprehension, before turning back to her work.

'Next one's a way away,' Daniel warned. 'Back down on the seafront, but right on the other side of town.'

I glanced at my watch. It was coming up to four o'clock, the hottest part of the day. Vast clouds hovered over the mountains but seemed unable to scale their peaks, giving no shade or promise of rain.

I wished I'd worn a hat. And put sunblock on my neck. And chosen more comfortable shoes. And stayed at home, instead of embarking on this futile mission.

Actually, what I really wished was that Andy had stayed at home in the first place, safe in his bijou apartment in Manchester, leaving voice notes for me on WhatsApp, so none of this palaver would have been necessary and I could have got the train up there and given him a massive hug and taken him out for afternoon tea at The Edwardian.

'Come on then,' I said to Daniel, shaking myself out of my thoughts. 'Let's do it.'

Daniel turned down the narrow street. Twenty minutes and eight cats later (I'd started counting them, after lunch. It seemed as good a way as any to pass the time, given neither of us had much to offer in the way of sparkling conversation), we reached the place.

The previous few had been modest establishments, small and inexpensive looking. This was something else again – a glitzy resort with its five-star rating prominently displayed on the low stone wall that surrounded it. We walked through glass doors into blissful, air-conditioned cold and were immediately approached by a waiter bearing a tray with two glasses of fruit juice on it, their sides frosted with condensation, flanked by napkins twisted into the shape of swans.

Welcome to honeymoon central, I thought sourly.

'We're not...' I began, but the waiter smiled and extended his tray towards us. The temptation was too much for me and I took a glass and sipped gratefully. The juice was sweet but also slightly tangy – passionfruit, maybe? Daniel downed the contents of his in a few long swallows, and together we approached the reception desk.

'Good afternoon.' The dark-haired woman behind it smiled as warmly as her colleague. 'How may I help you?'

'We're trying to find our friend,' I began the familiar spiel, taking out my phone and showing her the screen. 'Any chance he's been staying here?'

For the first time that afternoon, I felt a sense of genuine hope – this was Andy's kind of place. I hadn't been able to picture him in any of the modest two-star guesthouses, but I one hundred per cent could imagine him here.

But the woman shook her head, an expression of blank

puzzlement on her face.

Then her eyes widened, and she spun her wheeled chair around and said a few words in Turkish.

Another woman appeared from the back office, and the two of them conferred rapidly, their faces bent over the screen, their eyes occasionally flickering up to sneak a glance at Daniel.

'We think *maybe* we saw him,' the first woman explained. 'He's not staying here, but my friend thinks she might know where he was staying. It was one week ago, maybe more.'

Her colleague hurried away again, and we waited. I finished my juice and returned the glass to the waiter, then leaned my arms gratefully on the cool, polished wood of the reception counter.

The second woman emerged again, holding a printed brochure which she handed to her colleague with a few words of Turkish.

'We think maybe you could try here,' her friend explained, handing over the brochure.

It was an A4 sheet folded into three. On the front were the words 'Wild Maple Eco Resort'. I flipped it open and saw pictures of people hiking up a mountainside, a swimming pool that appeared hewn out of natural rock, hands massaging a woman's back. It was printed on the kind of recycled paper that has bits in it.

'Thank you,' Daniel said. 'You've been incredibly helpful. We'll give it a try.'

'It's up in the mountains,' the woman warned. 'Maybe five kilometres? They don't allow cars up there to protect the...' Her excellent English exhausted, she waved a hand vaguely towards the doors.

'The environment?' Daniel suggested.

'Yes. The ecology,' she said, smiling at him.

Daniel smiled back, and for a second, the two of them held each other's eyes. I felt a fresh flare of resentment. I was sweaty, sunburned and bedraggled, with blisters on my feet, while he still looked as fresh as he had at breakfast, his legs beneath his khaki shorts beginning to tan slightly, his white T-shirt unmarked by sweat.

'Please thank your colleague for us, too,' he said, handing over some cash.

The woman waved it away, but he insisted. I added my thanks, and we pushed the door open again, the heat meeting us like a slap in the face.

'This feels like progress,' Daniel said, grinning.

'Really? I'm not sure. Can you imagine Andy staying at a place like that?'

We looked at each other. I was remembering all the times Andy had joked about vegetarians being lettuce-botherers, moaned about climate-change protestors blocking the motorway when he was trying to drive from Manchester to London to see us, complained about the relentless tedium of sorting out his recycling.

'Well, people change,' Daniel said firmly. 'And anyway, maybe Ash is into all that stuff, and Andy went along with it to impress him. Anyway, let's get back. I don't know about you, but I'm not up for heading there today.'

'If Andy's there this afternoon, he'll still be there tomorrow,' I agreed, concealing my relief that I was to be spared more walking for the time being.

'I reckon this calls for a celebration,' Daniel said. 'Why don't we go out for dinner when it gets cooler?'

I was too hot, knackered and footsore to protest, and besides, Daniel was already striding away, the good news making him walk even faster than usual.

Forty-five minutes (and fifteen cats) later, I collapsed on my bed, kicking off my shoes to inspect my painful feet. What had the woman said – a five-kilometre walk and no cars allowed? But that was tomorrow's problem.

First, I had a celebration dinner with Daniel to look forward to (about as much as I looked forward to a session with the woman who waxed my bits).

But before that, I was just going to lie down, letting the cool air wash over my body, relishing not being in the sun, not being with a man who seemed to think it was his due to reduce women to simpering compliance by smiling at them, and not having to stop every five minutes to pet another bloody cat.

I closed my eyes, listening to the distant sound of gulls swooping over the water and the nearer voices of children playing in the pool...

A soft tap on the door woke me, and I sprang upright, bewildered. It was quarter to eight. I was due to meet Daniel in fifteen minutes and I was nowhere close to ready. And what if that was him knocking at my door, and he'd find me still sweat-stained and dishevelled, with sleep in my eyes and the dust of the road still on my blistered feet?

But it was only a delivery of fresh bottled water, which I gratefully accepted before hurrying to shower.

As soon as the first drops of water hit my shin, I knew I was in trouble. What I'd thought was a bit of sunburn was clearly much worse; even the lukewarm water felt like it was being poured on my neck and shoulders from a freshly boiled kettle. In the mirror, as I towelled off, I could see my skin was lobster-red. There was a stark line on my thighs where my shorts ended: pasty-white flesh above it and angry scarlet below.

'Shit,' I muttered.

I didn't care if Daniel found me attractive – quite the reverse. But there was no doubt that turning up for dinner looking like the love child of a cauliflower and a tomato would put me at a disadvantage. And, to make matters worse, I'd slept for so long that I had zero time to do my make-up and cover up

– I peered more closely at my reflection – the scattering of freckles that had emerged across my cheeks and nose.

Like I say, I didn't care what Daniel thought of me. We were here for the sole purpose of finding Andy. But that didn't mean I wanted him to see me looking like Darla from *Finding Nemo*. But even worse would be turning up late and fully made-up. That would reinforce Daniel's belief that I was high-maintenance, hard work and rude.

I was stuck between a rock and a hard place. But I was also hungry, and the prospect of an icy gin and tonic made my mind up for me. I dragged on a white cotton maxi skirt and a grey T-shirt that covered up the worst of the redness, and forced my throbbing feet into trainers, throwing my treacherous flip-flops into a corner of the room.

I opened my door at exactly the same moment as Daniel emerged from his room. He looked infuriatingly cool and composed. The tan I'd noticed emerging earlier had deepened, and I was sure there were even new, lighter streaks in his hair. He smelled faintly of some kind of juniper fragrance, and his pale pink linen shirt looked freshly pressed.

When he saw me, his face registered alarm. He reached out and eased the neckline of my top over my shoulder. His hand was cool, as if he'd been for another of his swims.

'Jesus, Kate. That looks really sore.'

'Yes, master of the fucking obvious,' I said. 'Sunburn hurts. Shall we go?'

'I knew you should have—' he began, and then stopped.

'Should have what?' *If you so much as utter the word 'hat', I'll go back in, fetch my flip-flops, and beat you to death with them*, I thought.

'Nothing.' Daniel headed down the stairs. 'Shouldn't you put aloe vera on it or something?'

'Probably, if I had aloe vera. Which I don't.'

'I'm sure we can get some in town.'

'Look, it's fine. I'll live.' *And be peeling like a human lychee in the morning.*

'Well, if you're sure. It's your skin. There's a place down by the waterfront that does decent seafood, apparently. Fancy that?'

'Sure, whatever you want.'

Although why he wanted to watch the sunset with waves lapping at our feet and eat shellfish like this was some kind of romantic date was utterly beyond me.

We walked together down to the shoreline. The sun was disappearing behind the mountain on the far side of the bay, only a golden sliver still visible, illuminating the banks of dark cloud with bands of amber and crimson. In the evening light, the sea had lost its intense blue and faded to a gleaming silver. Drifts of sand crunched beneath my feet on the cobblestones. The air was cooling.

We walked for about ten minutes, past bars and restaurants and coffee shops, merging with a passing parade of people heading out for the evening: couples strolling hand in hand, families with babies in buggies, groups of giggling teenagers.

It appeared to be the dinner hour for the local cats, too – outside many of the restaurants were bowls and plates full of food, furry heads buried deep in them.

At last, Daniel stopped. 'Will this do?'

'Looks great.'

As he'd promised, the restaurant was right on the water, a wooden jetty protruding into the sea set with white-clothed tables. I glanced at the menu by the entrance and could see nothing to complain about.

'Take a seat,' he said. 'Order some wine. I'll be right back.'

Relieved, I sank into a chair and waved over a waiter, ordering another bottle of rosé (because, after all, what other wine is there when you're abroad and it's hot?) and a gin and tonic for myself. I took a long, cooling gulp, then snapped a

photo of the scene to send to Claude and to the Girlfriends'
Club WhatsApp. I knew Claude wouldn't respond – he'd still
be at work, given the time difference – but my friends did.

*Kate: So we're here. No sign of Andy yet but a promising lead
to follow up tomorrow.*

*Rowan: But what we all need to know is... Have you and
Daniel killed each other yet?*

*Kate: Well, he hasn't killed me, otherwise I wouldn't be
posting.*

Abbie: Have you actually, like, made friends?

*Kate: Like I said, there's been no bloodshed. That's as good as
it's going to get, I reckon.*

*Naomi: God, that view! It looks heavenly. You lucky thing, on
holiday with a hot man.*

*Kate: Not a hot man. He's got wanky hair. Although every
woman we've seen today has been simpering over him like he's
Chris Hemsworth or something. Guess they like wanky hair
over here.*

Abbie: Harsh! I quite like long hair on a man.

*Rowan: And those biceps! If it wasn't for Alex, I so would.
Actually, if it wasn't for Alex and us having been mates for so
long. It would feel like fancying my own brother.*

*Naomi: Go on, Kate, admit it. You do fancy him, just a bit.
Don't you?*

Kate: Not one tiny bit. Gotta go, he's coming back.

But instead of sliding into the seat opposite mine, Daniel walked behind me – and stopped. I looked up and saw him reach into his pocket and take out a small, green-and-white plastic bottle. He snapped open the top, and a second later I felt blissful cold on my sunburned neck.

'Aloe vera gel,' Daniel said matter-of-factly.

His hands were gentle against my skin, spreading the soothing coolness lower down over my shoulders. Even the smell of it, herbal and medicinal, felt instantly healing.

'Thanks,' I muttered.

'Do you mind if I...' He eased my bra strap aside to make sure he didn't miss anywhere. Fleetingly, I caught myself considering asking him to do my legs as well, then cringed so hard at the idea I almost turned inside out.

'Thanks,' I said again. 'It's okay. I can do it.'

'Pretty much done now.' He recapped the bottle and put it on the table between us. 'Take that back with you and put more on before you go to bed. It won't actually do much, but it does take some of the heat out.'

'I appreciate it,' I said. I'd finished my gin, so I poured wine into both our glasses. The waiter approached to take our order, and we picked an assortment of random items from the menu, then clinked our glasses together in a tentative toast.

'So,' Daniel said. 'Tomorrow we find Andy. Hopefully.'

'Hopefully,' I echoed. 'Although I've got to admit, I'm not looking forward much to trekking up that mountain.'

I gestured inland. The sun had fully set now, and the hills reared up behind the town, dark and forbidding. It would be a whole lot more forbidding, I realised, in full sunlight.

'You don't have to go if you don't want to,' Daniel said. 'I can manage on my own.'

'Yeah, right. With your fluent Turkish.'

'Hey, I can use Google Translate just as well as you can.' He smiled, the corners of his grey eyes crinkling. 'And I can read a map.'

'Multi-skilled or what?' Then I added, almost thinking out loud, 'He must be with Ash. He'd never go to some eco retreat thing like that on his own.'

'Maybe. I guess we'll soon find out.'

'And Ash must be pretty special to him,' I went on. 'I can't actually remember the last time Andy was serious enough about anyone to spend more than a few nights with them, never mind travel halfway across Europe for them.'

'I could say the same about you.' Daniel wasn't smiling any more – his face was serious.

'What? What do you mean?'

Before he could reply, the waiter appeared with plates of food. There was salad made with ripe tomatoes, cucumber, feta cheese and olives. There was a basket of pillowy bread and bowls of hummus and taramasalata to dip it in. There was a vast platter of huge prawns with rice, fried potatoes and gauze-wrapped lemon halves.

'I don't think we ordered enough food,' Daniel joked, tearing a piece of bread and scooping up some dip.

'Yes, we'll starve for sure.' I speared an olive and ate it, then filled up our wine. 'What were you saying, just now? About me?'

Daniel shrugged. 'Just that you've been single for ages too. Same as Andy. No one serious in your life.'

I felt my face flame and reassured myself with the knowledge that there was no way he'd notice, thanks to the sunburn.

'Yeah, poor me. I lie alone every night thinking about getting old and shrivelled and then no man will ever want me, because what other purpose in life could I possibly have?'

'I didn't mean that. God, Kate, you don't have to be so defensive.'

'I'm not being defensive. Am I not allowed to question the idea that because I'm not half of a couple I'm somehow failing at life?'

'And I didn't say that, either.'

'I'll have you know there are plenty of men in my life, anyway. I'm dating a guy I met at my last job. He's called Claude. He's French. Lives in Chelsea.'

'That's what I've always admired about you, Kate. You're not one bit shallow.'

'And you're not one bit funny,' I retorted. 'He's also highly intelligent, successful and does triathlons for charity.'

Daniel peeled a prawn and ate it, then presented the head to a passing cat, which immediately stationed itself under his chair, hoping for more. Seconds later, three of its friends joined it.

'Wow. Sounds like a lovely guy. How long have you been seeing him?'

I gave the cats a prawn head, too, mostly so I could briefly hide my face behind the tablecloth. I felt like I'd walked into a trap.

'Umm, not long.'

'How long's not long? I mean, tell me to butt out if you want. I'm just making conversation.'

Which meant I now couldn't tell him to butt out without making it sound as if I didn't want to have a conversation.

'Like, a week. Only since I left my last job. But I've known him a while, because we worked together.'

'And how many dates? Two? Three? Just curious to know how fast the guy moves.'

'Only one. If you must know.'

'And how did it go? What did you do? I'm thinking coffee, bowling, movie?'

'We're not fifteen, you know. Actually, he took me on a hot-air balloon ride.'

Daniel's mouth twitched. 'Really? Bet that went down like a bucket of cold sick.'

I couldn't help laughing. 'It wasn't the best call ever, I'm not going to lie. But it's not his fault I can't stand heights. When I get back after... after this, I'll probably see him again and hopefully that won't be some death-defying extreme sport.'

'Hot-air ballooning's not exactly death-defying. Isn't it meant to be quite safe?'

'It certainly didn't feel that way,' I admitted. 'Anyway, you're single, too, so why are you judging Andy and me for being?'

'I'm not judging anyone. Just making conversation, like I said. Want that last prawn?'

'And now you're avoiding answering my question. I'm full – the cats can have it.'

Daniel shelled the prawn and carefully divided it into five – for by now there were that many cats milling around the legs of our chairs: one ginger and white, two black and white, a plain black and a tabby.

'Which would you choose, if you could only take one of them home?' Daniel asked.

'Which what?'

'Cat, obviously.'

'But I don't want a cat.'

'Just as well, because you're not getting one. It's hypothetical.'

'The tabby one, then.'

I reached over and nabbed one of the prawn pieces from Daniel's plate and fed it to the tabby cat. Its nose was soft against my fingers, but the nip of its teeth as it took the morsel was sharp.

'Why that one?' he asked.

'She's beautiful. Look at her white whiskers and her amber eyes.'

'Thought you didn't like cats.' He grinned, divvying up the rest of the prawn between the others. There was a tiny scrap left, which I gave to my new tabby friend.

As if they knew their run of luck had come to an end, the cats meandered off, tails in the air, searching for their next mark.

'Maybe I do, a bit. But you still haven't answered my question.'

'Want dessert? Coffee?'

'Not coffee. I'll struggle to sleep tonight as it is.'

'Because your neck hurts?'

I shook my head. 'I usually sleep badly. And tonight – I'll be thinking about what happens tomorrow.'

Daniel signalled for the bill, and the waiter brought it over with two shot glasses of some clear liqueur and a little plate of cubed Turkish delight. I took a piece, licking the sugar off one side before biting into it, while he settled the bill. I was fine with that; I'd paid for our first four nights' accommodation and we'd agreed we'd work everything out at the end – whenever that would be.

'This is amazing. Usually it tastes like soap,' I said.

Daniel gave a half-smile. 'You're in the habit of eating soap? I knew you were weird.'

'And I knew you were a dick. And you still haven't—'

'Answered your question. What was it again?'

I found I couldn't remember, so I asked a new one. 'Why are you single?'

'Haven't found the right person, I guess.'

'What went wrong with you and Carla, anyway?'

It wasn't like Daniel and I socialised together regularly, but I remembered him having turned up at the occasional get-togethers we'd both attended, over the course of two years or so, with a willowy blonde woman whose name – if you'd asked me five seconds before – I'd have said I had no recollection of.

'Carla wanted to get married and settle down, have kids,

stuff like that. I didn't. Not then, and probably – with her anyway – not ever.'

'Why not?'

'I just didn't feel that way about her. And it felt unfair to string her along, so we had a couple of tough conversations and called it a day.'

'Wow. So marriage and kids aren't your bag?'

'I'd love to get married and have kids, with the right person. Guess I'm just not prepared to settle – and no one's settling with me, so...' He spread his palms upwards in a shrug.

I blinked in surprise. Daniel wasn't my cup of tea – wouldn't be even if I was in the desert dying of thirst – but I'd seen the way all those women had looked at him today. I remembered my friends' casual mentions of his attractiveness, as if it was common knowledge. Even though I'd barely been able to recall her name, I could remember the adoring way beautiful blonde Carla had gazed at him as she hung on to his arm.

There'd be plenty of women willing to settle for Daniel, I reckoned. Ideally before they found out how infuriating he was, and after they frogmarched him to the nearest barber.

Then I noticed the waiter hovering by our table, and a small queue of people waiting to be seated. I picked up my shot glass and downed the contents, wincing at the strong aniseed flavour, and said, 'Come on – let's go.'

Daniel drank his too and we stood up. We walked back to our hotel through the balmy night in near-silence. I didn't know what Daniel was thinking about, and my own thoughts were a chaotic jumble of Andy, Claude, raki, food and sun. We said a brief goodnight outside our rooms and I fell into bed, only after smearing more aloe vera on my skin.

Its coldness and fragrance brought back the memory of Daniel's hands in a way that was strangely pleasant and totally unsettling.

TWELVE

Whatever miracle the gods of sleep had bestowed upon me the previous night, that night they were clearly off out on the lash somewhere – possibly with the sun god. Because the second I turned out the light, I knew that sleep wasn't going to come.

I lay in the air-conditioned room between the cool sheets and felt like I was burning up. Every inch of my skin felt tight and sore, so that when I closed my eyes, I could literally picture it peeling off me in sheets and had to switch the light on again to check that it wasn't. When I applied yet more aloe vera, all I could think about was Daniel's gentle hands and his concerned, yet slightly appraising, grey eyes – that and the fact that even beautiful Carla hadn't been good enough for him.

When I forced his face out of my mind, it was replaced by Andy's, his familiar mocking smile taunting me. *Haven't found me yet, have you? Doesn't look like you're trying all that hard, Katie babe, at least not from where I'm standing.* Not that I knew where that was.

And then my mind turned to the mission we had scheduled for the morning – the long walk up into the mountains. Daniel would be striding ahead, I was sure, those long, tanned legs in his stupid cargo shorts carrying him effortlessly upwards while I puffed along in his wake, getting hotter and hotter and falling further and further behind.

I'd probably get lost, and then Daniel would have two missing-in-action people to search for instead of just the one.

Damn it.

Questing for something pleasant and soothing to think about, I reached in my brain for Claude. Handsome, successful Claude, who seemed to genuinely fancy me in spite of me almost vomming on his Comme des Garçons trainers. Or did he still? If there was anything guaranteed to change his mind, it was that. Perhaps he'd told all my former team what had happened, and they'd tell other people in the industry and soon I wouldn't be able to find work at all, and if I did I'd be greeted on my first day with, 'Oh, aren't you the woman who spewed all over Claude Anjambé?' And then they'd laugh and – worst of all – I'd have to laugh too, to prove I was a good sport and didn't care what people thought of me.

If I was at home, I'd be able to get up and bake, filling my flat with the soothing smell of hot butter and sugar, my mind focusing on whisking egg whites to stiff peaks, crumb-coating, chocolate work or piping perfect buttercream rosettes. But I wasn't, so I couldn't.

I could only lie still, focusing on relaxing each bit of my body in turn (knowing that by the time I reached my toes, my forehead would have tensed up again and I've have to start over) and hope that eventually I'd get at least a little sleep.

I must have slept at some point during the night. I'd read enough about insomnia to know that people always overestimate the time during a restless night they spend awake. Certainly, when my alarm buzzed at six, I was deeply asleep, even if it felt like it had only been for ten minutes. But I had to get up – Daniel had insisted on an early start to get the long walk out of the way before it got too hot.

It had seemed like a good plan at the time. Now, not so much.

And when I met Daniel at breakfast, even less so.

I turned up a few minutes after our appointed meeting time of seven, having had a shot at erasing the black rings under my eyes with concealer, taming the Brillo pad my hair had morphed into overnight and sticking down the flakes of dead skin that had erupted on my neck, shoulders and legs with factor 50 sunblock.

In contrast, Daniel looked rested and positively glowing with health, tucking into a massive feed of what looked like spicy sausage with fried eggs on top of it, served in an actual frying pan. My mouth watered at the smell, but at the same time, my stomach churned queasily at the idea of so much saturated fat before I'd even got a coffee down me.

'Morning, Kate,' he said chirpily, once he'd swallowed a shovel-sized forkful of trans-fatty acid. 'Sleep well?'

'No.' I sat down opposite him and managed not to kiss the waiter who came over to take my order for coffee. 'What the hell is that you're eating?'

Daniel took another forkful. There was cheese in there too, I noticed – a melty string of it hung down off his fork. 'Traditional Turkish breakfast. Unpronounceable, but I showed it on my phone to the guy at the omelette station and they made it for me. Want to try some?'

He held out a laden fork, but I shook my head. 'It's way too early for me. I'll grab some pastries, and then shall we head off?'

Daniel nodded, still troughing away. I drank my coffee and ate my breakfast, looking out at the sun sparkling on the water of the pool and creating rainbows where the sprinklers arced over the green lawn. At last he was done, having mopped the last bits of cheese out of the pan with chunks of bread.

'Ready?' he asked.

'Ready as I'll ever be.'

We set off along the path that led to the beach. At first it was smooth and paved, leading through the manicured hotel gardens past lemon trees laden with fruit, golden on the side where the sun rose, still green on the other. There were olive trees too, gnarled and twisted, crowned with silvery-green leaves.

After a few minutes, the path divided. To our right, it continued smoothly towards the beach; to our left a gravel track led upwards into the hills. Almost at once, the manicured gardens gave way to a more rustic environment: chickens scratched and pecked in a wooden enclosure, birds sang in the trees overhead, the ground turned uneven beneath our feet.

Even in the shade of the tall sycamore trees that lined the path, the air was hot. The path led upwards, gently at first and then more steeply. Stones slid beneath the soles of my trainers. Ahead of me, Daniel's long brown legs powered easily forward. I could feel sweat snaking down my back and into my eyes, which stung as the sunblock melted off my face.

Daniel turned to me, his phone in his hand. 'Reckon we've come about a kilometre so far. Four or so to go.'

I nodded, not trusting myself to speak. *Come on, Kate. Woman up. It's just a walk.*

But the sleepless night, the pain of my sunburn and my ever-present worry about Andy made it seem more arduous than that. I felt almost disembodied, as if my legs were moving against my will, my feet treading where Daniel's did, my eyes focused on the ground in front of me, only occasionally looking up to see the strong V of his back, the lean lines of his glutes and thighs.

I could feel sweat stinging yesterday's blisters. Pressure that had been building behind my eyes threatened to turn into a proper headache, becoming more intense with every beat of my heart. As the path grew steeper, I could hear my breath moving harshly in my throat.

'You all right back there, Kate?' Daniel asked.

'Of course I am. It's just a hill – not exactly Mount Kilimanjaro.'

'Even so, we should have thought to bring water.'

I could see sweat darkening the back of Daniel's grey T-shirt and noticed how it clung to his muscular shoulders. *After we get to the top*, I promised myself, *I'll never have to look at his annoying, smug back ever again.*

Daniel came to another branch in the path and paused, taking out his phone again. I panted the last few metres to catch up with him. He was standing by a rustic wooden sign, three narrow boards fixed to its central post.

One pointed back the way we'd come, and onto the wood was burned the word 'Beach', followed by what I assumed was its translation in Turkish. To the left, 'Wild Maple Eco Resort' and a logo depicting a five-lobed leaf within a circle.

'That's where we're headed, right?' I panted.

'Yes, but...' Daniel pointed to the third sign. 'How can we not investigate that?'

The sign said: 'Cat feeding station'.

'Daniel, for God's sake! You don't know what it even is, or how far away it is.'

'Pretty clear, isn't it? It's where people feed cats.'

'If it's so clear then why do you need to go and look at it?'

'Because it'll be *interesting*. Come on, Kate.'

I glared at him mutinously for a second. We'd already been walking for almost an hour. If we followed the sign to our destination, we'd be there in the next fifteen minutes or so, and hopefully find Andy or at least news of him. But here was Daniel demanding we head off on some wild goose chase to look at a place where people fed cats, where there probably wouldn't even be any bloody cats because if they had an ounce of sense in their furry heads, they'd be having a nice sleep in the shade somewhere.

Then I saw the smile on his face. It was a simple, almost boyish look of pleased excitement at discovering something that might prove interesting, at exploring a new place and seeing something he hadn't expected to find. It was guileless and curious and oddly endearing.

'I didn't realise I was here with a bloody Boy Scout,' I said. 'All right, if you insist.'

Fired by enthusiasm, Daniel struck out along the path, walking even faster than before. This path was narrower than the previous one – and steeper. There were large rocks underfoot and the ground was covered in slippery pine needles. Gritting my teeth, I plodded on after him, with little hope of keeping pace.

After ten minutes or so, he'd disappeared around a bend in the path. Cursing silently, my eyes still fixed on the treacherous ground, I kept going – then rounded a corner myself and collided with his stationary back, sending him staggering forward and me staggering backward.

'Shit! I'm sorry about that.'

He turned and steadied me, his hands strong and firm on my shoulders. Up close, I could feel the heat coming off his body and smell lemon shampoo and hot man.

'Are you okay? Talk about an irresistible force meeting an immobile object.'

'You weren't immobile. I almost sent you flying.'

He smiled. 'But you're…'

'I'm what?'

'Never mind. Look at that.'

Daniel pointed. In a clearing off to the side of the path was a rough wooden structure – just a box on stilts, really, with a ramp leading up to a ledge running along its base. On the ledge I could see a few metal bowls, some filled with water but most empty. In the side of the box at the head of the ramp, a small doorway had been cut into the wood.

'So that's a cat feeding station,' I said. 'Very cute. Now can we—'

'Sssh.' Daniel put his hand on my shoulder again, and I stopped talking and stood still, watching the doorway.

A second later, a face peered out, all wide amber eyes, ears and whiskers. Then, tentatively, the rest of the cat emerged onto the ledge. It was grey and white, skinny and sinuous as a ferret, with a long, stripy tail.

'The cats up here will be properly feral,' Daniel whispered, 'not tame like the ones we saw last night in town. Let's try and not frighten it.'

The cat looked at us, its eyes alarmed and its body close to the ground, tail held low. Then it seemed to decide we were no threat, sat down and started to wash, taking its time, paying attention to every paw and every whisker. When it was done, it stood, stretched luxuriantly and padded down the ramp.

'Oh my God!' My whisper came out more like a squeak. 'Look at that!'

Following the cat was a small grey-and-white kitten. It was as round and plump as a cotton-wool ball, its tiny tail and four little legs looking as if they'd been poked onto its soft body. Its face was alert and curious, its legs still slightly unsteady as it followed its mother down the ramp.

'There's another one,' Daniel breathed.

We watched as a second kitten emerged, looked around, then followed the others. The mother cat had reached ground level now and, with a glance over her shoulder that clearly meant 'Get a move on, kids' she began to make her way into the forest. The first kitten reached the foot of the ramp and hopped off, hurrying after its mother. The second followed. And, as we watched, three more emerged from the shelter, scuttled down the ramp, did identical little hops off at the bottom and scampered away into the trees.

'Oh my God,' I said again, breaking into giggles. 'That was just so adorable.'

'Glad we came?' Daniel asked. His hand was still resting on my shoulder, I realised – but I didn't move away.

'One hundred per cent,' I said. 'How cute were they? Their little legs. Do you think they'll be okay here?'

'Who knows?' His hand left my shoulder, and he brushed his hair back off his face. 'Looked like the mum was doing her best – showing them where to find food and stuff. And with any luck they'll get tame enough to catch before they have kittens of their own.'

'And next time we come here, they'll be hanging around the fish restaurant in town,' I suggested.

And then I realised what I'd said: that there'd be a 'next time'. And that there was a 'we'.

'Anyway,' I added hastily, 'cat interlude over. Let's get moving.'

We turned to go back down the path. This time, I walked in front. I could hear Daniel's footsteps behind me and the even rhythm of his breath. We reached the signpost, and I took a photo of it to send to the Girlfriends' Club – Abbie, especially, would be obsessed with my story of the kittens, and I wished I'd thought to take a photo of them.

Watching Daniel when he saw the kittens had shifted something inside me, I realised. I mean, I'd never thought he was the kind of man who'd hunt foxes or pull the wings off flies for fun, or anything like that. But at the same time, I hadn't had him as such a complete and utter softie. There had been something in his face – a wonder, a tenderness – that had awoken a similar softness in me.

I found myself thinking, *This man would make someone an amazing father.*

He just had to find a woman who'd put up with his maddening smugness and infuriating hair first.

'So what do you reckon this eco resort place will be like then?' I asked as we turned back onto the path leading up the hillside.

'I checked out their website,' he said. 'Looks like peak woo. Lots of macrobiotic food and crystal healing and reiki and stuff. There's even a sensory deprivation chamber.'

'A *what* now?'

'Sensory deprivation chamber. It's, like, a tank you lie in, filled with highly salinated water, and they shut you in and you float in the dark.'

'God! Sounds like a recipe for a claustrophobic panic attack.'

The path had widened slightly, and Daniel increased his pace to walk alongside me. 'You don't like heights, you don't like enclosed spaces. There are lots of things that scare you, aren't there, Kate?'

Whoever ended up being the mother of Daniel's child would have to put up with a whole lot of annoying observations, too, I thought.

'There's nothing irrational about being afraid of things that are frightening,' I said.

'But why would you be frightened of lying in a tank of warm water for an hour?'

'Because what if they forgot you were there, and no one came to let you out? And it must be soundproofed because otherwise there wouldn't be sensory deprivation, so no one would hear you calling for help. And you couldn't drink the water because it's too salty and eventually you'd starve to death or suffocate or something. Obviously.'

'Wow. That's quite the leap.'

'Or,' I went on, 'there could be a zombie apocalypse while you were in there, and you'd come out and find that all essential services had shut down and only a few bands of survivors remained, scavenging for food amid the smouldering ruins of civilisation.'

'So you're scared of a zombie apocalypse too?'

'No, don't be ridiculous. That's not a real thing. When I do a risk analysis for a client, I literally never mention undead corporeal revenants.'

Daniel shook his head, making his hair flop down over his grey eyes. I heard the intake of his breath, as if he was about to say something – or laugh. But he didn't, because the path in front of us had abruptly widened and emerged from the shade of the forest.

'Looks like we're here.' I came to a relieved halt, waiting to get my breath back.

After the gloom beneath the trees, the light was suddenly brilliant, and we stood for a second, blinking in the brightness before lowering our sunglasses. Ahead of us was a garden similar to the one at our own hotel, yet entirely different. There was no lawn – instead beds of succulents and alpine plants and fine gravel filled the space between the flagstone paths. The pool looked as if it had been hewn out of the natural rock, its base and sides a deep ochre, striated with layers of grey and sandy gold. Low stone buildings were scattered up the hillside, brilliant magenta bougainvillea cladding their sides. The silver thread of a stream ran down from the mountaintop, ending in a small waterfall that I guessed fed the swimming pool below.

By the side of the pool, a woman was doing yoga on a wheat-coloured jute mat. At least, I assumed it was yoga – it was far removed from the effortful downward dog poses I'd suffered through when I'd given it a try in the gym a few years before, longing for the end bit where you get to lie on your back and examine your life choices.

She was wearing washed-out sea-green Lycra hot pants and a matching strappy sports bra. Her feet were bare, and I could make out white polish on her toenails. Her skin was an even golden brown, and a braid of almost-black hair hung down her slender back.

She glanced over when she saw us but didn't interrupt her routine – and I was glad she hadn't, because it was quite the spectacle. She did a thing where she balanced on her hands with her knees in her armpits. She bent over backwards until her palms were on the mat and then extended first one leg and then the other into a perfect, steady handstand. She stood on one leg with the other raised high above her head, her fingers gripping her toes. She dropped down into the splits, her legs extended to the front and back of her body as if it was the easiest thing in the world, her toes pointed like a ballerina's.

Randomly, I found myself remembering the last time I'd had sex, with a man I'd met on Bumble whose name I couldn't recall. At one point, he'd gripped my ankles and pushed my legs back to achieve deeper penetration (which, to be fair, was quite the challenge given that he hadn't exactly been well endowed) and I'd had to tell him to stop before I snapped a hamstring.

This woman would be able to get both feet behind her head, no problem.

Her body was incredible. She was small and slight, yet I could imagine how much strength those movements required. Her skin was as smooth as honey, but I could see powerful muscles flexing beneath it. She made it all look effortless, but there was sweat snaking down the hollow of her spine and darkening the pale fabric of her... sportswear, underwear, swimwear, whatever it was.

I sensed Daniel watching her too and heard him inhale in admiration at exactly the same points as my own throat took in a gulp of the hot air. It was as if we were watching some mystic ritual performed by a high priestess – even a goddess.

I wondered if Daniel was imagining what it would be like to fuck a woman so impossibly limber and strong, the entire *Kama Sutra* at his fingertips as they explored her silken skin and the steely muscles beneath it. I wondered if he, too, was thinking she could get her feet behind her head.

The idea made me flare with irrational hatred of her.

At last, she finished her workout, picked up a towel and swished it over her back and shoulders, then draped it around her neck, pulling her hair out over it. She grabbed an aluminium water bottle from the edge of the pool and took a few deep swallows, and I felt my own parched mouth attempt to water in sympathy.

Then she jogged towards us, her feet silent on the flagstones. Her face broke into a smile, and I noticed that her front teeth were slightly crooked. She didn't look like a goddess any more – just a regular, although exceptionally pretty, woman a couple of years younger than me.

'Hello, can I help you?' she asked. Her voice surprised me – it was a totally normal Liverpudlian accent. 'I'm the wellness manager here. My name's Ash.'

THIRTEEN

I looked at Daniel and Daniel looked at me. I couldn't see his eyes behind his sunglasses, but I was sure they were wide with surprise, as I knew my own were.

Actually, surprise was an understatement. I felt shocked, as if all the air had been driven out of my body and my stomach was whooshing upwards to fill the space it had left. I felt like I'd felt when the turbulence had hit us on the plane, or like I'd been standing on the jute yoga mat and some prankster had whipped it out from beneath my feet.

'Are you—' I managed to say, before running out of words.

'Do you know Andy Sinclair?' Daniel completed the question, although not the one I'd been about to ask.

The smile dropped off Ash's face, and frown lines appeared in the smooth skin between her eyebrows.

'Andy? Of course. Oh my God. Has something happened to him?'

'We don't know,' Daniel said. 'That's why we're here. We've come out from London to try and find him.'

'My name's Kate,' I said, my voice coming hoarsely from my dry throat.

'Daniel,' Daniel said.

Ash didn't offer to shake hands. She looked at us for a moment, concerned but wary.

Then she said, 'You'd better come inside.'

We followed her round the pool and into one of the low buildings. A bar stretched across its far side, a bright multi-hued woven rug covered the stone floor, and cream armchairs were arranged in groups around low tables. Ash gestured to one of them, and we sat down. A waitress appeared with a tray holding three glasses and a jug of iced water, cucumber and lemon slices floating in it.

'Would you prefer tea?' Ash asked. 'I'm afraid we don't serve alcohol here.'

'Water would be great, thanks,' I said.

Ash poured carefully, and Daniel and I took deep, thirsty swallows. I could see that her hand was trembling when she set the jug back on the table.

'So, you're friends of Andy's?' she asked.

I nodded. 'We hadn't heard from him in a while and he wasn't answering his phone. So we flew out from London to try and locate him.'

'How did you find... I mean, how did you even know to look here?'

Quickly, Daniel summed up the detective work we'd done so far.

'Andy left over a week ago,' Ash said, taking a sip of water. I imagined that her mouth must be dry with shock, too. 'I thought he'd be home by now. I mean, he said he was going home. He was going to hire a car and drive to the airport.'

'But what about his phone?' Daniel asked.

Ash flushed, spots of pink appearing on her tanned skin. 'We had a row. Andy – I mean, you must know what he's like. Impulsive. He threw his phone into the sea. That was right before he left.'

'He never made it home,' I said. 'That's for sure. He'd have been in touch with us if he had. He'd have got a new phone.'

The colour had left Ash's face now, and she looked almost grey beneath her golden tan.

'Shit,' she said. 'We're going to have to make some calls.'

She stood, hurried over to the bar and retrieved her phone, a notepad and a pencil, then sat back down with her legs tucked up under her.

'You speak Turkish?' Daniel asked.

'Sure. My mum's Turkish. I was born here, then we moved to the UK when I was seven because Dad wanted me to go to school and uni there. I'd only been back for holidays until I took the job at this place a couple of months ago.'

It was the answer to just one of about a million questions I wanted to ask her. But they'd have to wait – the worry about Andy's welfare, which had been simmering in the back of my mind for days now, was reaching boiling point.

I pictured the scene in my mind: Andy and Ash together by the water, heated words passing between them. Andy hurling his phone away from him in a rage, not thinking what the consequences might be, and then storming off, ending their relationship just like that.

I could see it. Since his recovery from addiction, Andy had become more serene, more at peace with himself. But that volatility had always been there beneath the surface: whatever dark side of him had driven him to drugs in the first place still erupted in fits of petulant ill-temper or bouts of morose silence that ended abruptly, like the sun coming out after a storm.

But there had been no end to this one. No moment when Andy had smiled his irresistible smile at Ash and said, 'God, I've been a dick, haven't I?' before taking her in his arms for a cuddle.

Instead, he'd gone. And I felt sick with fear at the prospect of him never coming back.

Ash had her phone pressed to her ear, speaking rapidly in Turkish. Daniel and I sat silently, waiting. There was nothing else we could do – we couldn't even listen in on her side of the conversation, because neither of us understood a word of what she was saying, only Andy's name, which she repeated several times before – I presumed – spelling it out for the person on the other end of the line, to whom it would be as unfamiliar as Turkey's version of the ABC was to me.

We waited while she finished the call, glanced at the numbers she'd written on her notepad, then dialled again. Another long conversation ensued, ending with her shaking her head, then dialling another number. This time, after repeating the query with which she'd begun the last call, the frown disappeared from Ash's face. She looked up at us, tentatively hopeful. Through her phone, I could hear tinny hold music playing.

Then she spoke again, listened, and spoke some more.

When she ended the call, she put her phone down in her lap, her hands trembling.

'I've found him,' she said.

I gasped.

'Is he...' I began.

'Is he okay?' Daniel asked.

'He's in hospital,' Ash said. 'They wouldn't give me any details, but it sounds like he's not in great shape, but not in actual danger either.'

'What happened?' I couldn't think of the words for my worst fear. 'I mean, he didn't... try to hurt himself or anything like that?'

'It depends what you mean by that.' Ash poured a fresh glass of water and drank it. 'He crashed the car.'

'Shit,' Daniel said. 'Was anyone else involved?'

'I don't know,' Ash said. 'Oh God, I hope not. This is all my bloody fault.'

'What? Of course it's not.' I reached over and touched her hand. 'Why would it be your fault?'

'He came here because of me. It didn't work out because of me. He left because the row we had was so awful I said I didn't want him spending another night in my apartment. It was night-time. I should have let him stay.'

'Ash,' I soothed. 'Trust me. I've known Andy for a long time, and I don't think what you're saying is right. Sure, he came here because you're here. But mostly he did it because he wanted to. And as for your argument – I don't know what it was about and it's none of my business. But when Andy's in a certain kind of mood, he could start a fight with himself in a locked room. And when he's being like that, no one would want him around.'

'And the way he drives when he's pissed off...' Daniel added. 'I had to make him pull over on a motorway once and tell him if he didn't slow the hell down, I was going to get out and walk. And that was just because Queens Park Rangers were three–nil down to Chelsea.'

Also, I thought – although I wasn't going to say it; Ash was perfectly capable of working it out for herself – that sort of behaviour, self-destructive but also capable of hurting others, was typical of Andy at his worst. *You've hurt me and so if I hurt myself, it'll be all your fault.*

Ash gave a watery smile. 'Thanks. Thanks for trying to make me feel better.'

Daniel said, 'We should go and see him. Find out what the deal is.'

'The hospital's in the city,' Ash said. 'Near where the airport is. I can take you to the road in a golf buggy and order a taxi for you, if you like?'

We talked back and forth about the logistics for a bit, and eventually decided it made more sense to walk back to our hotel and pick up our own hire car there.

'But don't you want to come?' I asked Ash.

She shook her head vehemently, so the long dark plait swished back and forth across her back. 'He said he never wanted to see me again. He meant it. I've got to respect that.'

'If he's changed his mind, we'll let you know.' I entered her number on my phone.

'And we'll drop you a line once we know how he is, if you like,' Daniel added.

There seemed to be no point in lingering after that. We thanked Ash and said goodbye and headed off back down the path towards the coast. This time, Daniel didn't power ahead of me as he had on the way up but walked more slowly alongside me, his shoulder almost touching mine, our footsteps on the gravel path sounding as if they belonged to one person, not two.

This time, he didn't suggest stopping to look at the cat feeding station.

FOURTEEN

'Here's what I don't get,' Daniel said, easing the car into a gap in the motorway traffic.

It was mid-afternoon; we'd returned to the hotel, showered and changed because we were both sweaty from our walk, and had a hasty lunch because we were starving – as Daniel had said, there was no point in going to see Andy if we were going to slip into hypoglycaemic comas and need medical treatment ourselves. I hadn't been able to resist pointing out that equally, if he drove like some kind of lunatic, there'd be three of us stuck in hospital beds rather than just the one.

'What don't you get?' I watched the red line on the satnav leading us onwards. Unlike the little aeroplane icon I'd watched on our flight out, which had felt as if it was leading us to the beginning of a journey, this felt as if, at last, we were nearing our destination.

'I mean, Andy's gay, right? Andy's always been gay. He's the gayest gay guy I know.'

'Some people are bi,' I teased him. 'Get over it.'

'Kate, stop!' I sneaked a look at him behind my sunglasses

and saw he was grinning. 'Come on. You know I'm not some kind of bigot. But if he'd fallen for a girl, why didn't he tell us?'

'Well, he didn't have to, did he? There's no rule saying you've got to disclose every detail of your love life to your mates.'

Daniel grimaced. 'Just as well. But he was always kind of cagey about the whole thing.'

'Yeah, he was. And I guess now we know why. It's a big thing to have to come out, even if you're already out as something else.'

It was his turn to look sideways at me. 'You don't seem particularly surprised about any of it.'

I shrugged. 'Nothing Andy does could surprise me any more.'

'Kate. Did you already know?'

'If I had, and Andy hadn't wanted me to tell anyone, I wouldn't have.'

'That's not an answer to my question.'

'Oh, for God's sake, Daniel. What is this, interrogation by the Stasi? No, I didn't know. But I'm fine with Andy not sharing the news with all and sundry.'

'I guess if it was the first time he'd fallen for a woman, it would be kind of a big deal,' Daniel mused.

'Yes, exactly. It would be a big deal. So totally understandable that Andy would've wanted to share it with people in his own way and his own time.'

'I wonder what they fought about.'

'Jesus, Daniel! It's none of our fucking business, is it? If Andy or Ash want to share every last detail of their relationship with us, I'm sure they will. But right now we don't even know whether Andy's in a fit state to share anything. He could be concussed or in a coma or – anything, really.'

'I was just making conversation,' Daniel said coldly. 'Don't you think you're overreacting just a touch?'

'If not wanting to discuss our friend's sex life in minute detail when we're on our way to find out whether he's suffered life-changing injuries is overreacting, then yes, I suppose I am.'

Daniel changed tack. 'You know I was asking why you're still single?'

Surprised, I turned to look at him. The clean line of his jaw was tight beneath the golden stubble. His hands were strong and competent on the steering wheel, and from what I could see of his eyes behind the wing of hair that hung over his temple, they were impassive.

'Yes. Why?'

'Think I might have figured it out.'

I subsided into furious silence, which lasted the rest of the car journey. I couldn't help noticing that Daniel was looking rather pleased with himself, chuffed to bits to have lured me into a trap and scored a victory in our silly little battle of words.

Absolutely insufferable, I thought. *Pity the woman who ends up with him – her life will be one long game of one-upmanship.* At least she'd get to shag him and then he might shut the hell up for a bit – I didn't have that option open to me.

At last, Daniel made a final turn, following the last in a series of signs reading 'Hastane', with the emblem of a cross alongside rendering translation unnecessary.

The building was modern, its curved sides clad in glass and aluminium. A small circular garden with a fountain at its centre stood before the imposing entrance, with a 3D model of the medical group's sweeping blue-and-green logo under the cascading water. With economical precision, Daniel reversed into a parking space.

'Looks like Andy's ended up getting five-star treatment, anyway,' he remarked.

I was tempted not to answer, but sulking wasn't going to get me anywhere. 'He'll have taken out travel insurance. He's reckless sometimes, but he's not daft.'

'Clearly whoever does their risk assessment is though, if they gave him comprehensive cover.'

'Just as well they did,' I said crisply. 'He's probably getting better treatment here than he would if he'd wrapped his car round a lamppost in Manchester. Shall we go in?'

'Sure thing.' Daniel pushed open the car door, swung his long legs out and stood.

The outdoor heat blasted immediately into the air-conditioned interior, and with it all my apprehension came flooding back. Sniping at Daniel had been a distraction, I realised – a way of avoiding thinking about the unthinkable.

I recalled Ash's words: 'not in actual danger'. That could mean anything – anything from being up and about charming the nurses and complaining about the food, to being kept on life support but not about to actually die. Until they switched it off, obviously.

The car door thunked closed behind Daniel. For a moment, I was alone in the cool, silent interior, not wanting to move. Learning how badly Andy had been hurt lay in front of me; I wanted not knowing to last as long as it could. Then the passenger door swung open, and Daniel extended a hand to me. I didn't need help getting out of the car, but I took it anyway.

'Come on, Kate. Sooner we get in there, sooner we'll know the score.'

I clambered out into the scorching heat, sweat immediately beading on my forehead. The tarmac surface of the car park radiated the sun's heat back upwards into the brassy sky. I took a deep gulp of air, but it was so warm it felt like inhaling through muslin.

'Daniel,' I said quietly. 'I'm scared.'

'Of course you are.' He beeped the remote-controlled key, and I heard the doors click locked. 'Me too. But you're scared of everything, so it doesn't count.'

I glared at him furiously for a second, and then laughed. He reached out and slipped his arm round my shoulder, gently pulling me close into something that wasn't quite a hug, but almost was. It was the closest we'd ever been to each other, and the strength of his body felt so comforting I had to resist the urge to bury my face in his chest and have a good old cry.

I didn't of course. I just leaned my cheek against his firm bicep for a moment, then pulled away.

'Thanks,' I mumbled. 'I'm pathetic, I know.'

He smiled – that gentle, tender smile I'd seen when he'd looked at the mother cat and her babies.

'Not pathetic. Just human. Let's go – we've got this.'

Shoulder to shoulder, we walked into the blissfully cool lobby of the hospital. Whatever had led to Andy being brought here, I thought, he'd apparently hit the jackpot. The place was space-age modern and spotlessly clean. Smiling staff in blue-and-green uniforms whisked about in a manner that appeared efficient without being rushed. The smell of excellent coffee wafted from a nearby café.

Daniel and I approached the front desk, ready to do the Google Translate thing on our phones. But the woman behind it spoke fluent English, and listened to our story with wide, concerned eyes.

'Of course,' she said. 'Let me check for you. Your friend will be happy you're here.'

She tapped the keys on her computer, her lips pressed together in concentration, then picked up her desk phone and dialled, speaking rapidly in Turkish.

'My colleague from orthopaedics will be with you shortly. Please take a seat.'

Daniel and I moved to a plush, sage-green sofa and sat down.

'Orthopaedics,' I said. 'So he's broken something.'

'Could be worse,' Daniel replied. 'At least she wasn't calling her colleague from the morgue.'

'Daniel! You can't say that.'

'I can now I know he's alive and I don't have to think it any more.'

I realised then how much effort it must have taken him to hide his own fears, to stay strong and support me through mine. And I realised how comforting his steady presence had been, preventing me from spiralling from worry to panic, which I could so easily have done if I'd been alone.

But before I could articulate any of this, or find words to thank him for being there, a tall, handsome man holding a tablet hurried to the front desk, conferred briefly with the receptionist, then turned towards us, a warm smile on his face.

He approached us with his hand extended, and we both stood and shook it.

'Hello, my name is Hakan Yilmaz,' he said, 'and I'm the senior nurse in the orthopaedics department here.'

Daniel and I introduced ourselves.

'The surgeon in change of Mr Sinclair's case is operating right now, but when he's free, he will be able to give you a full update on his condition,' Hakan said. 'But meanwhile, I'm sure you want to see your friend, yes?'

'Oh, yes please,' I said.

Daniel didn't say anything. His jaw was clenched, and I saw him swallow hard. I reached out and gently squeezed his hand, and he squeezed back with a force that almost crushed my fingers.

'This way, please.' Hakan led us into a glass-walled elevator and pressed a button, and we glided upwards. He made cheerful small talk on the journey to the sixth floor and during the walk along a few light-filled, clean-smelling corridors, past doors with sleek metal plates screwed to their surfaces and more calm, smiling staff.

Was it our first time in Turkey? Had we had a good flight

out? Where were we staying? Would we be taking the opportunity to enjoy the local sights while we were here?

I answered politely, managing to resist asking any of the questions that were crowding my mind. But one answer was clear already: he expected us to be here for some time, and that meant that Andy would be, too.

'And here we are.' Hakan pushed open a door, wide enough to admit a hospital bed. 'Mr Sinclair, you have visitors.'

Beneath the window in the cool, fresh-smelling room, its walls painted a restful pale blue, was a bed, and on the bed was Andy.

His blonde hair had grown out from his usual on-trend side-parted quiff and was held back from his face with a kirby grip. Whatever tan he'd acquired since arriving in Turkey had faced to a yellowish pallor. He was wearing a blue-and-green hospital gown, and a clear tube led into his arm, its end covered with a dressing.

'I'll be just down the corridor if you need me,' Hakan said. 'Feel free to buzz.'

Andy looked at us, his face breaking into a familiar, dazzling smile. 'Well, look who's here. If it isn't Mulder and Scully. Or maybe not – the two of them actually got along. You took your fucking time, didn't you?'

'Yeah, we had to check the twelve-islands cruise, the Bronze Age rock tombs and the butterfly safari off our itinerary before we could fit in seeing you,' Daniel deadpanned.

'We had to get our priorities straight, you know.' I felt a bubble of laughter rising in my chest but didn't let it out, because I knew it was dangerously close to tears. Then I dropped the pretence of indifference and hurried to Andy's bedside. 'Jesus Christ, Andy. You had us worried there for a bit.'

'Careful.' Alarm flashed over his face. 'I can't actually move. And a hug might just finish me off.'

'Okay.' I squatted down next to the bed and took Andy's

hand. Daniel pulled a chair over to the other side and sat down. 'So, do you want to tell us what happened to you?'

'A slight disagreement with the side of a mountain,' Andy said. 'Weirdly, the mountain won. Entirely my fault, of course. I was driving like a prize pillock. The mountain was an innocent bystander and will probably take me to the cleaners.'

'I dunno, mate,' Daniel said. 'I reckon those dodgy ambulance-chasing lawyers that keep cold-calling me about a car accident I never had could probably be persuaded to take on a mountain. What's the damage, anyway?'

Andy shifted uncomfortably in bed and reached for his water glass. 'They had to sort out the serious stuff first. The internal bleeding. Make sure that wasn't going to finish me off.'

'Internal— Oh my God. That sounds awful.' The cold feeling was settling inside me again.

'Sure was. But – once I could say anything, that is – I told them my liver's taken far more punishment over the years than a crushed Renault Fluence could inflict on it in a few seconds. They took me to the state hospital first, then moved me here once they realised my travel insurance was legit. And then they operated to patch up my pelvis. It's a vertical shear fracture, apparently – the worst kind.'

'Well, you never did do things by halves,' Daniel said.

'Nope,' Andy agreed. 'There's a bunch of pins and plates and shit in there now holding it all together. The surgeon assures me that I'll be able to fuck again, but I don't fancy it somehow, can't think why.'

'Why didn't you get in touch with anyone?' I asked.

'For the first couple of days I was pretty out of it, I'm not going to lie. I mean, it really was nip and tuck. I've got more donated blood sloshing around in here right now than my own stuff. I couldn't have told you my own name, but fortunately they found my passport, so they worked it out.'

'And after that?' Daniel adjusted his position in his chair, wincing as if he was imagining what a vertical shear fracture of the pelvis might feel like.

'I didn't have my phone – long story with which I'll regale you in due course – so I couldn't get in touch with any of you lot. I don't think I've remembered a phone number since I did my A levels. And like a total idiot, when I took out the travel insurance, I put Mum as my emergency contact.'

'So why didn't they contact her?' I asked.

'I'd completely forgotten, but she's off in Northumbria doing one of her silent retreats. No talking, no technology for a fortnight. Bit of a gift to humanity that they can get her to keep her gob shut for that long – Dad certainly never managed it. So as an emergency contact, she was a total non-starter. And, like I say, I've been pretty much out of it until the past couple of days. They've still got me on some seriously good drugs though, mind.'

Daniel and I met each other's eyes. Seriously good drugs might be necessary for someone in Andy's position, but for Andy himself they could spell a load of trouble down the line.

'And there's no need to look like that,' Andy went on. 'What do you expect me to have done while they were hammering steel rods into my sacroiliac joint – bite down on a stick?'

I laughed, but dodged his question. 'Seriously, we're just relieved you're okay. How long do they think you'll have to stay here?'

Andy shook his head wearily. 'Trying to get them to commit to that has been like trying to get that Ronan boy I went out with a few years back to commit to a date on a Saturday night. They've got some physiotherapist woman coming in twice a day to torture me, and they say she and the surgeon will let me know when they think it's safe for me to fly. I can't actually bend anything right now. How did you find me, anyway?'

Quickly, Daniel summarised the detective work we'd done

trailing round hotels. 'And then we showed your picture at this swanky resort on the edge of town, and they recognised you.'

Andy's face paled slightly, so the yellow tinge of his skin looked almost khaki. 'Oh. They remembered me, did they?'

I nodded. 'And they told us where to find Ash – I guess they thought wherever she was, you'd be too. So we went there this morning.'

'You spoke to *Ash*?' Andy asked. The bright flippancy he'd maintained up until that point seemed to be draining away pretty rapidly. I wondered whether it was because he was in pain, or something else.

'We spoke to Ash,' Daniel confirmed. 'She made a bunch of calls, and because she speaks Turkish, she found out pretty quickly from the police that you'd totalled the car, and from the state hospital that you'd been moved from there to here. So we came right away.'

'And a right pair of guardian angels you are too. Did Ash – did she say anything to you about what happened?'

'Just that you two had had a row,' I said. 'She told us you'd said you didn't want to see her again – that's why she didn't come.'

'Can't say I blame her, if I'm honest,' Andy said. 'Let's just say what happened between us – well, it wasn't my finest hour.'

'You don't have to talk about it if you don't want to,' I said, putting my hand on his.

'Main thing is for you to get better,' Daniel said.

Then the door opened and Hakan bustled in, saying that it was time for Andy's medication, and that the physiotherapist would be along straight after that.

'Oh God, not that bloody woman,' Andy said. 'I bet she beats Conservative politicians with paddles in her spare time.'

Clearly, Hakan was already used to Andy's little ways. 'If you want to get home, we have to get you mobile, Mr Sinclair. You know that.'

'So you say.' Andy sighed theatrically. 'All right. Hand over the good shit and then summon Mistress Whiplash. Are you two going to bugger off home now you've reassured yourselves I'm not going to be boiled down for cat food just yet?'

'Of course not,' Daniel said. 'We're going to stay until you're fit to come home with us. Aren't we, Kate?'

I gawped at him. We were? He and I? Staying here for what could become a matter of *weeks*, together?

Andy, I noticed, was gawping too.

'Hold the phone,' he said. 'You two, together in a romantic hotel – don't raise your eyebrows at me, Katie babe; I know you wouldn't have booked a Premier Inn unless the only alternative was sleeping in a tent – until I'm better and can go home? Wow, you must really like me.'

'Yeah,' I said. 'I think you can take my word for that.'

FIFTEEN

Daniel and I didn't say much to each other on the drive back to the hotel.

He remarked that it was a relief to find Andy in one piece at least, and I agreed. I said it was such a good thing he'd taken out travel insurance, because without it he'd have been stuffed, and Daniel half-joked that as someone who derived much of their income from insurance firms, I would say that, wouldn't I. Then he said something about the afternoon seeming to be getting even hotter, and I agreed that it only really seemed to start cooling down once the sun had set.

And then we lapsed into silence and stayed that way for the remainder of the journey, until Daniel reversed into a parking space, opened the door and pointed out that we were here. I thanked him for doing the driving, and together we climbed the stairs to our separate rooms and opened our separate doors.

'See you later, Kate.'

'See you.'

I entered the cool of my room and immediately stripped off my clothes. Without even pausing to check on my sunburn, I lay down on the bed, arms and legs extended like a starfish, and fell asleep almost immediately.

I was woken by a familiar, discreet tap on the door.

Shit. My watch told me it was seven in the evening – I'd slept for more than two hours. My mouth tasted sour and my body felt sticky. I snatched a towel from the bathroom and wrapped it hastily around myself before opening the door, just a crack, enough to accept my delivery of bottled water from the waiter.

But it wasn't the guy with the water. It was Daniel, carrying a bottle of wine and a bag of pistachio nuts. He looked at me in surprise. 'Been asleep?'

I nodded. 'Like I said, I didn't sleep last night. How about you?'

I opened the door wider. I was going to have to let him in, and I'd realised that the towel I'd grabbed in my haste was a small one, barely long enough to cover my modesty and unfortunately not wide enough to wrap all the way round myself.

Basically, my naked arse was sticking out the back, like Andy's no doubt would in his hospital gown. Damn Daniel's unerring ability to make me feel at a disadvantage – and my ability to put myself at one.

'I walked into town and checked out the local supermarket, then had a swim and a shower,' he said. 'I thought we could have a drink on your balcony, then decide where to go for dinner. But if you'd rather leave it, or come next door when you're ready...'

The offer was tempting. I could send him and his Provence rosé and salty snacks packing, and spend the evening on my own. But then, in the morning, he'd still be there and so would I. And the morning after that, and however many more mornings it took before smiley Hakan and Mistress Whiplash and their colleagues at the hospital declared Andy fit to travel – or Daniel and I fell out so badly that one of us couldn't stand it any longer and decamped home.

'You may as well come in,' I said ungraciously, edging aside while taking care to keep my back to the wall. 'Take a seat out there.'

I waved him ahead and followed him through the bedroom, waiting until I could see he was safely installed on the balcony before reversing back towards the bathroom.

'You know they do have normal-sized towels, as well as those tiny ones,' he said, with a faux-helpful smile. 'Bathrobes, too. All the mod cons.'

'Thank you for sharing that helpful intel. I believe *Condé Nast Traveller* are looking for reviewers,' I snapped.

'It's not just the hotel I can review. I'd give your arse at least five stars.'

Fuming, I shot backwards into the bathroom, locking the door and dropping the inadequate towel to the floor.

I took my time in the shower, washing my hair and shaving my legs, cursing the fact that the short notice we'd given ourselves of our trip hadn't afforded me the time to get every bit of me waxed, have gel polish put on my finger- and toenails and – crucially – book in to have the roots of my hair tinted. I smoothed scented body lotion on my skin, paying particular attention to the burned bits. My shoulders were a total war zone, coated in flaking skin and peppered with freckles. My legs weren't much better – still tomato-red from mid-thigh down and bone-white above that. Wearily, I slapped on some make-up, smoothing concealer over my nose and cheeks where yet more freckles had appeared, seemingly while I slept.

Then I hung up my towel and stepped out of the bathroom, almost colliding with Daniel.

'Jesus Christ! What are you doing?'

'Sorry. They brought your water.' He held it up, two bottles in each hand. I noticed his eyes begin to travel down my body, then snap back to my face. 'You smell nice.'

I ducked back into the bathroom and pulled the door closed.

'I'd appreciate it if you could wait outside while I get dressed,' I said. 'Unless you were planning to offer to fasten my bra strap or something?'

'I'm sure you can manage that yourself.'

I heard his footsteps retreating across the stone floor. Then he said something else I couldn't quite catch, because his words were drowned out by the swish of the door to the balcony sliding open. I dressed hastily, pulling on jeans, although it was too hot for them, and a vest top, although it exposed my flaking shoulders. I slipped my feet into ballet pumps, hoping a bit of fresh air would help the now scabbed-over blisters to heal.

Then I gave my reflection in the mirror a long, hard stare.

'A sight for sore eyes,' I told it. 'As in, anyone looking at you would be instantly struck down by a nasty case of conjunctivitis.'

I stepped out onto the balcony, just as Daniel was easing the cork out of the wine he'd brought.

'What did you say?' I asked.

'Nothing.'

'Yes, you did. Just now, when you were going outside. I didn't quite catch it.'

He smiled. 'Never mind.'

'Look, just tell me.'

'If you insist. I only said I wouldn't mind if you didn't wear a bra. No sane person would.'

He said it quite casually, pouring wine into the two glasses he'd put on the table next to the coffee mug full of pistachios and the saucer he'd put out for the shells. I found myself sitting down and taking a swallow of wine, but I didn't raise my glass to him.

'Look, Daniel,' I said, 'I don't appreciate pervy, non-compliments from you. I don't need you to come round here and serve us drinks on the balcony like we're on holiday. I especially don't want you wandering round my room when I'm half naked, or in the shower.'

He raised his eyebrows. '*Okaay*. I didn't mean to offend you. I was just being friendly.'

'That's the whole bloody point.' I prised open a nutshell with what the Royal Society for the Prevention of Cruelty to Pistachios would consider unnecessary force. 'We're not friends, are we? Come on. We're civil to each other when we're with the rest of the group because we never wanted to cause ructions. I'm glad we never have. And we've managed to be civil to each other while we've been here, and that's fine too. But believe me, if I didn't have to be here with you, I wouldn't be. If it wasn't for Andy needing us, I'd be gone. And for that matter, I don't appreciate you signing me up to stay here as long as it takes.'

He shrugged and sipped his wine. The sun was setting behind me, and golden light illuminated the planes and angles of his face, reflecting off his sunglasses and making his expression unreadable. On the balustrade of the next-door balcony, I could see his swimming shorts hung out to dry, and I was reminded again of how his body had looked with the turquoise water of the pool sliding over it like a caress.

'Fine, Kate,' he said. 'Forgive me for assuming you'd want to stay – it seemed like the right thing to do. And forgive me for thinking, since we're stuck here for the duration, we might as well make an effort to be pleasant to each other. I don't mind what we do when we get back home, but spending however many weeks sniping and point-scoring just strikes me as a whole lot of effort for zero reward.'

'Fine. We're staying – that decision's made, thanks to you. But making like we're bessie mates strikes *me* as a whole lot of effort for zero reward.'

'I don't know.' He sighed. 'Back when we were friends, I found it kind of rewarding. I got the impression you did, too.'

'More fool me.' I knocked back some more wine and ate another nut. 'That was a long time ago. We've all moved on. Especially Andy – and thank God for that.'

'Yeah, Andy. I take it you want to go and visit him tomorrow?'

'Of course. Now he's out of danger, he'll be going out of his mind with boredom. I thought we could sort out a new phone for him, maybe take him some – I don't know, magazines. Grapes. Flowers. Shit like that.'

'Fill your boots, Florence Nightingale.' He stood up. 'I'm off to get some food. I'll meet you down in reception at four tomorrow afternoon and we can go to the hospital. Unless you'd prefer to get the bus there on your own?'

'I...' I hesitated.

If this had been a game of chess, Daniel would have just made a move that meant me having to sacrifice my queen to avoid checkmate. Of course I could get the bus to the hospital. But I didn't know where the bus stop was, and I didn't feel confident in my ability to navigate public transport that worked in a language I didn't understand. I could get a taxi, but that would mean explaining to Andy why I'd come alone and cause him unnecessary distress in his fragile state. Daniel had me over a barrel and he knew it.

'Four sounds good. Thank you for offering to drive. And for the wine and stuff, obviously.'

'You're welcome. I hope you enjoy it.'

He pushed open the balcony door and disappeared into my bedroom. Seconds later, I heard the door to the corridor open and close, and after a minute or so I saw him emerge into the garden and set off round the pool, out onto the road leading to town.

Fine, I told him silently in my head. *Fuck you. Hope you have a fun evening feeding your dinner to the local cats.*

And then I thought, *He'll have a whole lot more fun doing that than you'll have eating nuts and drinking wine on your own, smart arse.*

It was true, of course. Without Daniel, I was on my own, adrift. I could go into town myself and find somewhere to eat. But the idea of bumping into him while I was there was excruciating, and the prospect of being chatted up by random men thinking that I, as a woman out alone, was fair game was even worse. And, I realised, without Daniel, it wouldn't be the same. Cats wouldn't come to me and demand to share my dinner. I'd have no one to talk to. I'd be lonely.

So it looked like I'd just signed myself up not only for an indeterminate stay but also for a string of solo dinners in my room. Go me.

You made your bed, Kate, I told myself. *So lie on it. It's not for much longer.*

I moved inside and sat on the sofa, eating pistachio nuts, drinking and scrolling idly through my phone, just like a billy no mates or a desperate single woman, which at that point I supposed I was.

By ten o'clock, I was in bed, alone, waiting hopelessly for sleep to come.

SIXTEEN

I spent a predictably restless night plagued by guilt about the hurtful way I'd spoken to Daniel and doubts about how we were to get through the next however long, co-existing here but not speaking. But every now and then the guilt would fade and be replaced by righteous indignation – he'd had no right to comment on my body like that, or hang about outside the bathroom while I was in the shower, or assume that I'd be willing to stay here with him – never mind all the stuff he'd done before, years ago, which had wrecked our friendship.

If we ended up spending a couple of miserable weeks here, not talking, that would be on him. I'd just have to deal with it.

At last, just as dawn light was beginning to trickle through the gap in the curtains, I fell asleep, only to jerk awake again what felt like five minutes later but was actually four hours. I was conscious of a sense of misgiving – of something having gone wrong – and then I remembered what had happened and lay staring at the ceiling for a bit, all the feelings of remorse and anger returning.

But I couldn't lie there for long. My wine-and-pistachios

dinner had left me ravenously hungry and even more thirsty, and breakfast would be over in half an hour.

I sprang out of bed, necked one of the bottles of water Daniel had taken in for me the previous night and checked my sunburn. The angry red was fading to pink now, and the worst of the peeling looked to be over. I couldn't hope for a tan – I never tanned. I'd just have to keep slathering on the sunblock and hope I hadn't given myself a malignant melanoma.

I dressed quickly and opened my door, feeling the heat of the morning blast my face. As I hurried towards the dining room, I felt a knot of apprehension forming in my stomach.

What if Daniel was there, calmly stuffing his face with eggs and sausage and drinking coffee? Was I supposed to join him, or say good morning but sit at a table on my own, or blank him, or what?

But there was no sign of him. I ate slowly, sipping my way through three cups of coffee, until at last the staff clearing up around me made me realise I'd outstayed my welcome. It was ten o'clock – six hours until I was due to meet Daniel to drive to the hospital.

But I felt restless, with no idea how to fill the time. I returned to my room and sat on the balcony for a bit. The prospect of Daniel appearing on the other side of the wall, so close but as distant as he'd ever been, made me edgy – but the prospect of him not appearing made me even edgier. I'd got used to the idea of him being here with me, I realised, and now that he wasn't I felt at a loose end.

It was almost as if I was missing him, which was clearly so preposterous as to be impossible. Far more likely I just had PMS, or indigestion from breakfast.

I stood and looked down at the pool – only a few sunloungers were occupied, none by him. So I put on my swim-suit, slathered on factor 50 sunblock and headed down.

But I couldn't relax there, either. Even in the shade of a

parasol, I was worried about burning, and it was too hot to be pleasant. I could swim, but a family with three small children were enjoying a noisy and splashy game in the water. I could stare at my phone, but the bright light and my sunglasses made it difficult to read the screen, and when I tried to reply to a text from Claude (I'd left him on read for almost twenty-four hours, I realised guiltily) and suggested meeting for dinner when I was back in London, I typed 'my twat' instead of 'my treat' and had to hastily delete the message and try again.

After half an hour or so, I gave up, got dressed and walked into town. It was midday now and the heat was so fierce it felt like hands pressing down on my body. Melting sunblock stung my eyes, and I could feel perspiration running down my back and thighs beneath my clothes. Even the local cats seemed listless, lying splayed out in the shade and refusing to come and be petted when I invited them.

Or perhaps, I thought, I just lacked whatever magic touch Daniel possessed – the quality that had made all the hotel receptionists smile at him, that brought cats flocking to rub themselves against his ankles, that had made even me – much against my better judgement – believe it might be possible for us to be friends again.

I left the waterfront behind and headed into the side streets, hoping to find a shop where I could purchase a phone for Andy. But all the signage was in Turkish. I didn't understand how a contract would work and felt too shy to try using Google Translate to ask about pay as you go. In a newsagent, I found a copy of the previous weekend's *Sunday Times* and bought that; in a supermarket, I stocked up on fresh fruit, random local sweets and four unfamiliar flavours of Fanta, because Andy loved Fanta.

And then, too hot to explore further, I returned to my room, lay on the bed and stared at the ceiling some more.

Then I reached for my phone, scrolling automatically to the

Girlfriends' Club WhatsApp. I'd updated my friends the previous day on Andy's condition, telling them that yes, it looked as if he would be okay but no, I had no idea when he would be strong enough to return home, so I had nothing further to report. But I found myself craving the company of my friends, even if it could only be through words on a screen.

Kate: I miss you guys. Looks like I'm stuck here for the duration, or at least until I have to start my new job.

Naomi: And how's it going with Daniel?

I could almost see her fingers hovering over the screen, wondering whether it was okay to ask. The bad blood between the two of us was acknowledged only obliquely, if at all.

Kate: Okay. I mean, I'd rather be staying in a luxury hotel in Turkey with him than with Jeffrey Dahmer, but only just.

Abbie: Aw, I was kind of hoping you'd have the chance to talk things over – you know, make friends again.

Rowan: Dan's such a sweetheart really, I've never understood what went wrong between you two.

I could tell my friends anything – of course I could. But the whole sad saga felt too complex and too inane, too far in the past and too raw, all at once.

Kate: It's fine. We're rubbing along all right. We'll just get Andy home and then we can go back to normal.

But what was normal? Seeing each other once or twice a year, exchanging polite nothings and then gravitating to opposite ends of the group, like a couple of magnets with their negative faces turned towards each other.

Even that would be better than the no-contact approach I seemed to have instigated.

Abbie: If you really can't stand it, just come home. Daniel will be able to manage on his own. Or Matt can fly out and take over.

Kate: It'll be okay. I promised Andy I'd stay, so I'm staying.

Although, of course, it was Daniel who'd made that commitment to Andy on behalf of us both, not me. He didn't need me here – he was the one who could drive, could communicate his breakfast order using the power of Google Translate, could even charm the bloody cats on the street. So why did he want me here? And if he hadn't made the decision that we were both staying, would I have decided the same?

When four o'clock approached, I gathered the things I'd bought for Andy together and went downstairs to wait for Daniel by the car. I could have knocked on his door, but I didn't know if he was in his room, and besides, given the boundaries I'd laid down, that felt almost like an imposition.

But the car wasn't there. I looked around the car park, wondering if I was mistaken. There was a similar-looking red sedan over by the fountain, but as I watched, a man and a woman got in it and drove away. I looked at my watch – it was two minutes to four, so I wasn't late. I checked my phone, but there was no message.

Feeling hot and foolish, I waited, my mind already churning through possible scenarios: I'd offended Daniel so badly that he'd gone off to visit Andy without me, or even gone home, in which case I'd be stranded here on my own with no means of transport. He'd had an accident of his own, and I'd be stuck with two injured men to get home somehow. He'd forgotten our arrangement and I'd have to make my own way to the hospital somehow, or risk leaving Andy abandoned, alone and in pain.

But at five past four, the car swung through the gates and pulled up next to me. Daniel leaned over and opened the door.

'Sorry to keep you waiting, Kate. I took a wrong turn coming through town and got stuck in traffic. Had a good day?'

I slid into the passenger seat. 'All right, thanks. You?'

'Yeah, great actually. I went paddleboarding and lay on the beach for a bit and had lunch in town. I sorted a phone for Andy – bought a handset and got a pay-as-you-go SIM card. There's Wi-Fi in the hospital so he'll be okay. What have you been up to?'

He pulled smoothly away, turning the car onto the now-familiar road leading past the town.

'Oh, I spent most of the day in bed with the hot man I pulled last night,' I said.

'That's nic— Hold on, you *what*?'

'Not really. I had breakfast and lay by the pool a bit, but it got too hot so I went indoors and... just hung around, really. I got some stuff for Andy, too. Cherry-flavoured Fanta and a few other bits.'

But not the main thing he needed – with his competence and confidence, Daniel had cracked that one, in between his sightseeing and swimming. I felt both annoyed and inadequate.

'Cherry Fanta?' Daniel said. 'That sounds totally minging. But I bet he'll love it.'

I laughed and felt the atmosphere between us thaw. But we didn't get to find out Andy's reaction to our purchases that day, because he was fast asleep. Hakan said he'd had an 'uncomfort-able' night, which I took to mean that the pain he was in must have been severe, barely touched by the strong drugs. In sleep, his face looked peaceful, though, almost childlike.

Daniel and I sat by the bedside for almost half an hour,

looking down at Andy but not speaking so as not to wake him. At last, by silent mutual agreement, we stood up to leave. I reached out and gently smoothed Andy's pillow.

'Guess we come again tomorrow,' Daniel murmured.

I nodded, and we stashed our purchases in Andy's locker, then trooped despondently back to the car.

'How long do you think this is going to take?' I asked.

Daniel shrugged. 'Your guess is as good as mine. Hakan reckons it's all down to how well the physio goes and whether the next scan shows the fracture's healing as it should.'

'Do you think he'll ever be okay? I mean, properly okay again?'

'Kate, I've got no idea. If he had any plans to run a marathon or go on *Strictly*, he might want to put them on hold. But as for normal day-to-day stuff – no one seems to be suggesting he won't.'

'And the – the medication he's on...' I hesitated to use the word 'drugs', even though Andy had used it so glibly himself. 'Do you think it'll...'

I tailed off.

'I don't know,' he said, glancing at me and noticing my face. 'Guess we just have to trust the process.'

'I guess. Hey, where are you going? Have you lost the ability to map read as well as drive on the correct side of the road?'

Daniel had turned off the motorway a stop sooner than usual, and instead of driving through the tunnel beneath the mountain that led to Alsaya, he was steering up a narrower road that wound steadily upwards, the ground dropping precipitously away beneath it.

'You all right with this? We can turn back if not.'

'I'm fine.' So long as I kept my eyes fixed on the road ahead of us and the side of the mountain rising upwards to my right, as opposed to falling downwards on Daniel's side. 'Where are we going?'

'Just wanted to show you something I discovered when I was out earlier.'

I didn't say anything more, letting him focus on driving. His steadiness and skill impressed me: he navigated the hairpin bends slowly, yet with enough power to keep the car gliding smoothly up the ever-ascending road.

As last, with evening beginning to fall, we reached the summit. Daniel swung the car into a lay-by and got out. I followed him, cautiously, but a sturdy guard rail stood between us and the edge of the mountain.

On three sides of the escarpment, the sea spread out to the horizon, so pale a blue in the light of the dying day it was almost platinum. The beach was a narrow gold ribbon lying along its edge, bordered by an even thinner line of white surf. The sun was slipping down over the western horizon, a disc of brass in the cloudless sky. The small sprawl of the town lay beneath us, picturesque in the silence, the bustle of its streets stilled by distance. Faintly, the call of gulls reached us on the breeze, and I could hear the song of birds I didn't recognise closer by.

'I came this way for a change, to see what it was like,' Daniel explained. 'What do you reckon?'

'It's beautiful. More than beautiful. It's breathtaking.'

We spoke softly, but our voices sounded loud in the stillness.

'Kate,' he said. 'I don't know what's going to happen. Not tomorrow, not next week, not in a month or a year. Neither of us does. But I do know it's all going to be a whole lot harder if we're at each other's throats the whole time. This isn't about you and me.'

'No,' I admitted. 'It's not.'

Beneath the vast dome of the darkening sky, the two of us felt very small. My anger and resentment seemed as distant as the three-quarter moon I could see beginning to edge upwards over Daniel's shoulder.

'So how about we call a truce? We don't have to be best mates, but can we not—'

'Land each other in hospital with minor stab wounds?' I joked.

'Yeah, that. Or major ones. Although I guess at least then we'd be company for Andy.'

I laughed. 'Okay, fine. Truce it is.'

He reached out a hand, and I shook it. His palm was dry and warm, and I could feel calluses on his skin.

'Dinner in town tonight?' he suggested.

'Okay. But you're going to have to do the cat-whispering. None of the buggers would talk to me when I tried earlier.'

'Can't think why, given your warm and easygoing personality.'

I laughed again. It felt easier this time, more natural. And once we'd returned to the car and Daniel was driving carefully down the other side of the steep pass, I found I was barely afraid at all.

SEVENTEEN

'I am so fucking hungover,' I moaned into my coffee the next morning. 'So hungover. Legit dying.'

'I blame you,' Daniel said. His face was pale under the golden stubble, and he sipped his coffee cautiously, like it was an emergency kill-or-cure situation. 'You suggested the raki shots.'

'Yeah, but the second bottle of wine was all on you,' I countered. 'And we weren't to know that they'd give us two extra rounds of shots on the house.'

'They liked us because you fed most of your seabass to the cats. Therefore, it's mostly your fault.'

'But the cats only came to our table in the first place because you were there. If I'd been on my own, they'd have left me alone, seabass or no seabass.'

'I don't know if I can risk that cheese and egg thing today.' Daniel pushed his sunglasses up on his head and winced at the bright morning light. His eyes were red-rimmed with dark hollows under them, and I was pretty sure mine looked much the same.

'I thought you were all about taking risks? Living life to the max. All that mad shit.'

'There's living life to the max, and then there's spewing up my breakfast.'

'You know what?' I said, standing up and gripping the edge of the table for a second as the room wheeled giddily around me, then came to a stop. 'I'm going in. If it doesn't break me, it'll make me stronger.'

'Fair play,' Daniel said. 'All right, I'll join you. But if it all goes horribly wrong...'

'You'll blame me. Heard and understood.'

Giggling like idiots, we made our way up to the counter. Daniel ordered for both of us, showing the guy the picture of the dish we wanted on his phone and repeating its name in Turkish, laughing as his pronunciation was repeatedly corrected. A few minutes later, we returned to our table with laden frying pans.

'Genuinely, Kate, I'm not sure about this.' Warily, Daniel poked the food with his fork, lifting a long string of melted cheese.

I followed suit, raising a mouthful cautiously to my lips. It smelled deliciously of spicy sausage, perfectly runny egg yolk, butter, cheese and some sort of peppery seasoning. I gave my queasy stomach a moment to get used to the idea, then ate it.

'Oh my God, that's good.' I took another forkful, tearing off a piece of bread and dunking it in the pan. 'I reckon this is going to sort us out, I really do.'

'If you say so.' Daniel dug in, eating one large forkful and then another. 'Okay, I believe you might just be right.'

'I'm always right,' I said. 'You ought to know this by now.'

'Must be hard work being so perfect.'

'Sure is. Especially when there are people in the world who refuse to acknowledge my effortless superiority.'

Daniel laughed. 'So what, in your infallible judgement, should we do this morning?'

'We could lie down in a darkened room,' I suggested. 'And wait and see whether we feel much, much better, or we die.'

'Or we could go to the beach?'

'It's too hot.'

'You can lie in the shade.'

'It's too windy.'

'But the sea breeze will keep us cool.'

'It's too sandy.'

'Kate! It's a fucking beach, what do you expect? Fitted carpets?'

I started to giggle again, and he did too, and moments later the two of us were helpless with the kind of stupid laughter that only seems to happen when you're severely hungover.

When we'd recovered our composure, I said, 'Okay. Beach it is. But you'll have to put sunblock on my back before we even leave our rooms.'

'Deal.'

I was in front of the full-length mirror in my room, wearing my bikini, scrutinising myself from every angle, when Daniel tapped on the door. I craned my head to look over my shoulder at my bum one final time, then turned sideways and sucked in my tummy. Not great – not great at all, to be honest – but there was literally nothing I could do about it between now and three seconds' time.

And anyway, I reminded myself, I didn't give a toss what Daniel thought of me or my bum. Did I?

I opened the door.

Daniel looked at me appraisingly, grinning. '*Swit swoo*. Oh sorry – I'm not meant to be objectifying you.'

'No, you're not. And besides, I'm nothing to *swit swoo* about right now – too much work and cake in the past few months, not enough reformer Pilates. Still, at least my sunburn's fading.'

'Let me take a look. Yes, it definitely looks less angry today. Here, I'll do your back.'

I heard the farting sound of suncream squeezing out of the bottle, and stood still while he smeared it over my shoulders, the nape of my neck and the curve of my lower back. His hands felt strong and capable, rubbing the cream in briskly and efficiently, with none of the tenderness I'd felt when he'd applied aloe vera gel to my burns a few days before, but even so his touch felt intimate, and the coldness of the cream – *definitely* the coldness of the cream – caused a shiver to run down my spine. In the mirror, I could see his head bent over me, a frown of concentration on his face. And I could see the way his muscles moved in his chest and arms as he worked – I bet the man had never been near a Pilates reformer in his life, but whatever he did seemed to have been pretty effective.

'That's cool, thanks,' I said. 'I'll do my front, then I'll do you.'

Daniel turned obediently and waited while I slathered sunblock over my chest, legs and stomach. Then I squeezed a thick worm of it onto his back and smoothed it in with my hands. God, he had some seriously impressive muscles going on under his smooth, tanned skin. I could clearly feel lats and traps and deltoids and a whole bunch of others I didn't know the names of.

'Looks like you've been putting in some gym time,' I said.

'Nah, haven't been near one in years. I run sometimes, and cycle, and still play footie when I get the chance. But you've got to be fairly strong in my line of work, lugging wood and finished pieces of furniture around.'

'Well, whatever it is, it's working for you.'

'Are you objectifying me, by any chance?'

'I wouldn't dream of it.'

'Pity. Maybe next time?'

'As soon as I feel an objectifying moment coming on, I'll be sure and let you know so you can enjoy it to the full.'

We laughed. I snapped the cap back on the factor 50 and put it in my bag, along with a bottle of water, my phone and the paperback book I'd bought to read on the flight but been too freaked out to open. I slipped on my flip-flops – the walk wasn't long, and my blisters were healing well – pulled on a loose white cotton shirt, and plonked on my hat and sunglasses.

'You look like you're off on an expedition to the Dark Continent, not a five-minute walk to the beach,' Daniel teased.

'I'm not taking any chances with that sun. It got me once – it's not getting me again.'

He looked at me curiously. 'You've got dark hair. Why is it you don't tan?'

I felt myself flushing. 'Just don't. Celtic genes or something. My default is milk bottle, and the most I can ever hope for is weak tea.'

We left the room and walked downstairs, past the glittering swimming pool and onto the path leading to the beach. It was hot, but as we approached the shoreline I could feel a cool breeze coming off the water, threatening to flip my wide-brimmed hat off my head and carry it away. I clutched the brim determinedly. We collected fluffy, sand-coloured towels and made our way to a pair of sunloungers beneath a parasol.

'So what do we do now?' I asked.

'Duh. We lie on the beach.'

'But...' I stopped, determined not to quarrel and spoil the new-found good vibes between us. I spread out my towel, peeled off my shirt, adjusted the backrest of my sunlounger and lay down. Next to me, Daniel was doing the same.

The waves were lapping against the front feet of my sunbed. The breeze was blowing gently, cooling my skin. Between my outstretched feet, I could see an expanse of blue water stretching away to the horizon where it met the deeper blue sky. A few people were in the water, paddling or swimming. Two children were earnestly working on a sandcastle with plastic buckets and spades. A yacht edged slowly through the water; other boats were anchored and still.

There was nothing whatsoever to do.

At first, I felt edgy and restless. I checked my phone, but I had no new emails and Claude had replied only vaguely to my message about dinner. I opened my book, but the first page failed to engage my attention. I sipped some water. I applied sunblock to the tops of my feet. I checked my phone again.

'What's wrong, Kate? You're acting like you're lying on a bed of nails or something.'

'I'm not great at relaxing.'

'Really? Wow, I would never have guessed.'

'Don't take the piss.'

He grinned. 'Sorry. But seriously, give it a try – you'll like it. Want a cocktail? I can't, because I'm driving later, but there's nothing stopping you.'

I assessed the status of my hangover. Breakfast had definitely helped, and I sensed that a small amount of alcohol, judiciously applied, might just complete my recovery.

'Go on then.'

'What kind?'

'You know.' I gestured with my hand, sketching a tall glass and something sticking out of it. 'A beach cocktail. Surprise me.'

Daniel sprang to his feet and jogged the short distance to the bar. A few minutes later, he returned with a pink drink filled with ice, a paper umbrella sticking out of its top and a strawberry balanced on its rim.

'What's this?' I asked.

'No idea, but it looks the part.'

'It certainly does.' I thanked him and took a sip. 'Oh my God. That's the right stuff.'

'Glad I could help. Now, we relax for a bit and then we'll go for a swim.'

'But won't the water be too—'

'Kate. Behave.'

'Sorry.' I looked sideways at him and a smile flashed between us, our earlier giggles threatening to return. 'Right. Relaxing in three, two, one...'

I sipped my drink and stretched my toes in the sun. I closed my eyes and watched the splashes of colour the sun left on my eyelids, like a stained-glass window. I listened to the rhythm of the waves and the whisper of the breeze. When my cocktail was finished, I laid my sunbed flat and shut my eyes again, imagining all the tension draining out of my body, through my towel and down into the sand.

I was woken – or jerked back to consciousness at any rate; I wasn't sure if I'd fallen asleep or just sunk into such deep relaxation that it was almost indistinguishable from sleep – by Daniel's voice.

'Hey, Kate. How's doing nothing coming along?'

I sat up, taking my hat off my face and putting it back on my head. Every bit of me was relaxed – almost limp. I felt more soothed than I had in years – maybe ever. 'Surprisingly well, actually.'

'Always knew you were a woman who could turn her hand to anything. Well, almost anything.'

'What's that supposed to mean?'

'You never were able to keep a house plant alive, I seem to remember.'

'How do you know I haven't changed? How do you know my flat's not a total urban jungle bursting with lush-leaved yuccas and cheese plants and... er... other green things?'

'I just do.'

I laughed. 'As it happens, you're right.'

'But only sometimes. Not like you.'

'Anyway, you didn't spoil my nap to remind me of my lack of green fingers. What's up?'

'I'm going for a swim.' He swung his long legs off the sunbed, and I watched his tanned feet sink into the sand. 'Coming?'

'Isn't that a bit, you know, active?'

'God, it really is amateur hour round here. You go in the water so you can lie in the sun a bit more without getting too hot.'

'Fair enough, beach coach. Let's do it.'

I followed Daniel the short distance to the water's edge and stepped in. The sea felt shockingly cold at first, but he didn't seem to notice. He strode in until the water was at his chest level, then extended his arms and dived, swimming away like a porpoise, the graceful arching of his body and powerful strokes of his arms the same as when I'd watched him in the pool, only now it seemed even more like he was in his natural element.

Well, good for him. If he wanted to get wet through, cold and covered in sand, that was his look-out. I proceeded with more caution, feeling the cool water inch up to my knees and then my thighs, reluctant to get my bikini bottoms wet. Daniel paused, quite far out now, and trod water, extending a hand to me in a wave. I waved back and stepped forward, the water washing up as far as my hips.

Then, suddenly, the ground dropped away beneath my feet and water rushed up as far as my armpits. I gasped with the shock of the cold, then felt the sea lift me gently off my feet, and I was swimming.

Well, paddling through the water in a pathetic breaststroke, determined to keep my face dry and my sunglasses mostly unsplashed. Still, I stayed in until the water felt the same temperature as my body, turning over to float on my back for a bit, gazing up at the sun and the sky, content and at peace.

When I'd had enough, I waded back to dry land, towelled

the sand off my feet and lay back down on my sunlounger, watching as Daniel finished his swim and returned to flop down next to me, shaking water out of his hair.

'So this is how it's done,' I said. 'Rinse and repeat. Literally.'

'Rinse and repeat,' he agreed. 'I don't know about you, but I'm not even a bit hungover any more.'

'Same, which is just as well. I'm not sure Andy would cope with seeing us like we were this morning.'

'How do you reckon he'd feel? Smug or envious?'

'Oh, envious. One hundred per cent.'

'Stay here for another hour, then head in and change?'

I nodded, groping in my bag for my phone. Guiltily, I realised I'd barely given Andy a thought while I basked in the sun and swam in the sea. The purpose of our trip had been entirely forgotten; it had just felt like a holiday. A romantic one, even. With Daniel. Perhaps I was actually still a little bit drunk.

Then I said, 'Hey, Daniel?'

'What?'

'I've got a message from Ash. She wants to talk to us. She's asked if we can go round to her apartment tonight.'

EIGHTEEN

That afternoon, Andy was petulant and miserable. The mahjong set Daniel presented him with was greeted with, 'But there's no one to play with me, except when you guys are here.' And the bottle of piña colada Fanta I'd brought for him to try earned me, 'What are you trying to do, give me rotten teeth as well as a mashed pelvis?'

Still, we stayed until Hakan chucked us out so Andy could have his medication and his physio. But, by silent agreement, neither of us mentioned that we were going to see Ash that evening.

'What do you reckon?' Daniel asked when we left the hotel at seven o'clock, heading on foot along the now familiar route into town. 'Should we have said something to him?'

'I don't know.' I fell into step next to him. 'It kind of feels like anything that makes him feel less positive is probably a bad idea, right?'

'And depending on what she has to say about it all, we could update him tomorrow.'

'Exactly. We don't know what went on between them. Hakan seemed fairly positive, at least.'

'Yeah, it sounds as if he might be able to travel home in a week or so.'

'Although who knows what will happen once he gets there,' I said. 'I mean, he won't be able to work for a while. He probably won't be able to go home unless he gets a stairlift installed or something.'

'God! Andy with a stairlift. Can you imagine?'

I could, all too easily. The tantrums that would ensue, born out of frustration at his lack of independence, would be epic. I could almost hear Andy saying, 'What am I, a fucking OAP?'

'We'll cross that bridge when we come to it,' I said firmly. 'And speaking of bridges, is this where we turn?'

Daniel glanced at his phone and nodded. We crossed a humpbacked stone bridge that led across a stream, heading away from the touristy part of town. The busy restaurants and bars, with their menus displayed outside in English as well as Turkish, gave way to small coffee shops and then to ordinary stores selling everyday essentials: sacks of chickpeas, tubs of baby milk, bottles of cleaning products. Instead of hotels and guesthouses, the streets were lined with apartment blocks, two or three storeys high, tiled pathways leading to their entrances, washing hanging on their balconies.

There were still cats everywhere, of course, lounging in doorways, splayed out on windowsills, helping themselves from plastic food bowls set out on the pavement. Daniel paused to fuss a few of them, but mostly he was focused on his phone, plotting our route through the narrow streets.

'I think this is it.' We stopped outside an ochre building, the plaster falling away from its walls in places, a creeper winding around its door. Daniel raised a hand to press the buzzer, and we waited. There was the sound of hurrying footsteps, and Ash swung open the door.

'Welcome! Come on in,' she said. 'It's just up the stairs and to your left.'

As we squeezed past her in the narrow hallway, I could smell her perfume, like she'd been rolling around in a meadow full of flowers. She was wearing a simple white broderie anglaise shift dress, and I felt hot and frumpy by comparison in my rolled-up jeans and vest top, conscious of the sweat that had soaked through on my back, which she must have been able to see as she followed me. I couldn't help wondering whether Daniel, walking behind Ash, was also aware of the contrast between her almost balletic grace and my clumsy ascent up the steep flight of stairs.

The apartment was small: just one room with a kitchenette at one end and a sofa at the other, which I guessed folded out into a bed. A door led to what I presumed was the bathroom, and a second, glass-paned one led to a tiny balcony where fuchsias grew in hanging baskets. Plates, glasses and cutlery (an eclectic mix that looked like it could have been bought from a market stall or charity shop) were laid out on a low coffee table, and three cushions were set on the floor around it.

For the life of me, I could not picture Andy here. Yet here he had lived, for several weeks, and presumably intended to live for longer, if things hadn't gone wrong.

'Thanks for coming.' Ash gestured to the cushions. 'Grab a seat. I'm sorry – it's a bit of a step down from where you're staying, I know.'

'Thanks for inviting us.' As politely as a little boy attending a birthday party, Daniel handed over the bottle of wine we'd brought.

I lowered myself to the floor, crossing my legs and leaning back against the sofa. I looked around, trying to imagine Andy making coffee on the worn melamine countertop, Andy's designer clothes hanging in the rickety pine wardrobe, Andy emerging from the bathroom with a towel round his waist.

Where I was sitting, he and Ash would have lain in bed together in the light cast by the streetlamp outside, their bodies tangled in sweaty sheets, happy – until they weren't. That was even harder to imagine than all the rest of it.

Ash placed three glasses of wine on the table and sat down opposite me, lowering herself effortlessly to the floor without using her hands. Her prettiness struck me again: her hair was loose down her back today, slightly kinked from the plait it must have been in earlier, falling almost to her tiny waist. Her eyes were an impossible shade of aquamarine. Her lips were a rosy pink that looked like lipstick but couldn't be, because she wasn't wearing any other make-up. No wonder Andy had fancied her. How could it be possible that Daniel wouldn't fancy her too?

'So how is Andy?' she asked.

'Physically, surprisingly okay,' I said. 'Like I told you in my text, he had surgery to pin the broken pelvis, and it's apparently healing well. Mentally, he's finding it tough, of course. He can't wait to get home, but at the same time, he knows it's going to be a while before he's anything like back to normal.'

'Did he... ask about me?'

Daniel said, 'We didn't tell him we were coming. We weren't sure if you'd want him to know, and he wasn't in a great mood earlier so we thought...'

'I understand.' Ash sipped her wine, her eyes lowered so the long lashes cast shadows over her smooth cheeks. Then she said, 'What kind of a hostess am I, anyway? Let me get you guys some food.'

She performed the sinking-to-the-floor manoeuvre in reverse and took the few steps to the kitchen counter, returning with dishes of salad, bread, dips and cheese. It all looked and smelled delicious, and I wondered how long she'd spent preparing it, and whether it meant she'd been as nervous about having us here as I'd felt about coming.

'I don't eat meat,' she said. 'So I hope you don't mind it all being veggie.'

'Of course we don't,' I assured her. 'This is amazing, thank you. Honestly, we've had such incredible food since we've been here. We've been really spoiled, haven't we, Daniel?'

'The breakfast at our hotel is off the scale,' Daniel agreed, and the conversation moved politely on to the virtues of Anatolian cuisine for a few minutes.

I could sense Ash relaxing, and so after a bit I decided to risk asking, 'So how did you and Andy meet?'

She raised her remarkable eyes to meet mine. 'It was at a meeting in Manchester. Not a formal thing, more just a get-together – a support group, I suppose you could call it – for people doing twelve-step programmes.'

I blinked in surprise. Of course, Andy had made no secret of his regular attendance at Narcotics Anonymous meetings, and AA ones too because, as he'd said once, 'Coke might have been my drug of choice, Katie babe, but let's be honest, a lovely dry Martini ran it a close second.'

But Ash? I couldn't picture this clean-living, yoga-practising woman indulging in anything more intoxicating than the wine she was sipping, or maybe a particularly decadent fruit salad.

'I attend Overeaters Anonymous,' she explained in answer to my unasked question. 'I had – still have, although I'm in recovery – a binge eating disorder. I lost most of my twenties to it.'

'I see,' I said, although to be honest I struggled to see. 'That's – uh, very brave.'

'It's a long story.' She smiled. 'And I won't bore you with it. But the support from people who are on the same journey is a huge part of the healing process. I've found a group to attend here, too, although meetings aren't as frequent as they were back home. So, anyway, that's where Andy and I met.'

'And you hit it off right away?' Daniel asked.

'I guess, yeah. I fancied him right away.' A flush spread over her cheeks like someone had dusted them with Nars Orgasm. 'I mean, wouldn't anyone?'

Yeah, I thought, *you would. And any man alive would fancy you.* Across the table, I saw Daniel watching Ash intently.

'Sorry if I'm oversharing,' Ash went on. 'It's just, I know how close you are. Andy talked about you all the time. You and – Abbie and Matt, is it? And Rosie, with the teenage daughter.'

'Rowan,' I corrected her, smiling.

'Oh yeah, of course. I felt almost as if I knew you. I hoped I'd meet you sometime, although obviously not like this.'

'It's good to meet you anyway,' Daniel said gallantly, and I thought, *You would say that, wouldn't you?*

'I...' Ash began, and then she tailed off before trying again. 'I know Andy will tell you his version of what happened. But I guess I wanted to share it from my point of view, too, because it's important to me and I'm still figuring it all out in my head. And I feel, like, really bad, actually.'

'It's okay,' I said. 'You can tell us as much as you want to, and we'll tell Andy, or not, whatever you prefer.'

'Thanks.' Ash's shoulders visibly relaxed under the crisp white cotton of her dress. She took an olive and ate it, nibbling round the stone as if eating an apple. 'Yeah, so, like I said, I fancied him right away. But I assumed he was gay. I mean, why wouldn't I?'

Daniel poured the rest of the wine into our glasses, listening silently.

I thought, *Of course. Didn't we all?*

'So we kind of made friends,' Ash went on. 'This was late last year, like October time. We went for a couple of coffees, saw a movie together, stuff like that. Went shopping. It was nice. I've always wanted a gay best friend. But all the time, I felt this... *thing*. You know. When you're attracted to someone and you feel like you wouldn't be *that* attracted – not that intensely – if there wasn't something there on their side too.'

I felt a stab of something that was part sorrow, part envy – but mostly a feeling I couldn't begin to name.

'I get that,' Daniel said, smiling, and I thought, *You do? How come?*

'Then one night,' Ash said, 'it all just happened. Just like that. It was Bonfire Night, and we'd been to see a firework display. I took a flask of mulled cranberry juice, so Andy could have some, and we had jacket potatoes from a food cart, and he was really cool about finishing mine when I said I'd had enough. And then when we were walking home – we lived quite near each other at the time – he held my hand.'

I listened. I could picture them there together, on a drizzly autumn evening in the north-west, far more clearly than I could imagine Andy here. I could almost feel the damp air on my face, smell the sulphur from the fireworks blending with the whole-some fragrance of baked potato, feel the pressure of a hand through a woolly glove.

'He told me he had feelings for me,' Ash said. 'He said he couldn't hide it any more. He said he'd always been bi, but he'd never been out. I didn't know what to make of it, really, but if I'm honest, I didn't think it through that much. I was just so happy he felt the same about me as I did about him.'

'Of course you were,' I said, nodding.

'And after that,' Ash continued as if I hadn't spoken, 'it all kind of went from nought to a hundred. I'd already been applying for jobs out here, and then I got the one at Wild Maple. I was made up, but I was also gutted because it meant leaving Andy behind. But he said he'd come out and join me – he'd take all the annual leave he'd built up and he'd come. So I moved out here in January and we FaceTimed and Whats-Apped and stuff the whole time. And then he came, and I was so happy. He moved in here with me and it was like the begin-ning of something magical.

'I'll make tea,' she said abruptly, standing up in a way that was less graceful than before, more of a scramble. She rapidly cleared the remains of the meal from the table, and I heard the hum of a kettle before she returned with glass cups in metal holders, stuffed with fresh mint, over which she poured boiling water.

Daniel and I thanked her, knowing the tea was just an excuse for her to collect her thoughts before finishing her story. She sat back down, this time hugging her knees to her chest.

'It was my fault,' she said. 'All the stuff I've had to deal with – around my body image and everything – I'm still working through. And when Andy was here, with me, it should've all been great. But I kept quizzing him, about what he'd been doing back in Manchester, about whether he'd slept with anyone else – and he knew I meant men, not women.'

I nodded again sympathetically. Next to me, Daniel was listening, silent and still.

'It wasn't cool,' she went on. '*I* wasn't cool. And after a bit, Andy got fed up. He totally lost his rag with me. He called me all sorts of horrible names. That was when we were out for dinner at that swanky place on the waterfront – that's why they remembered us, and they knew I was working in the area. I feel so ashamed. He's right – it was bigoted of me, or bi-phobic or whatever.'

'Hey,' Daniel said. 'You know you're allowed to feel insecure in relationships. It's not the crime of the century.'

'Yeah, I know. But it was *why* I felt insecure that was the real problem.'

I said, 'So if you could go back and change things, keeping in mind what you just told us, would you somehow not feel insecure any more?'

Miserably, she shook her head.

'Insecurity doesn't come out of the blue,' I said. 'Were there things that happened to make you feel like that with Andy specifically, or is it a regular thing you've experienced in other relationships?'

'It was more a thing he said.' Ash looked down miserably

into her tea. 'He said he wasn't sure our relationship would last, like, forever. I mean, no one can be sure of that. But I was falling for him, and he said he wasn't sure he could only be with one person forever. He said monogamy isn't natural. And he said he'd only ever been in love the once, and it wasn't with me.'

We said what we could to reassure her – that she was allowed to have boundaries, that Andy probably hadn't been the right person for her, that you're allowed to end things with a person for whatever reason, if it doesn't feel right.

I'm not sure our words reassured her, but we'd done what we could, and we left shortly afterwards.

Walking back along the seafront to our hotel, Daniel paused and gazed out over the sea. 'Hey, look at that.'

'What? The boat?'

'Yeah. It's a new one. It's not the same superyacht that was there before.'

'New day, new oligarch,' I said.

Daniel laughed. 'That's not just any oligarch, though. It's my oligarch.'

'What, you keep one as a pet?'

'Don't be daft. That's the *Meridia*. It's the boat I did the cabinetry on. Belongs to an Estonian tech billionaire. He's actually a decent guy – I might drop him a text and let him know I'm in the area.'

'Wow,' I said. 'Friends in high places, or what?'

We turned away from the water and carried on walking, shoulder to shoulder, falling into step with each other.

After a bit, Daniel said, 'What she said about Andy only having been in love with one person. Who do you reckon he meant?'

NINETEEN

THEN

2009

It was a Sunday in January – one of those miserable days when Christmas seems like a distant memory, but winter still feels as if it will last forever. In fact, the following day was the much-vaunted Most Depressing Day of the Year, so at least there was that to look forward to.

Andy and I had arranged to walk over to Tate Modern to see an exhibition there, not because we particularly wanted to, but because at that stage practically anything that would alleviate the smothering tedium of the endless, cold, drizzly month had to be worth trying. But he'd texted me at about eleven in the morning to say he wasn't feeling well, and could he just come and hang out at mine instead.

Which was fine by me – I had a cold, too, and the prospect of not leaving my cosy flat, flopping on the sofa drinking hot chocolate and watching *Antiques Roadshow* (of which Andy was passionately and bafflingly fond) seemed like a pretty decent plan to me.

But when he arrived that afternoon, I realised instantly that it wasn't a cold that was the problem. He was white and shaking, with deep lines of tension around his mouth and dark circles under his eyes that looked like they'd been gouged out of his face by an overenthusiastic 1950s housewife wielding a melon baller. He wasn't dressed in his usual quirky style, but in grey tracksuit bottoms that had seen better days and were far too long for him, a jumper with Snoopy on the front, and an equally oversized tweed coat. When I opened the door, he headed straight for the sofa, clutching a two-litre bottle of Fanta and unwrapping a scarf from round his neck.

'Jesus Christ, Katie babe, I feel like all kinds of shit. Don't know where I ended up last night but I lost my coat and I must've fallen over because the knees of my trousers were all shredded and covered in oil.'

'Did you not make it home?'

'Didn't I tell you? Mum and Dad have sold the flat. I'm crashing at Tall Matt's. These are his.'

He gestured to the tracksuit pants. That explained the length, at least – Matt was six foot five, a good eight inches taller than Andy.

'Ah. I thought it was a fashion statement. Next up, clown shoes.'

He laughed, but it turned into a shudder. 'My jaw aches like hell. No word of a lie, I ground my teeth so badly last night I woke up with a mouth full of grit from my own teeth, like when they do that sandblasting thing at the dentist. Any chance of a glass?'

I fetched one from the kitchen, and he splashed Fanta into it, his arms trembling so badly he could hardly lift the bottle.

'I don't think Abbie's best pleased with me,' he continued. 'I got in after four and ruined their Sunday lie-in. So I said I'd get out of their hair this afternoon, even though getting out of bed just about killed me. Why does it have to be so arsing cold? Will it ever end?'

'In about two months' time,' I said. 'You see, there's this thing called spring, which generally follows on from winter. There'll be daffodils and the clocks will go forward, and the next thing you know we'll be drinking gin and tonic in the park.'

'Oh God, Kate.' He put his glass down and slumped over, his head in my lap. 'What would I do without you? You do know how to make me feel better.'

'Have you eaten?' I asked sternly. 'Low blood sugar will only make you feel worse.'

I felt his head move on my thighs in a shake. 'I was going to get a Maccers, but my card was declined. I'm absolutely fucking brassic.'

If Andy not only contemplated ordering McDonald's but couldn't afford it, things must be even worse than I'd realised.

'What do you want? An omelette?'

'Too much like proper food.'

'Doritos?'

'Not enough like proper food.'

'Fucking hell, Andy, it's like having Goldilocks over for lunch. Dippy eggs and soldiers?'

'Oh my God, yes! With loads of butter on the toast. You're an angel.'

'Move your bloody great swede off my lap then.'

As we ate, I saw some colour come back into Andy's cheeks, and I decided to risk asking him why his finances were in such dire shape.

'The last job didn't last. I chucked one sickie too many and they let me go. It all seems so damn pointless, doesn't it? You get up every morning and go and sit in some ghastly office for eight hours, and then you have two days off for fun and then it all starts again. Over and over and over until eventually you're too clapped out to be any use any more and then you retire and die.'

I thought of my own career stretching ahead of me, challenging but relentless. While it gave me moments of satisfaction and was certainly more lucrative than any job Andy had ever had, I could kind of see his point.

'At least you get to stop and have babies,' he went on.

'In theory. But I'm not sure if I actually want them, and there's certainly been no sign of anyone wanting to have them with me.'

'You know what, we should get married. It would be lovely. We could host fabulous parties and read the papers in bed on Saturday mornings and have a talking parrot in a cage.'

'We could teach it swear words. And make our own pasta.'

'We'd have a grand piano in our living room and books everywhere. I'd learn how to arrange flowers.'

'We'd rent villas in Sardinia in summer, and all our friends would come and stay.'

'We'd play croquet on the lawn and have tea under a chestnut tree.'

'Our children would have fat little dapple-grey ponies and go to gymkhanas.'

'A boy and a girl. Called Sebastian and Seraphina.'

'Or Peregrine and Persephone.'

'Or we could have four and use all the names.'

'Unfortunately, I see one flaw in your cunning plan,' I said.

'What's that? We don't have the dosh for a house in the country with a chestnut tree and stables?'

'Yeah, that, obviously. But also, you know, you like boys.'

'Kate,' he said, his face suddenly serious. 'If I tell you a secret, will you promise never, ever to tell anyone else?'

I felt a knot of tension inside me, where the warm, happy feeling had been a second before. I knew secrets were powerful – and dangerous. I knew they could drive people apart just as often as they joined them together. But when someone asks another person that question, is there ever a different answer to the one I gave?

'Of course,' I said.

'I don't just like boys. I've never told anyone except you.'

My mouth felt dry and I could feel my heart beating hard. The tension under my ribs felt different now – less like dread and more a kind of wild excitement.

I said, 'Is that because... because you...?'

'Because I like you, Kate. I've been fucking smitten with you from the moment I first saw you.'

My voice came out in a whisper. 'Same.'

And then, as if a powerful elastic band was pulling us, we cannoned into each other's arms on the sofa, kissing and kissing as if we'd never be able to stop.

TWENTY

NOW

I don't know why, because I certainly hadn't expected to need it, but when I'd done my packing two weeks before, some deep-rooted instinct, or force of habit, had made me include a little black dress. It wasn't much – just a mid-thigh-length slip in stretchy polyester, with shoestring straps and a cowl neckline, that I'd had for years and hung on to because it was versatile, had never gone out of fashion (probably because it had never been *in* fashion in the first place) packed down to a tiny roll and never creased.

I thanked my years of travel experience as I took the dress out of my wardrobe and pulled it on, adding a pair of dangly silver earrings, loads of mascara and bright red lipstick. I didn't exactly look glamorous, but I hoped I'd be able to fake it until I made it – or that everyone else would be too drunk to care what I looked like, which was far more likely. I was piling my hair up with a claw clip – it was too frizzy from the sea air to wear down – when Daniel tapped gently at my door.

'How insane is this?' I said as I opened it. 'We're going to a *literal* party on an *actual* yacht!'

'Not that insane. I texted Maksim and told him I was here;

he was having some people over and said we should join. What's insane about that?'

'Urgh, don't be such a spoilsport. What shoes should I wear?'

'Doesn't matter.' Daniel looked as if he'd been putting in some serious effort with the hotel-room iron – his pink linen shirt was pressed so crisply I could almost hear it crackle, and his chino shorts looked freshly laundered. 'You'll have to take them off anyway. The decks of those boats are tens of thousands of pounds' worth of teak, and the owners are understandably a bit fussy about them.'

'Oh. Shit. Then I'm going to have to paint my toenails. Hold on. There's beer in the minibar fridge if you want one.'

I grabbed what I needed from the bathroom and perched on the end of the bed, soaking off the old polish on my toes, which was chipped round the edges from walking on the beach. Daniel cracked open a beer and lounged in the balcony door-way, half looking out at the view, where *Meridia* dominated the skyline, and half watching me.

I finished removing the old nail enamel and held out two bottles towards him. 'Inside Scoop or Go Overboard?'

'What? Inside what?'

'That's what it's called,' I explained with exaggerated patience.

'Do people seriously get paid to think up bollocks like that? And would you seriously wear something called Go Overboard to a party on a boat?'

'Fine. Inside Scoop it is. And don't laugh – I bet you buy paint that's called equally ridiculous things. And at least I didn't bring Sandy Bum.'

'I dunno. I feel I could get behind Sandy Bum.'

Did he mean that literally? Looking down so he couldn't see me blushing, I shook the bottle and began carefully applying the polish. Daniel kept watching me, a faint smile on his face.

'What's so funny?' I asked.

'One, I can see your knickers, Kate. And two, this is a foot fetishist's dream.'

I laughed. 'Stop distracting me. You're not a foot fetishist, are you? That's so gross. I had one message me on online dating once.'

'Really? How do you bring that up in a profile? "Likes fun nights out, cosy nights in and knocking one out over your bunions"?'

'Actually, he asked me if I do that thing of dangling my high heels off my toes when I'm sitting on a tall bar stool.'

He raised his eyebrows. 'Well, at least he was up front about it.'

'Exactly – and gave me a clear heads-up to ignore and block. I mean, there's nothing wrong with feet as such.'

'You've got nice feet.'

The compliment surprised me. 'Come on, no one's got nice feet. There are gross ones and not-so-gross ones. Mine are average at best.'

He shrugged. 'If you say so. Are you ready yet?'

'Nope. I need to put on another coat and then let them dry for ten minutes before I can risk my flip-flops.'

'God, it's a bit of a pain being a woman, isn't it? All that maintenance.'

'Hey, at least I didn't have to get the iron out.'

'Glad you noticed I put a bit of effort in.'

'You look very smart. Shame about your hair.'

'What?' He raised a hand and ran it through his barnet, which was almost all corn-gold now from the sun. 'What's wrong with my hair?'

'Too long,' I said. 'It looks wanky.'

'Want me to take your nail scissors to it before we go?'

Quite suddenly, I realised I didn't. Objectively, Daniel's hair might be wanky. But subjectively, it was quite another story. Looking at it, I found myself wondering how it would feel to run my fingers through it, to bury my face in it and breathe in its fresh-lemonade scent, to feel its ends tickling my face if he kissed— What? What was I even thinking?

Feeling my face flame, I swung my legs down off the bed. 'You're all good. I expect lots of people on yachts have wanky hair.'

'Ah, thanks for the vote of confidence.'

'Don't mention it.' I slid my feet into my flip-flops and gave myself another quick glance in the mirror.

'Kate?' Daniel appeared, his reflection close behind mine.

'That's me.'

'You look stunning. Just saying.'

I couldn't have been more surprised if he'd slapped me on my (not sandy) bum. In the mirror, I saw my eyebrows shoot upwards and a delighted grin spread over my face. *He thinks I look nice.* The knowledge made me glow with pleasure, and a tiny thrill of something else – something far more potent and exciting.

'You're not so bad yourself. Wanky hair notwithstanding of course.'

Gently, he punched my upper arm. It was the briefest touch, a friendly bump and no more. But it felt as intimate as a caress. It felt like the mark of his knuckles would stay on my arm all night, clear as the lipstick imprint of a kiss. Hastily, I fumbled my room key into my handbag along with my phone.

'Are you sure we don't need to take anything?' I asked. 'Flowers for the hostess? Bottle of wine? Something like that?'

'Don't be daft. They'll have laid on enough booze to float the entire yacht and got a team of florists in. We'll send a thank-you message tomorrow.'

We emerged into the hot night and walked downstairs. The sun was just beginning to slip behind the mountain, and the sea was turning the familiar silver it took on in the evenings. After tonight, I knew I wouldn't see it again.

Over the past ten days, Andy had made what the medics said was significant progress. He could get himself along the corridor and (with difficulty) up and down the stairs on his crutches. The pain relief was doing its thing. X-rays showed the fracture was healing as it should. And so, tomorrow, he was to be discharged and fly home – or at least to London – accompanied by Daniel and me as his carers.

It was a massive relief in almost every way. I wouldn't have to delay starting my new job. Andy had recovered better than the medical team could have hoped. Daniel and I wouldn't be stuck paying for the none-too-cheap hotel accommodation for the foreseeable.

But. There was a but so massive I could hardly articulate it – not to myself and certainly not to Daniel. There'd be no more strolls into town in the evenings, no more sharing our dinner with the local cats, no more seeing Daniel's face across the table at breakfast. No more going for drives into the surrounding countryside together, half-bickering over whether Daniel was adhering to the speed limit. No more combing the local shops for soft drinks and English newspapers to take to Andy when we visited him in hospital. Our holiday, which was never meant to have been a holiday but had somehow become one, was almost over. This strange intimacy that had built up would be at an end – replaced by the easy friendship I'd taken for granted for so long if I was lucky, and with our more recent animosity if I wasn't. A few days ago, I'd have felt only relief about that. Now, I didn't – I felt a hollow sense of something I thought might be loss.

In silence, we walked down to the pier. A few glamorously dressed people were milling about, chatting in a language I didn't recognise. One of the women was wearing a floaty midi dress that I could have sworn was Balenciaga; her husband's shades were branded Cartier. A stunning twenty-something woman had on a diamond bracelet that must have been worth as much as the deposit on my flat, and her boob job had probably cost close on as much. I hung back with Daniel, suddenly over-whelmed with shyness in my Topshop dress.

It's vintage, Kate, I told myself. *You're saving the planet, one twenty-pound outfit at a time.*

Then a motorboat pulled up, a wake of sparkling water following it.

'Going to *Meridia*?' the driver – or captain, I supposed he was – asked, alighting easily from the boat onto the pier.

'*Eks, aita,*' said Cartier Shades.

'*Meeldiv tutvuda,*' Daniel said. '*Minu nimi on Daniel.*'

Cartier Shades pumped Daniel's hand enthusiastically before breaking into a flurry of words in the same language. Daniel shook his head, smiling, and responded haltingly. Cartier Shades laughed and slapped him on the back.

'Please?' The captain extended a hand, and Diamond Bracelet took it, stepping onto the boat like she did this sort of thing all the time, which she probably did. Balenciaga Frock, who I guessed was her mother, was next, stepping more cautiously in her towering heels. Either she hadn't got the memo about going barefoot, or she was going to rock her Manolos until the last possible second.

It looked like I was next. I reached out for the captain's hand, which was warm and crusted with calluses, trying to look as if I, too, had done this countless times before and wasn't one bit afraid of capsizing the boat. All the same, when I stepped in and felt it lurch on the water, my hand gripped the captain's for dear life, visions of me toppling into the Mediterranean Sea and having to be hauled back to shore (possibly by passing fishermen with nets, as if I was the catch of the day) flashing before my eyes.

But I didn't fall in. Seconds later, I was sitting next to Balenciaga Frock, who smiled warmly at me and told me in fluent English that her name was Sofia, her daughter was Lisandra and her husband Andrei.

As we chatted, the boat pulled away from the jetty and moved swiftly towards the yacht. It had looked pretty big from a distance, but as we neared it, I revised my opinion. The thing wasn't pretty big – it was bloody enormous. Against the dark water, it blazed like a lit-up Christmas tree, lights of all colours shining from its decks: one warm gold, one brilliant white, another cycling through pinks and purples and blues. I could hear music and laughing voices drifting towards us across the water, faintly but clearly audible over the roar of the boat's engine.

'All right, Kate?' Daniel laid a hand on my shoulder. 'You're not going to get seasick, are you?'

I turned around to glare at him, but his excited grin made me smile instead. 'Of course I'm not going to get seasick. It's a five-minute ride on calm water. Don't be mental.'

'I just thought...'

'That because I'm scared of flying, I'd also be scared of boats? That's completely illogical – like saying because you like cats, you'll also like dogs.'

'As it happens, I do like dogs.'

We held each other's eyes for a long moment. I felt something lurch inside me, as sudden and unsettling as the list when I'd stepped into the boat. Then we both started to laugh, so giddy with shared excitement that anything could set us off. The boat came to a stop, right next to an expanse of varnished wooden deck. The captain jumped gracefully out, and we all alighted behind him.

We were ushered through to an upper deck, where waiters circulated with trays of champagne glasses. Our new friends immediately spotted people they knew and disappeared into the crowd. Daniel and I helped ourselves to drinks and moved to the edge of the space, looking down to the aquamarine swimming pool beneath us and the vast expanse of the sea beyond it, as dark as the pool water was bright.

'I could get used to this,' I murmured.

'Not bad, is it?' Daniel flashed a grin at me, and we touched the rims of our glasses together in a silent toast. 'But I'm surprised you've never been on a yacht before. I'd have thought a high-flyer like you would do this sort of thing all the time.'

'Oh, yeah. My last boyfriend had a yacht a bit like this one, only bigger.'

'Really?' The smile faded slightly from his face.

'No, of course not. Come off it! I'm more booze cruise on the Thames than yacht on the Med level – you know I am.'

Daniel laughed. 'I thought you'd have been a bit more blasé if you'd done this before.'

'I never have. Should we find our hosts and then explore a bit?'

'Sure.'

We drained our glasses and replaced them on a passing tray, then made our way into the crowd. The music had been turned up, and it was too loud to talk, almost too loud to do much more than shout introductions and thank-yous to our host and hostess when we eventually located them. But Maksim pumped Daniel's hand with genuine warmth and immediately whisked us off to show us the master stateroom where Daniel's marquetry headboard had been installed.

'Your partner is a true craftsman,' he said to me. 'Your home must be full of beautiful pieces.'

I didn't say that Daniel wasn't my partner, and my flat was more IKEA than *Ideal Home*.

Glowing with pride, Maksim showed us the en-suite bathroom with its whirlpool bathtub; the downstairs gym with sauna, steam room and beauty treatment area; the hot tub on the upper deck; the boardroom and cinema room. The level of luxury was insane – I allowed myself a little daydream about what it would be like to be so wealthy you never had to give a second's thought to where your next mortgage payment was coming from. Instead of worrying whether there was enough money on your debit card to pay for your Tube fare to work, you'd be deciding whether to buy a Bentley or a Jaguar, before plumping for both. When you opened your fridge, you wouldn't be worrying that the best-before date on your ready-meal lasagne was yesterday and deciding to risk listeria anyway, you'd notice that you were down to your last jar of caviar and tell the housekeeper to order more. If you were running out of space in your wardrobe, you wouldn't stick some clothes on Vinted, you'd buy a new house.

'But enough of the guided tour,' Maksim said at last. 'You're here to enjoy yourselves. Come!'

He led us back into the thick of the crowd on the main deck, magicked up a waiter with more champagne, and disappeared into the crowd, glad-handing and backslapping his guests.

'What do you reckon?' Daniel asked. 'Like it?'

'It's nuts. Imagine living like this. You could literally go anywhere in the world, have whatever you wanted.'

'Is that what you want? To have more money than you knew what to do with?'

'I mean, it would be kind of nice. Wouldn't it?'

'Only if you could overlook the environmental impact a boat like this has, and the appalling levels of global inequality it represents.'

'God, you're no fun.' I leaned in towards him, our heads close so we could hear each other, and caught a whiff of the lemony scent on his hair. 'Why not forget the state of the planet for a second and enjoy yourself?'

'Sounds like a reasonable suggestion. More champagne?'

'Why not? Be a shame to let it go to waste.'

. . .

By midnight, I'd eaten more lobster than I'd known existed in the world, and drunk more champagne than I'd have dreamed was possible without literally floating away like a helium-filled balloon. I'd chatted to my fellow guests at such random, drunken length that I felt some of them were my new best friends. I'd actually told one of the barmen that he was the kindest man I'd ever met, after he made me a perfect dry Martini.

I'd come to the conclusion that a no-shoes policy on a dance floor was an absolutely outstanding idea that should be adopted everywhere, because even after almost two hours throwing shapes (admittedly very amateur shapes – I'd always been a crap dancer), my feet didn't hurt at all.

And, I suddenly realised, I'd lost Daniel.

I tried to remember when I'd seen him last. Certainly, we'd raided the buffet together an hour or so earlier. He'd been dancing just a few feet away from me. And then we'd taken a brief break and sat by the swimming pool, dangling our feet in the water.

But now, looking at the laughing faces around me, lit by the slow arc of the mirror ball, I couldn't see him anywhere. I let the press of bodies edge me to the side of the rainbow-lit dance floor and stepped off, back onto the teak of the deck. The pounding music vibrated through my feet. Above me, the stars wheeled as if they too were some high-tech lighting effect.

Kate, you're drunk, I told myself. *It's time to go home, before you snog some random stranger.*

Blinking mascara out of my eyes, hoping I didn't look like I was Maksim's pet panda that had escaped from its living quarters, I made my way to the bar and claimed a bottle of water, taking a few deliciously cold gulps. I walked carefully down the smooth, varnished stairs to the buffet, which had been replenished with miniature burgers and chips in paper cones. But I wasn't hungry, and Daniel wasn't there.

I descended to the next deck down, where the main swimming pool was. The yacht was huge – in my less-than-sober state, I could easily get lost. And more to the point, finding Daniel would be like some ridiculously posh game of hide and seek. I'd look on the bottom deck, I decided, and if he wasn't there, I'd call him and say I was ready to leave.

And, at last, there he was, sitting on the end of the deck where the motorboat had moored, dangling his feet in the sea, looking out at the view of the town spread out in the distance.

It was quieter here, but still he didn't turn when I padded towards him on my bare feet.

'Hello.' I sat down next to him, lowering my feet into the water next to his. 'Ooooh, that's cold.'

'You'll get used to it. Having fun?'

'So, so much fun. The very best time. Isn't this crazy?' I asked, gesturing around us.

'Bonkers.' He smiled. He had a half-full bottle of beer in his hand, and he took a sip before offering it to me.

'I'm all good.' I held up my water bottle. 'Cheers, anyway. I thought it was time to slow down on the booze.'

He looked at me, and I realised his face was swimming in and out of focus. I pressed my fingers to my eyes and pushed my sweaty hair back off my face, then tried looking at him again. Better, but still blurry.

'What's up, Kate?'

'Nothing. Just the drink catching up with me now I'm not dancing any more.'

'You were really going for it a while ago. Never knew you had all the moves.'

'Oh God. I'm going to have the worst Fear tomorrow, aren't I?'

'Make the most of not having it while you can, then,' he advised.

I lay back on the deck. Daniel was right – my feet had

grown used to the temperature of the sea and now the water felt pleasantly cool. The smooth wood was hard beneath my back; I could feel the barest sway as the yacht gently rose and fell in the current – or possibly it was just my brain swaying. Above me, the night sky was thick with stars.

Daniel's head appeared next to mine, his hair spreading out to meet mine. I could smell beer on his breath, and whatever cologne he'd used earlier – fresh with juniper, like a gin and tonic.

'I wonder if we'll see a shooting star,' I said, but my words came out slightly garbled and slurred.

'I can think of things I'd rather look at.' He propped himself up on one elbow and smiled down into my face. 'You're cute when you're pissed, you know. All your sharp edges and corners are rubbed away.'

'Oi. You leave my corners alone.'

Above me, his eyes were very close. The water was reflecting off his face, creating dancing patterns on his skin and making his eyes look more blue than grey. I could feel his hair tickling my collarbone.

He reached out and cupped my face with his warm, dry hand, then ran his thumb lightly over my lips. I felt a smile stretching across them in response.

'Kate? You know how you always snog random men on nights out?'

'I do not *always* snog random men on nights out.'

'Yes, you do. It's a well-known fact. And it would be a shame to break with tradition, don't you think?'

And then he kissed me. I'd known the kiss was coming; it had felt inevitable from the second I sat down next to him. But still, in that moment, it took me by surprise. Everything about him was so familiar: his grey eyes, his broad shoulders, his sun-bleached hair. But his kiss was alien, like arriving in a foreign country.

But the strangeness only lasted a second – before I was able to articulate the thought, kissing him felt like something I'd always been meant to do. Like our lips had been designed to fit together. Like my hands had always wanted to twine themselves in the softness of his hair, and his jaw had grown that dusting of stubble especially to rub against my cheeks.

I don't know how long that first kiss lasted. It might have been only a minute or so but, with the stars wheeling in their trajectories above me when I opened my eyes and looked past the closeness of his face, it felt like forever. His lips tasted so good against mine. The length of his body pressing lightly down on me made me want to hold him closer and closer until we merged into one person. My beating heart seemed to be drumming out a rhythm that filled the night, drowning out even the pounding bass from the dance floor above us.

And then I realised the sound was more than just my heart – it was the throb of the approaching motorboat.

Daniel said, 'Shall we go home?'

I nodded. I couldn't say anything – I had no breath for words – but I knew he could feel the movement of my face against his. He stood, and for a second I gazed up at him in wonder, feeling like I was seeing him for the first time. Then he reached out a hand and helped me to my feet, and I let my body melt against the warmth and strength of his.

We were the only two to board the boat, which had been steadily ferrying guests back to shore for the past couple of hours. We gasped out a couple of words of thanks to the skipper, then sat together, our hands clasped, our thighs pressed together from hip to knee. Then, without saying anything, as if it was the only possible thing for us to do, we started to kiss again.

All the short journey back to land, sea spray misting our faces, the sky huge and spangled above us, the water close enough to dabble our fingers in, we kissed and kissed. We stopped only for the few seconds it took to step off the boat onto the pier, and then our bodies fell together again, and we kissed some more.

We kissed when we paused for Daniel to take out his key card at the entrance to the hotel grounds. We kissed at the foot of the stairs. We kissed outside my bedroom door.

And then, barely breaking the kiss, I spoke. 'Do you want to come in?'

'Of course.' I could feel his lips against mine, saying the words I'd hoped to hear.

I opened the door and we stepped into the familiar coolness of the room, not bothering to switch on the lights. I barely registered that this was probably the last time I'd enter the space that had become home.

Our lips didn't break contact as I moved slowly backwards towards the bed, letting Daniel lower me gently onto its softness. Briefly, I remembered sitting there earlier, painting my toenails, in what felt like another world.

Then he lay next to me, and I forgot everything except his lips, his hands, his breath and mine coming faster and faster. I unbuttoned his shirt, the linen feeling rough against my fingers in contrast to the skin on his shoulders, satiny smooth like polished wood. He pulled the straps of my dress down over my arms, and I heard him give a rasping gasp as he touched my breasts for the first time, my nipples hardening instantly beneath his hands.

His lips moved from my mouth down to my throat, then lower. I heard my own gasp as his tongue found my nipple, teasing the skin around it until I felt like I'd scream if he didn't touch it. And then when he did, I felt like I'd scream with the pleasure of it. Together, we moved higher up the bed, so I slid fully out of my dress and lay there in my pants on the white duvet, smiling up at him. The muscles in his arms supporting his body above me were hard and defined in the dim moonlight that filtered through the curtains. His hair hung down towards my face. His smile was intoxicating.

I trailed my fingertips from his shoulders over his chest then down to his abs, feeling them tense under my touch, the line of soft, fine hair guiding me unerringly to the fastening of his shorts. Fumbling slightly, I undid the button then pulled down the zip, releasing the hot, springy hardness of his erection in his boxer shorts. I slipped my hand between the fabric and his skin, wondering again at its softness, then closed my fingers around his cock.

'Jesus, Kate. This is...'

'I know it is,' I murmured. 'I know. Don't stop.'

He kicked off his clothes and lay next to me, and we kissed again, exploring each other's bodies with our hands and mouths. His buttocks were firm and smooth. I could feel the separate muscles on his thighs, and the point where they dipped in towards his groin. I could smell the musky man-smell of him.

His hand moved between my legs and he stroked me, the merest brush of skin on skin at first, then deeper, searching, parting me and feeling how wet I was, how much I wanted him. A finger found my clit, and my hips arched involuntarily upwards towards him.

I moved onto all fours and crouched above him, leaning in for another deep, endless kiss as I guided his cock towards where we both yearned for it to be, sliding my body downwards until the entire hard, hot length of him was inside me and we were moving together, our lips and tongues and hair and limbs intertwined, even our breath mingling in the cool air.

TWENTY-ONE

I slept so deeply that night it was like falling into warm, dark water and not needing to come up for air. I slept more deeply than I could remember ever sleeping before. When I woke a few hours later, roused by the unfamiliarity of Daniel's body next to me in bed, I rolled over and embraced him, fitting myself tightly against him, and that woke him, and we had sex again in a somnolent, almost dreamlike way. Then I slept again and stayed asleep until the sunshine woke me.

Daniel was up already. He was standing in the balcony doorway, a towel wrapped round his waist. I could smell coffee and hear the regular spurts of the sprinklers watering the gardens outside and the early-morning birdsong. The outline of sky I could see framing Daniel's shoulders told me it was another dazzling, perfect day.

But I didn't feel dazzling or perfect. My hangover had descended with a vengeance, blotting out all the giddy happiness of the night before. My mouth was dry. I could smell stale perfume on my sheets – and something else as well. I closed my eyes and pieced together the events of the previous night: the yacht, the endless flow of champagne. The kisses. The rest of it...

How could I have been so utterly stupid?

'Daniel?' My voice sounded dry and croaky when I said his name. He turned around, his face still.

'Morning. You all right, Kate?'

'Not really. Daniel, last night – we didn't use a...'

'No,' he said. 'We didn't.'

'Shit. Why the hell didn't you...?'

'Bring condoms on a trip abroad to find my missing friend, with a woman who can't stand the sight of me? I can't imagine.'

'Total lack of foresight on your part,' I said, in a lame attempt at a joke. 'I should have expected it. Rank incompetence.'

'You didn't either, did you, Ms Shit Hot Risk Manager?'

'I think that was what in the trade we call a black swan event,' I said. 'Unexpected and unprecedented.'

'And presumably unique.'

'I'll need to get to a pharmacy,' I said. 'Thank God we're flying home today. I wouldn't fancy navigating that in Turkish.'

'I'm sorry, Kate. I should have thought...'

'There wasn't a whole lot of thinking going on back there though, was there?'

He shook his head. 'Like I said, I'm sorry.'

'Not as sorry as I am.'

My stomach gave a queasy lurch, and I tasted acid in my mouth. 'Fuck. Going to be sick.'

I pushed the duvet aside and stood up, pressing my palms against the wall as the room wheeled around me. It steadied just in time for me to make it to the bathroom, where I dropped down onto the tiled floor and retched, feeling like the tide of nausea would never stop.

When at last it did, Daniel was there, fully dressed, passing me a cold flannel and a glass of water.

'Are you okay?' he asked.

'Never been better. What does it look like? I should shower – we're meant to be at the hospital at ten and I still need to pack.'

'I guess you won't want breakfast?'

My stomach churned horribly again. 'No chance.'

'Sure I can't bring you anything?'

'Please just leave me alone. Sorry about this, but I'll get sorted more quickly on my own.'

'If you're sure...' He hovered in the doorway. 'Kate...'

'I'll be fine. Just go. I'll see you downstairs at nine.'

He waited another moment, then shrugged, reached out a hand to brush my naked shoulder and turned and left. Moments later, I heard the door of his room open and close again.

Shakily, I got to my feet and looked in the mirror. Last night's make-up was smeared around my eyes and lips; my foundation had collected around my jawline in greyish, grubby smears. My hair stood up around my head in a parody of a halo, damp with sweat and smelling faintly of sick. And the rest of me was pretty rank, too. Stale perfume, stale sweat, stale Perrier-Jouët and stale Daniel seemed to be oozing from every pore.

I pointed a finger at my reflection and told it, 'You are a complete and utter fucking tit.'

My reflection nodded, with no choice but to agree.

I stepped under the shower and sluiced my body and hair with tepid water, then went in big time with the free toiletries, squeezing out the last of the mandarin shower gel and the dregs of the lemony shampoo I'd smelled so often on Daniel's hair. I used my own conditioner, although my hair was so brittle and dry from seawater and sun that I knew it would have little effect – a serious go with the Olaplex would be needed as soon as I got home.

As soon as I got home and had been to a pharmacy and dry-swallowed the morning-after pill the second they handed it over.

'What a dick,' I muttered, stepping out of the shower and upending the almond-scented body lotion into my palm before smearing it over my legs and shoulders, where the new red skin was fading to pink. 'What an utter prize idiot you are.'

I was castigating myself but, as I crammed my toiletries into my wash bag and quickly slapped on some make-up before stowing that away too, I realised that the description could equally apply to Daniel.

I'd been drunker than him, last night. He'd let it happen just as much as I had. The fragile truce we'd achieved had been blown apart, turned into something full of recriminations and blame even worse than it had been last time.

One of us should have stopped it. *I* should have stopped it – I was the risk-averse one, the sensible one. Only I'd been the one begging him *not* to stop. I could hardly blame the man for not guessing that I wasn't on the pill.

I remembered the kisses, the touches, the way our bodies had fused together like we were one person, all our messy, complicated history seeming to have vanished in a tide of booze and lust – or be somehow amalgamated into a shared thing.

And then I remembered him saying, *You always snog random men on nights out*, and felt my insides curling up with shame. It was true. I did always snog random men on nights out. Well, not always, but often enough for it to have become a thing – a joke. Was that what he thought last night had been? Just a casual shag between two drunk people who wanted to prove they'd still got it?

And what had I been *thinking*, anyway? I didn't even like Daniel. Sure, I had, back in the day. And certainly, we'd reached a kind of accord, out here, so that we could get ourselves and Andy back home without the wheels falling off big time. But this had not been part of the plan. One-hundred-arsing-per-cent not.

I pulled some clothes from the wardrobe to wear today and chucked them on the bed, then put my suitcase on the opposite side and began throwing things into it, not bothering to fold or roll anything properly, cramming my trainers on top of the pile instead of carefully stuffing them with socks and tucking them in the bottom, then sitting on the lid to get it closed.

The way Daniel had reacted to me this morning, his half-hearted attempt at banter barely concealing the deep remorse that mirrored my own, told me that last night hadn't been part of his game plan either. He hadn't hugged me. He hadn't said it was okay. He knew we'd screwed up big time, same as I did. Except it was me holding the potential consequences of our screw-up inside me, hidden under the innocent-looking black cotton of my knickers.

I was furious, with myself as much as with him. I couldn't even pretend that I'd been an innocent victim in it all – I'd consented, not just enthusiastically but avidly. I'd been gagging for it. The fact I'd been pretty drunk was neither here nor there – for all the dark thoughts I'd had about Daniel over the years, I knew for sure that last night would never, ever have happened if he'd been in any doubt at all that I'd wanted it to.

Only, now that it had, I wished with all my heart it hadn't.

Because now that it had, with the memory of those hours as fresh in my mind as the sheets on the bed would be once we'd gone and the chambermaid had been in to do her thing, I knew how hard it would be not to want it to happen again. Because it had been fucking amazing.

Amazing fucking.

I couldn't see a way for Daniel and me to go back to being friends. If he ever rubbed sunblock on my back again, or took my hand to help me into a boat, or hugged me when I was upset, I knew the memory of how his body had felt close to me, over me, inside me, would come rushing back and I'd be lost.

Friendship wasn't on the table any more, so enemies we'd have to be. Frenemies, if I was really lucky.

Wearily, I gave the room a final scan, pulling open drawers, glancing inside the wardrobe, tugging back the shower curtain. There was nothing of me left in this room where I'd stayed for two weeks. Only a few stray hairs in the bathroom sink, a couple of cotton pads smeared with my eye make-up in the bin and the stack of notes and change I'd left for the cleaning staff showed I'd ever been there at all.

I shouldered my bag, set my suitcase on its wheels and pocketed the key card for the last time, then trundled my case to the lift – which we hadn't used since our arrival – and made my way down to the ground floor, blinking as I emerged into the sunshine.

Daniel was waiting outside the reception area, his backpack at his feet.

He handed me something wrapped in a white paper napkin. 'I saved you one of those spinach pastry things you like from breakfast.'

'Thanks, but I'm not hungry.'

'Maybe not now, but I one hundred per cent guarantee you will be in about half an hour. Better for you to eat this than chew your own hand off.'

I knew he was right. Reluctantly, I tucked it into my bag, but I didn't smile at his lame joke.

'Shall we settle the bill?' I asked.

'Done it already.'

'But what about—'

'It's okay, Kate, we can sort it out when we're home. Want me to carry your stuff to the car?'

'I can manage. It's got wheels, you know.'

Still, once he'd opened the boot and stowed his own bag, Daniel lifted mine up for me and slotted it in. Then he walked round to the passenger side and opened the door for me.

'I can manage. I've got hands, you know,' I said.

He turned away, just too late to conceal the smile that had flashed over his face. Then he got in the driver's side and started the car.

'Well,' he said. '*Sayonara*, Alsaya. Or should I say "*Gule gule*"?'

Smug git. In the two weeks we'd been here, he'd learned how to say loads of things in Turkish, from 'May I have a mushroom omelette please?' to 'He's always complaining about doing his physio', while I was pretty much stuck on 'Hello' and 'Thank you'.

I fastened my seat belt, and Daniel swung the car out through the stone gateposts. I looked behind me for the last time at the low, pale-gold buildings, the riotous magenta blanket of the bougainvillea, the glimmer of the sea beyond. *Meridia* was still at anchor, gleaming white against the blue sky. I wondered if there'd be another party on board soon, another ill-judged drunken shag, another woman heading home with a heart full of regret.

At the hospital, it was all action stations. Andy had already been helped out of his private room and was lying on a stretcher in the corridor. His luggage had been fetched from wherever it had been stored for safekeeping, and a nurse was ticking items off a list on a clipboard. The consultant, Hakan and a paramedic were conferring earnestly in Turkish over a tablet.

Andy should have been the centre of attention, but he wasn't. All that remained now for the staff who'd cared for him twenty-four/seven was to complete their administration, hand him over to the team that would be looking after him on the flight home and see him on his way.

'Now I know how cows feel when they get loaded up to be taken to the abattoir,' he said when he saw us.

'They won't get much of a rump steak off you, mate,' Daniel commented. 'You should've worked harder at your physio.'

'Mistress Whiplash is very proud of me, I'll have you know. I got her a bunch of flowers to say thanks. If I ever get back to full working order, I'll declare the Leyla Turan memorial shag under way.'

'I'm sure she'll be honoured,' I said. 'Will you send her a video?'

'She already follows me on TikTok,' Andy said smugly. 'We're basically new bessie mates. What's up with you anyway, Katie babe? You look like you're the one that drove into a mountain, not me.'

'Yeah, I'm kind of tempted to check myself in,' I joked. 'Next-level hangover. Next time someone invites me to a party on a yacht, I'll say I'm washing my hair.'

'I'll keep that in mind,' Daniel said, unsmiling.

Andy's eyes swivelled from him to me.

Damn it, I thought. *That came out snappier than I meant it to.* And then I thought, *Come on, Kate. Either you want to be all friendy-friends with him or you don't. Make up your mind.*

'You can come in the ambulance with me instead, if you like?' Andy said. 'It's highly exclusive. They say there's only room for one.'

'Well, since I'm the only one who can drive the car back to the airport, that's a done deal,' said Daniel.

'Unless you'd rather I...' I began.

'What? Have you along for the pleasure of your company?' Daniel asked. 'By all means come if you want to, but I'm not going down on bended knees to ask.'

'Fine, I'll go with Andy then,' I said curtly.

The medics appeared to have finished their procedure-checking. Two of them took charge of Andy's stretcher, I picked up one of his bags and Daniel took the rest. We thanked everyone profusely, and the little retinue proceeded along the corridor, into the lift, through the main entrance and out into the sunshine without Daniel and me saying a word to each other.

I didn't even give him a final telling-off about making sure he drove on the correct side of the road.

A few minutes later, I was ensconced in the ambulance, perched on a small seat next to one of the paramedics, who didn't appear to speak any English.

'So you slept together,' Andy said as soon as the doors were closed.

'What? No, I... we...'

'Don't try and pull the wool over my eyes, Katie babe. I've seen enough mornings after nights before in my time, and it's as plain as the nose on your face. Both the noses on both your faces.'

'Okay, fine. Yes, we did.'

'So what went wrong? Sneaky one up the bum, no harm done? Hung like a chipolata? Can't be that – I've seen our Daniel in the shower enough times to know he's got decent equipment. Did he call you Mummy at the crucial moment? Or did you call him—'

'For God's sake, stop it. Nothing like that. It was fine. It just shouldn't have happened in the first place, and I think we've both realised that.'

'On the contrary,' Andy said. 'I'm not going to lie, I always thought there was something there with you two. Obviously, there were reasons why nothing happened, but come on. Now it has, why aren't you going with the flow?'

'What do you mean?' I asked, the urge to know like the urge to pick a scab. 'Something there?'

'Back in the day, you two got on like a house on fire. Then

you fell out, and you were all like *nim nim nim* at each other like a couple of old maids quarrelling over a cup of sugar. At the time, I wondered whether you'd had it off and that's what had caused the ruction, but there wasn't the... thing there was today, so I ruled it out.'

'What are you, Sherlock bloody Holmes or something?'

'Unlike most people, I just notice what's there. No special skills involved. So are you friends again now, or what?'

'No,' I said. Then I blustered, 'Not friends. Not going to happen.'

Andy turned his head on the pillow and eyeballed me astutely. 'Whatever you say. But now time, the great healer, plus a party on a yacht with copious amounts of— Go on, what was it? Make me jealous.'

'Perrier-Jouët.'

'Perrier-Jouët, has worked its magic, and here we are. Your eyes met across a crowded sloop deck and the next thing you knew sparks were flying and you ended up in the scratcher. And you should be getting ready to live happily ever after, but you're not. Why not? Tell Uncle Andy.'

'There's nothing to tell, Andy. He doesn't want to and neither do I. End of story.'

'Oh, I don't think so, somehow. You mark my words, there'll come a time when you—'

But before he could finish speaking, the ambulance pulled gently to a stop. We heard doors opening and closing. The paramedic unstrapped herself and stood up, and the back doors swung open, letting in the sunlight.

Whatever Andy had been going to say would have to remain unsaid for now, and I was glad of that. Because, I told myself, for once my friend's unerring instinct for human nature had erred. I'd had enough experience of making mistakes with the men I got involved with (hell, when had I ever *not* made mistakes?) not to let myself get sucked into another cycle of potential (or more likely actual) heartbreak. What had happened between Daniel and me was in the past now, and the past was where it would stay.

It would be in good company there, along with all the other things I'd resolved to put behind me forever.

TWENTY-TWO

THEN

2009

So it began.

And once it had begun, I couldn't see a way to end it – although, most of the time, I didn't want to. Most of the time, when Andy and I were alone together, it was like the instant connection I'd felt the night I first met him was still there, still the same, only more intense and expressed differently. The mental connection I'd felt now had a physical aspect too, I told myself.

We were still friends, but now we were friends with benefits.

Those early months were kind of like a honeymoon. Andy was still at Abbie and Matt's place, but he didn't stay there every night. He spent at least two nights a week at mine. Sometimes we went out together. We went to watch obscure art-house films, taking a hipflask of sherry in with us. We went to rummage through charity shops in the most expensive areas of London, where Andy found me a bouclé Chanel jacket and I managed to persuade him not to buy a real fox-fur stole.

Neither of us had much money (actually, Andy had almost none, and I was saving furiously for my next step up the property ladder), so when we went out to eat it was to places in Chinatown that did duck tongues and chicken gizzards, or to Polish cafés where we'd drink shots of vodka and stuff ourselves with pierogi, or to greasy spoons for hungover breakfasts.

More often, we just hung out in my flat. Andy was addicted to TV shopping channels, and he'd spend hours glued to the screen, occasionally saying, 'Oh my God, just look at that ghastly tat!' or, 'Katie babe, you've got to see this right now, come here!' and I'd drop whatever I was doing to laugh with him over a DIY crochet tea-cosy or an obviously retouched before-and-after image or a presenter's orange fake tan.

I hadn't expected him to stop using drugs, so I couldn't allow myself even a flicker of disappointment when he didn't. He didn't use that much when he was with me, anyway, just the occasional joint on my balcony or a sneaky line on a night out. I told myself that this, too, would change – that when Andy felt more at ease with me, with himself, with his complex sexuality, he'd feel ready to quit.

Like I say, it was like a honeymoon, only it was one no one but us knew we were on. When we saw our friends together, we kept up a careful pretence of just-friendship. But we didn't see them that often, Andy insisting that he wanted to be alone with me. When I tentatively asked when we were going to tell people, he said we would, definitely, but not just yet.

'I want us to be our secret for now, Katie babe. I want you to be my little secret.'

Not always, but often, we'd have sex. It was different from what I was used to with other men – more simple, more innocent, almost chaste. I knew Andy felt desire for me, but I also knew he didn't feel the same passion I felt for him. It would come in time, I told myself, and if it didn't, that was okay – our love was different; it was based on friendship, which was why it would last.

I knew Andy was still seeing other people. I assumed they were exclusively men, although he never said. And I was too, although admittedly with a lot less enthusiasm than him. It would all be fine, I promised myself. I wasn't going to become jealous or possessive – I wasn't going to ask for more than he was willing to give.

I was going to be the ultimate cool girl.

So, when he confided in me about his chequered dating life, I laughed and sympathised and gave advice. When he didn't turn up when he said he would and I didn't know where he was, I told myself it was fine – I was his friend, not his keeper; he was entitled to a life apart from me. When our friends saw us together and noticed something – because, despite our best efforts to pretend everything was still the same as it always had been, we must have let slip some signals that things had changed – I denied everything.

But there was one thing no one could deny.

One Saturday afternoon, I got a call from Abbie, asking me to go round to her and Matt's flat, where Andy had been staying as a lodger or houseguest – I wasn't sure of the details of the arrangement. But as soon as I arrived, it became clear that whatever it had been was now over.

Matt let me in and then, stony-faced, said he was going out. Abbie was sitting at the kitchen table, clutching a mug of tea, surrounded by soggy tissues.

'Hey.' I hurried over and folded her into a hug, which made her immediately shake with fresh sobs. 'What's the matter? Are you okay? Did you and Matt have a row?'

'No,' she said, her voice muffled by my shoulder. 'I mean, yes. We did, but that's not... that's not...'

'Something else has happened? What was the row about?'

Gently, I extricated myself and sat down opposite her. She

was blank-faced with shock, her hands shaking as she lifted the mug of tea, sipped and grimaced.

'God, that's stone cold. And I haven't even offered you a drink. I keep making tea and forgetting about it. I went to work yesterday and ended up at the office we moved out of six months ago, and then I realised I wasn't in any fit state to function, so I came home.'

'I'll put the kettle on, then you can tell me what's up. Are your mum and dad okay?'

Only a death, I thought, could trigger a reaction like this. But I was wrong.

'It's Andy,' Abbie said, once she was able to speak again after a fresh storm of tears.

My whole body went cold. Had she found out about Andy and me? Was she angry as well as hurt by what she knew? And then I realised that would be relatively trivial, easily dealt with somehow or another. There was a far worse prospect.

'Has something happened to him?'

'No. Not as far as I know. But right now, I wouldn't care if something did. I don't care if I never see him again.'

Then the whole story came pouring out: how Andy had first not paid rent, then started stealing things from Abbie and Matt – cash, a new mobile phone, a watch. Small things and then bigger ones. And now, finally, he'd wiped out their savings from their online bank account.

Hearing the words from Abbie's trembling lips made me feel like I'd swallowed a stone.

'I can't believe he'd do that,' she sobbed. Anger would come, I knew, but for now Abbie was blindsided by shock. 'We're his oldest friends. We were at school together...'

'It's the drugs,' I said. 'Isn't it?'

'Obviously. God, Kate, at this point I couldn't care less if he'd used the money to buy Pokémon cards. But yes, it'll be drugs. Or debt from buying them, which amounts to the same thing.'

'Do you know where he is now?'

She shook her head. 'He didn't come home last night, unsurprisingly. I doubt he'll come back. He knows what this means to us.'

I knew, too. It was a betrayal almost too huge to contemplate. In spite of how devastated I felt for Matt and Abbie, I couldn't help imagining how Andy must be feeling – the vast weight of guilt, shame and regret he'd be burdened with; the fear and desperation that must have driven him to do such a thing.

'I can help,' I offered. 'I got a decent bonus at work this year. I can pay you some of it – maybe not all, but some. It would be a gift, not a loan.'

'We can't take your money, Kate. Absolutely not. And anyway, the money – I mean, it's a big deal. But it's not the biggest deal.'

I nodded, squeezing her damp, icy hands across the table. No matter how large the sum, it was a pittance compared to the loss of trust, the end of a friendship that had endured for so long. We talked around it for almost two hours, knowing that no resolution could be found, and by the time Matt came home, Abbie was calmer, able to make plans to save harder, forgo holidays, put off having a baby for a few more years until they were financially stable again.

It was evening by the time I left, making my way home through the spring rain, my thoughts in turmoil. What Andy had done was unforgivable – but also not entirely his fault. He would never have chosen to do this. He was in the grip of an addiction that was bigger than friendship, more powerful than loyalty, stronger than Andy himself. It was far, far bigger than I'd allowed myself to admit.

Abbie had made it clear that her friendship with Andy was

over, and I didn't blame her for that. Of course, she hadn't suggested that I follow suit and cut him out of my life too, but I could see why someone in my position would do just that. On the other hand, though, surely the desperation Andy must have felt, which had led him to steal from his friends, meant that he needed people on his side now more than ever?

By the time I got home, I still hadn't decided what the right thing to do was – but in the event, the decision was taken out of my hands.

Andy was sitting, huddled, on the steps leading up to my building. He had just one blue IKEA bag with him, containing what I presumed were his worldly goods. He was greasy-haired and unshaven. His clothes looked like they'd been slept in.

'Come on – let's get you upstairs.' I hustled him into the lift. I could smell alcohol on his breath and stale sweat on his body. He was shivering, and as soon as the lift doors closed, he started to cry.

'I've fucked up so badly, Kate,' he said. 'I don't know what to do. I had nowhere else to go.'

'Yep, you've made quite the hash of things,' I agreed.

'Have you spoken to Tall Matt and Abs?'

I nodded. 'I've just come from there.'

The lift stopped at my floor, and Andy followed me out into the corridor and then through the front door of my flat, hangdog and humble.

'Thank you,' he said. 'I thought you'd tell me to sling my hook. I wouldn't have blamed you if you did.'

'Get in the shower and I'll order some food. Pizza?'

'Anything. I haven't eaten since yesterday morning.'

'Okay.'

I waited until I could hear the shower running, phoned in the pizza order (extra-large meal deal with a stuffed crust, a tub of Häagen-Dazs and a two-litre bottle of Fanta) and poured myself a glass of water instead of the large white wine I so badly wanted.

I knew I had to act fast and decisively. Now, with Andy fragile and remorseful, he would probably listen to what I had to say; tomorrow, after a meal and a good sleep, his usual bravado would return and with it what had become his usual behaviour. Hunched over my laptop, I embarked on a rapid research session, and by the time Andy emerged from the shower, already looking significantly brighter, I had a plan.

Abbie and Matt had been too kind, too trusting – they'd let themselves be taken for mugs. I wasn't going to let that happen to me.

'Thanks for letting me stay, Katie babe,' Andy said, curling on the sofa with his feet up. 'You're an angel in human form.'

'I'm not letting you stay.' For the second time that day, I said, 'I got a decent bonus at work this year. I'm paying for you to go to rehab.'

Andy laughed and sang the line from the Amy Winehouse song, ending with an only slightly half-hearted, 'No, no, no.'

'Yes, yes, yes. You know it makes sense, Andy. You can't go on like this. You'll lose all your friends. You could end up killing yourself.'

'I wouldn't lose you, would I, Katie babe?' He looked up at me, his blue eyes imploring.

It took every ounce of resolve I had to say, 'If you did to me what you did to Abs and Matt, you one hundred per cent would. And if you don't do what I'm asking, it's one hundred per cent done between us. Game over.'

I saw his face slacken with acceptance, and I realised he really, really believed I meant it.

At the time, I even believed it myself.

TWENTY-THREE

NOW

It was raining when I arrived home. It was a typical London spring day – blustery and showery, the sun promising to put in an appearance any minute now, just not ready to do so yet. Still, in contrast to the dazzling sunshine, endless blue skies and baking heat I'd grown used to after a fortnight in Alsaya, it felt positively miserable.

Besides, I had that grim Sunday night, back-to-school feeling you get at the end of a holiday, even though strictly speaking my time in Turkey hadn't been a holiday at all. I felt out of sorts and miserable, the last cobwebs of my hangover still not blown away, my stomach still tight with anxiety after the four-hour flight, which I'd had to endure with resolute cheerfulness because I was meant to be looking after Andy, not needing to be looked after myself.

But now Andy and Daniel had gone. We'd parted at the airport, Andy returning to Daniel's home, where he'd stay until he was sufficiently recovered to return to his own life in Manchester. Our goodbye had been cursory – the ambulance was waiting to transport Andy and my train was due to leave, so

I'd kissed Andy and said I'd see him soon, knowing that seeing him would certainly mean seeing Daniel too.

And Daniel had only looked at me, smiled briefly and said, 'Take it easy, Kate.'

Coming from him, it had sounded like some kind of sarcastic accusation – *Like you ever take it easy, you uptight diva.*

Wearily, I wheeled my suitcase up to the front door of my apartment block, conscious of the washing that needed doing, the emails that needed answering, the catch-up with the Girlfriends' Club that needed arranging – and the limits of what I was willing to tell them about what had happened between Daniel and me on our last night in Turkey.

Last night. It barely seemed possible to believe that just twenty-four hours before, Daniel and I had been friends. That we'd been getting on well again, after so many years. That I'd imagined being able to tell my friends that the coldness between us was gone and everything was going to be all right.

Just twenty-four hours ago, he hadn't kissed me. I hadn't known I'd need the little blister pack in its purple box, containing one pill I needed to take as soon as possible, which I'd picked up at the pharmacy outside the Tube station. I'd felt like the most shameful cliche of a single woman returning from holiday after an ill-judged one-night stand, needing emergency contraception to put the mistake behind her and move on with her life.

And I supposed that was exactly what I was.

The door buzzed open at the touch of my key fob. I stepped into the lift, noticing a trace of the smell of cigarette smoke, which wasn't usually there. When I emerged on my floor, the smell was stronger – and there was another smell, too, of stale beer. I turned the corner and stopped in my tracks.

The corridor was normally a pretty bland space. Some

designer, sometime, had clearly decided 'corporate hotel lobby' was the look to aim for, and achieved it with faithful enthusiasm. There were abstract prints in pastel colours on the sage-green-painted walls. There were fleshy-leaved plants in brass holders, whose leaves a plant-care company came and dusted with damp sponges every couple of months. There were hexagonal cream tiles on the floor. It wasn't exactly characterful, but it felt safe and familiar.

Only now, the floor was littered with empty bottles and scattered with fag ash. There were cigarette butts in the plant pots. There was a cock and balls, complete with pubic hair and spurting ejaculate, drawn on the wall in what looked like... lipstick?

My first thought was that somehow, while I'd been away, squatters had moved into my flat. But I realised, kicking the bottles aside so I could wheel my case to my own front door, that was impossible. The doorbell app on my phone would have alerted me if anyone had tried to gain entry, and anyway, my door looked as secure as it always was.

I unlocked and carried my stuff inside. The flat smelled slightly musty, as places do when they've been left locked up and empty for a time, but otherwise everything seemed normal, exactly as I'd left it. The coat I'd decided against taking with me but not hung up in my haste to leave was still draped over the back of the sofa. The cake tin I'd washed after reclaiming it from Mona was still by the side of the sink. The imprint of my suitcase was there on the bed.

It was the same orderly, quiet place I'd left. The same lonely place.

I unpacked and put a load of washing on. Then I grabbed a couple of recycling bags, went out and collected all the empty bottles and took the bags downstairs. I picked up the cigarette butts and disposed of them, too. Normally the block's cleaner, Lucia, would have seen to this in the morning – I guessed she was off ill, and no one had noticed the mess until now.

Order restored, I went back inside, powered up my laptop and sat down at the dining table, which served as my desk when I was working at home. I opened the door to the balcony and heard the cries of gulls wheeling over the river, feeling fresh air blowing through and dispelling the mustiness.

It was five o'clock. Too early to pour a glass of wine, and too early to order a takeaway. Too early even to have a shower, because then I'd want to go ahead and do the other things, and soon it would be too early to go to bed. I replied to a few emails, placed a supermarket order for essentials (bagged salad, chicken breasts, cleaning products, baking parchment, wine, white chocolate Magnums), and flicked desultorily through Tinder on my phone.

It was just the same as any other evening at home. Just the same as things would have been if I hadn't gone away with Daniel. And yet, what would have felt like ordered serenity before now felt hollow and empty. There was no Daniel on the next-door balcony, his feet up on the balustrade, his swim shorts drying in the sun. There was no prospect of a walk and dinner in the evening, no cats to fuss and provide with titbits.

There was only me. And, I realised, there'd been only me for the longest time. I had my career, my friends, as many dates as I could be bothered to go on, even Claude waiting in the wings. I had my chats with Mona when I dropped off the results of my late-night baking. I had my beautiful home, everything in it arranged just the way I wanted it.

Before, it had been enough. Now, it wasn't.

It's just the post-holiday blues, I told myself. *You'll settle back into a rhythm and it will all be fine.*

It was true – I knew that. But the rhythm had been the same, unchanging bar a few minor dramas in my and my friends' lives, for years and years. The way things were looking, it would be the same for even longer – as long as I lived, perhaps.

I was used to solitude. I'd chosen it – I'd never had a relationship with a man I could imagine settling down with, and my university flatshare days were long past. But this didn't feel like solitude. It felt like loneliness. It felt horrible.

I imagined someone else ending their working day round about now. Someone to whom I could suggest a walk along the river, stop for a pint in a pub with, decide on a whim to go out for pizza with. Someone with whom I could have a minor argument about whose turn it was to take the bins out, discuss whether we needed to get someone in to replace the loose floorboard or if we could try doing it ourselves first, plan a weekend away at a nice hotel with a spa.

First world bloody problems, Kate. I pushed back my chair and stood up – it wasn't too early to have a shower any more. *If you want a weekend at a nice hotel, book one for yourself.*

But it wouldn't be the same.

I had a bath (which took the best part of an hour, versus fifteen minutes for a shower – bonus!), hung my washing on the airer and put another load on, turned on the telly and flicked through the channels looking for something to binge-watch that had at least five seasons so would keep me going for the best part of a week. I ordered prawn and cashew udon and poured a glass of wine. I messaged Claude to ask how things were going and let him know I was back in town.

I tried to suppress the waves of emptiness that kept washing over me, with a rhythm as steady as the breakers on the Alsaya beach but, just as inexorably, they kept coming.

By nine o'clock, I reckoned I could safely go to bed. I'd watched three episodes of the first season of *Westworld* (three more seasons to go! More than thirty episodes left! It might as well have been sent by the gods of bored, lonely people and, if I paced myself, should just about see me through until my new job started in ten days' time).

I brushed my teeth, cleansed my face with micellar water,

rosehip oil and more micellar water before applying an overnight resurfacing mask, smeared castor oil on my eyelashes, wrapped my hair in a silk turban, slathered moisturiser on my cuticles, put on my pyjamas and got into bed. The ritual was important – without it, I knew I wouldn't sleep.

With it, I might not sleep either, but I was going to give it my best shot.

I slid under the duvet, plugged in my AirPods and found a relaxing sound bath on my phone. Not waves on a beach – that was too triggering. Not the wind through pine trees, for the same reason. Rain on rooftops would have to do.

And, to my drowsy amazement, it worked. I felt my thoughts drifting away from reality, into absurd and random channels, a sure sign that sleep was approaching. The rain sounds swished comfortingly in my ears, my own mattress felt pleasingly firm beneath me, the cool breeze coming through the open window lightly fanned my face.

I was asleep.

Except I wasn't. I was on the yacht with Daniel. We were dancing together, the music filling our bodies, its pounding bass thrumming through me, willing me to move to its rhythm. Only I didn't want to be on the dance floor – I wanted to be alone with Daniel on the still deck with the cool seawater kissing my feet.

But I couldn't get away. The music was insistent, deafening, compelling me to keep dancing. Shrieks of laughter came from the other guests. There was the sound of beer cans being crushed and the smell of cigarette smoke. There was a resounding crash as a bottle shattered somewhere, and a woman's voice screaming, 'Fuck, what did you do that for, you utter plank?'

I sat bolt upright, sleep banished. I wasn't on the yacht – I was in my own bedroom. And the noise was coming from the next-door apartment.

Jintao, my neighbour, had always been as quiet and well behaved as I (mostly) was. When I had friends round, I slipped a note through his letterbox warning that there might be noise and thanked him with a bottle of something for his forbearance the next day, and he returned the favour. But, I remembered, Jintao had told me a few weeks back that he'd been seconded to his firm's New York office for six months and would be renting out the flat in his absence.

Clearly, his tenants weren't the quiet and respectful sort. And clearly, I was stuck with this party for as long as it went on. I got out of bed, pulled on my dressing gown and walked through to the living room. The noise was louder there, and louder still out on my balcony. Cigarette and weed smoke was drifting through from outside, so I retreated and closed the door, which made little difference to the noise level.

I considered knocking on the door and asking them to pack it in but rejected the idea almost immediately. I didn't want to be a fun sponge, and I didn't want to risk stirring up bad feeling when I was going to have to live next door to whoever these people were until Jintao's return.

I poured myself a glass of water and went back to bed, putting in earplugs and lying back down again. But I knew it was a lost cause. I was fully awake now; bands of tension had wrapped themselves around my shoulders and across my forehead. Sleep was a distant memory, and my earplugs barely dented the sound of the throbbing bass, which I was sure I could actually feel vibrating through my bedroom wall. Too enraged even to attempt baking, I lay in the darkness waiting for it to end.

They had quite the playlist. Over the next five hours, I listened to '80s pop, '90s rave, '00s rap and '10s grime. Show tunes seemed to be a particular favourite; at one point I could hear the partygoers shrieking tunelessly along to 'I Know Him

So Well'. I pulled my pillow over my head with a silent scream and wished I was dead – or deaf.

At last, the music subsided. I could hear voices in the street outside, laughing as they piled into Ubers and departed. There was a rattling crash as someone knocked over what sounded like a crate of empty bottles. And then silence descended, just before the dawn light began to filter through my curtains.

And it was then, in the darkest part of the night, hours of loneliness and anger and tiredness pressing down on me, that I weakened and texted Daniel.

TWENTY-FOUR

Andy opened the door on crutches. He'd had a haircut, and the long fringe that had been tied back from his face when he was in hospital was now flopping artfully over his forehead. His shirt looked like it had been ironed, which I guessed was Daniel's handiwork, unless he'd figured out a way to iron while sitting down. Although he'd only been discharged a day ago, the hospital pallor seemed to have gone from his face, and he was cheerful and smiling.

'Well, look what the cat dragged in.' He stepped carefully into my outstretched arms and I hugged him tightly. 'Did you get the unwaxed lemons and capers?'

'Every item on your extensive shopping list has been faithfully purchased,' I assured him. 'And the weight of these bags is about to drag my arms out of their sockets, so let's get them inside, unless you want to stand nattering on the doorstep all afternoon.'

He turned and I followed him inside, not offering to help him, because apparently Mistress Whiplash had been insistent that he should learn how to get himself around safely on his crutches before discharging him from hospital.

'You're looking good,' I said. 'You'll be training for the Paralympics in no time.'

'Maybe. But I still can't stand for long enough to cook, so you'd better take direction like a good little proxy chef. In here.'

He led the way into a large open-plan kitchen and living room. A sofa bed had been made up under the window, and various bottles and blister packs of pills stood on the kitchen counter. I'd never been to Daniel's home before, and I couldn't help being impressed by how beautiful it was: the floor polished, golden parquet, one wall painted a deep moss-green, a huge abstract cityscape hanging over the mantelpiece. A bureau made from some pale, glossy wood stood against the wall, a pottery jug crammed with peonies resting on it – the flowers a gift from the Girlfriends' Club to Andy, I knew from Whats-App. Two closed doors led to what I guessed must be the bathroom and bedroom – but I didn't want to think about Daniel's bedroom, now or ever. It was bad enough that I could almost detect the smell of lemon shampoo in the air.

'All settled into the convalescent home, then?' I asked.

'Getting there. Thank goodness our Daniel was able to have me to stay, because I could never have managed at home. That spiral staircase up to the mezzanine's a death trap, even when you're sober with two working hips, and the front room's not big enough to swing one of those cats he's so fond of.'

'Is he...?' I began.

'Through in the workshop. I'll unpack the shopping while you go and say hi.'

He propped his crutches up against the kitchen island, and I deposited the bags of food. I hesitated, feeling the need to gather my courage before seeing Daniel. But Andy winked at me and said, 'Off you go – it's through that door there. He won't bite. Not unless you want him to, anyway.'

I followed Andy's pointing hand and the faint hum of some sort of machinery to a door on the far side of the kitchen, and pushed it open. The workshop was large and bright, one long wall of steel-framed windows letting in the late-afternoon sun, which spilled in even squares on the polished concrete floor. Each beam of light looked almost solid, because of the sawdust that hung suspended in the air. The fresh smell of wood and the chemical smell of varnish was everywhere.

Around the perimeter of the room, pieces of furniture were arranged. There were elegantly proportioned sideboards, their polished surfaces glowing in the golden light. There were graceful bentwood chairs, each strip of timber evenly spaced, their curves so sinuous I wanted to stroke them. There was a drop-leaf dining table, its sides lowered to save space, leaving the marble-like grain of the walnut clearly visible.

At the far end of the room, Daniel was working. He was wearing paint-spattered overalls, the top down and the arms tied around his waist. I could see the contours of his back, chest and arms clearly in the low sunlight, the dusting of hairs on his chest glinting gold, his Turkish tan making him look as if he, too, had been carved from some rare wood.

The urge to run over and fling my body against his was as powerful as it was sudden. But I resisted, instead strolling over with a casual, 'Hey. How's it going?'

He lifted his head from the workbench. He'd been bending low over what looked like a chair or table leg, carefully smoothing its tapered surface with fine sandpaper. He pushed down the mask that covered his nose and mouth, and I could see that the skin surrounding it was lightly coated in sawdust.

'Good,' he said. 'I'm almost done here, then I'll grab a shower and come and join you guys. Andy tells me you're cooking for us?'

'Well, strictly speaking *he* is. He chose the recipes and sent me the shopping list. I'm just doing what I'm told. Kind of like one of those robots that performs operations, controlled by a surgeon on the other side of the world.'

'Quite the dream team. Everything all right at home?'

'Not really. That's why I messaged you at stupid o'clock to invite myself round today. Turns out the next-door flat's been turned into an Airbnb, and it's party central.'

'Fun times.'

'I had Barbara Dickson and Elaine Paige blaring through my bedroom wall at four in the morning.' I don't know what possessed me, but I heard myself break into song – the bit about it being madness he couldn't be mine. Then I tailed off abruptly. 'Sorry. It's been going round in my head all day.'

Daniel laughed. 'So what are you going to do about it?'

'No idea. My neighbour says the tenant he let the place to isn't living there – clearly she's decided she can make a fast buck renting it out. He's sent her a cease and desist but there's not much he can really do apart from give her notice, and that could take months.'

I moved a few steps closer to him – close enough to smell his body over the scents of wood and beeswax. I felt as if every cell of me was reliving the memory of our night together, every muscle longing to reach out and touch him again.

Instead, I reached out and touched the piece of wood he'd been working on, tracing my finger lightly over its hard length, from base to tip.

'This is pretty,' I said. 'All your stuff – it's stunning. I had no idea this place was so...'

'So what? Dusty?'

'Nah, I was expecting it to be dusty. But it's... I don't know. Like being in another world.'

'That's kind of how I feel, when I'm working,' he said. 'Like nothing really exists except me and the wood. It's got a life to it, even though some of it was last alive eighty years ago. When a piece has been hanging around in someone's garage or loft or whatever and it's knackered and warped and basically only good for the scrap heap, and you get the chance to restore it, it's... Well. Pretty amazing.'

'A bit more rewarding than drafting prudential risk frameworks, anyway,' I said.

Daniel laughed again. God, the way his white, even teeth flashed in his tanned face and his grey eyes sparkled almost silver. I wished I could bottle the way that laugh made me feel.

Then his face became serious again and he said, 'Is everything okay? Did you sort the... you know? The *thing*.'

'The emergency contraception?' He could pussyfoot around it if he wanted to, but I wasn't going to. 'Yes. It's been freely available in pharmacies for over twenty years.'

'And did it...?'

'Work? I assume so. I mean, I won't know until...'

Now it was my turn to be coy.

'Are you feeling okay? You're not – I don't know, sick or anything?'

'Actually, I feel rough as a bag of spanners. But two hours' sleep will do that to you, morning-after pill or no morning-after pill.'

'Kate, like I said, I'm so sorry about what happened.' He gave the piece of wood a final caress with the sandpaper and laid it down on his workbench, then untied the sleeves of his overall and wiped his face with one cuff before shrugging it back over his shoulders. 'I feel responsible.'

'You don't have to. There's nothing to feel responsible for. It happened, it won't happen again. It's done. End of.'

Daniel's face flickered in something that was almost a wince then became still again. 'Okay. If you're sure.'

'If anything changes, you'll be the first to know.'

But something has changed, my mind screamed. *It has! I just need to find a way to unchange it.*

Except there wasn't a way. I could only ignore the seismic shift that seemed to have affected the way I saw not just Daniel but my entire life. Ignore it, and hope it went away, the tectonic plates settling back into their old pattern, or me making peace with the new landscape I seemed to be inhabiting.

'Come on, then. I'm done for the day – let's get to this dinner you and Andy have been bigging up.'

While we were talking, the sun had dipped below the rooftops opposite and heavy grey clouds had descended, dimming the light in the workshop to a blueish, twilight glow. The dancing motes of dust in the air were invisible now and the squares of light on the floor had become elongated, silvery oblongs.

Daniel gestured 'after you', and I walked slowly back across the room, my trainers silent on the concrete floor; his work boots louder behind me. I pushed open the door to the living room and we walked through.

'Christ, you two took your time,' Andy said. 'I was beginning to worry you'd chopped Katie babe up with a bandsaw, mate.'

'I'm still in one piece,' I assured him.

'Well, you'd better get your skates on. That wild Alaskan salmon isn't going to cook itself, you know.'

'I'll just jump in the shower,' Daniel said (and, right on cue, my brain conjured up an image of his naked body, water sluicing down the chiselled planes of his torso, flattening the sun-bleached hair, coursing over his ridged abdomen towards —). 'I'll be out in five minutes.'

'No rush. Kate's got parsley to chop and lemons to zest, and her knife work's always been shit.' Andy picked up a glass of wine from the kitchen island and took a long swallow. 'Drink for the sous chef?'

'Andy.' Alarm filled me like icy water. 'Are you sure you should be—'

'Babe, have you seen the dose of tramadol I'm on? A drop of

Pinot frigging Grigio is neither here nor there. Now peel that garlic – we'll need four plump cloves.'

Daniel and I looked at each other, then I looked at Andy and the glass of wine in his hand. I wanted to snatch it, pour the contents down the sink and follow up with the rest of the bottle for good measure. But I couldn't police him forever – or even for the rest of the night. He might not be a hundred per cent steady on his crutches, but he was more than capable, once I'd left to go home, of getting himself down the road to the off-licence – or persuading Daniel to go for him.

I turned back to Daniel, who gave an almost invisible shrug before opening the door to the bathroom and closing it behind him. But I knew he'd realised, same as I had, that the consequences of Andy's Turkish adventure and our impulsive rescue mission would be more far-reaching than any of us could have predicted.

TWENTY-FIVE

There was no contact between me and Andy, or Daniel, for a couple of days after that dinner. I met Abbie and Rowan for drinks (Naomi sending her apologies, because Patch was visiting his grandmother, and her usual babysitter had gone on strike), and I updated them on Andy but said nothing about what had happened between Daniel and me.

The Airbnb guests left, or checked out or whatever, and I had a night of blissful peace and decent sleep before a new group arrived. On their second evening in Jintao's apartment, they had a barbecue on their balcony, filling my flat with a miasma of burning meat. Normally, I'd have gritted my teeth and told myself to unclench and be more tolerant, but their music had kept me awake all the previous night (clearly, whoever had been designated DJ this time round had a major penchant for power ballads, and I'd woken up after three hours' sleep with 'I Will Always Love You' looping relentlessly through my aching head). And also, I'd actually gone to the trouble of ironing a dress to wear on my date with Claude that evening, and it had acquired a smell of grilling sausages that clearly wasn't going to shift in time.

By the time I'd selected something else to wear, taken the pink polish off my toes and replaced it with green, because the skirt I'd picked to wear was pink and I'd had a wobble about the overall effect being too matchy-matchy, done my make-up and blow-dried my hair, I was running late. Resisting the temptation to position a speaker against my bedroom wall with the Dead Kennedys playing at full volume, I locked the flat and hurried out.

There'd be no hot-air balloons involved in this date – I was confident of that, because I'd booked the restaurant myself. And not just any restaurant – a swanky French place in a newly opened City hotel so exclusive I was willing to bet even Claude hadn't been there before. I'd only managed to get a table through what had felt like the blindest stroke of luck – I'd gone onto the booking engine with scant hope and predictably found there were no tables to be had. Then, on a whim, I'd checked back two minutes later and *voilà* (as Claude might say) a table for two at seven thirty had appeared. It was located close to where Claude and I used to work, and close enough to home for me to walk. But I was wearing high heels in honour of the occasion, and besides, I no longer had time, so I summoned an Uber and reached my destination only ten minutes late.

And there, waiting in the lobby, was Claude.

He greeted me with a slightly shame-faced smile. 'I'm so sorry, Kate. My last meeting overran and I didn't get a chance to change. I basically sprinted here from the office.'

'I'm late too, so I'm not about to judge you for it,' I assured him, taking in his broad shoulders in his immaculately cut suit, his sharply barbered hair, the scent of expensive cologne that came off his skin even after a day at the office and a last-minute rush through the hot, crowded City streets.

He was seriously attractive; everything I wanted in a man: smooth, successful, sexy. So why could I not help thinking of how Daniel had looked in his workshop, the sun shining on his dusty skin?

'The twelfth floor, right?' Claude gestured to the doors of a lift at the far end of the lobby.

Hold on – a lift? The twelfth floor? In my frantic haste to secure a table, I had neglected to find out the exact location of the restaurant. And none of the reviews I'd glanced at had mentioned that the damn place ought to come with a health warning for acrophobics. My knees began to tremble as I followed him into the lift – and not in a good way.

As we whooshed upwards, I tried to make cheerful conversation while wondering when my stomach, which I appeared to have left behind on the ground floor, was going to join the rest of me.

'We've put you outside on the terrace,' the maître d' said, leaning in conspiratorially. My stomach reappeared abruptly, with a queasy lurch. 'Since it's such a beautiful evening. You've got the best view – it's the table everyone asks for.'

'Impressive work,' Claude murmured to me. 'Friends in high places?'

High places? Please don't remind me we're in one right now.

I gave what I hoped was an alluring and mysterious smile and said, 'Maybe,' even though I'd just made the reservation online as I usually did.

But when we reached our table, I felt my mysterious allure fade away. It was right at the edge of the terrace, next to a glass barrier. The view over London was spectacular – I could see why it was a popular spot. But all I could think about was the view straight down. Next to me, if I so much as glanced sideways, was a sheer drop to the street far below. Cars and buses crawled along, tiny as toys. Commuters hurried along like a swarm of ants making their way home to their nest. Pigeons flew past at my eye level.

Looking at it made me feel sick and dizzy, so I forced my

eyes upwards and looked straight ahead, at Claude, which was certainly no hardship. But even when I couldn't see it, I knew that the precipitous drop was there, just a chest-high pane of glass away.

'You okay, Kate?' Claude asked. 'You've gone a bit pale.'

Poor bugger's probably worried I'm about to spew all over his shoes again, I thought. And who could blame him?

'I'm great.' I forced a cheerful note into my voice. 'Would you like a cocktail, or shall we move straight on to wine?'

'I couldn't resist taking a look at the wine list online earlier,' he said, his toothpaste-commercial-perfect smile flashing out. 'They've got some bin ends that are fantastic value. The sommelier knows his thing.'

'Why don't you choose?' I slid the leather-bound menu across the table. It felt weighty as a telephone directory; if I dropped it over the edge, I'd probably kill a pedestrian in the street below. 'I'm no expert.'

'I'm sure you know the most important thing,' he said, 'which is what you like.'

'I suppose we should decide what we're eating first.' I opened the food menu, my mouth instantly salivating at the prospect of langoustines cooked in Pernod, roast turbot and peach soufflé.

'You order food for us both, then,' he suggested. 'And I'll pick the wine.'

'Deal.'

A waiter appeared with a board of bread (not just any bread – four different kinds, each with accompanying whipped, flavoured butter) and I ordered our food: tomato salad and turbot for me, langoustines and roast lamb for him. Claude frowned down at the wine list for a moment, then placed an order in fluent French.

It seemed to go on for a long time – inside my handbag, I could almost hear my credit card giving a sharp intake of breath and felt vastly relieved that it wouldn't be long before I was back working and earning money.

Minutes later, a waiter appeared with two glasses of champagne and a tripod holding six oysters on a bed of ice.

'I hope you don't mind,' Claude said. 'I feel like no meal is complete without oysters. You don't hate them, do you?'

'Love them.'

'*Bien.*' He smiled, squeezed lemon onto an oyster, added a grind of black pepper, eased it loose from its shell with a fork and passed it across the table to me.

I slurped, tasting the delicious briny saltiness – like being hit in the face by a wave. I was instantly, fleetingly transported back to Alsaya, and swimming in the sea with Daniel. But I pushed the thought aside – I was back home now, with another man; a man with whom I could imagine a real future.

As we ate and drank – Claude, it turned out, had ordered not one wine but three: the champagne, a flinty Riesling for the salad and seafood, and a carafe of peppery, fruity red to accompany his lamb, which of course he insisted I share – he asked me about my time away, and I filled him in on the edited highlights of Andy's situation.

'He's staying with a friend of ours, just while he gets more mobile,' I explained. 'Then he'll be able to go back home and back to work. I'm glad we went, even though he'd have probably been okay without us.'

'You're a good friend,' Claude said. 'He – Andy – is lucky to have you. I hope I'll meet him one day; he sounds like a character.'

'He certainly is,' I said.

I felt a spark of pleasure at the idea that Claude might one day want to meet my friends. I imagined Rowan, Abbie and Naomi's glowing approval of him. My mind briefly wandered into a fantasy future with him: the stylish house we'd have, perhaps in South West London, with a garden and a vast kitchen where I'd learn to bake croissants. Our children would be bilingual, and I supposed I'd have to learn French as well, so I could charm his mother when we visited her during our regular trips to Paris. We'd honour their Cameroonian heritage of course, visiting Africa with our children and connecting them to their roots.

Whatever those looked like – I realised I had no idea. But still: we'd be a power couple, successful and attractive, utterly in synch and smitten with each other. Our careers would go from strength to strength, but we'd always have time for our friends, our family and each other.

Even Daniel, my imagination provided optimistically, would get on well with Claude.

Two hours later, I spooned the remnants of the intoxicatingly sweet purée from the bottom of my soufflé dish and sipped the last of the pudding wine Claude had ordered. The sun had set and the lights of the city beneath me looked positively benign, the sheer drop rendered invisible in the darkness. At some point, Claude's ankle had reached beneath the table, made contact with mine and stayed there. Our hands had brushed when we'd shared spoonfuls of dessert. Our eye contact had become longer and more intense as darkness fell.

'Would you like anything else?' I asked. 'A brandy or something?'

'I can seldom say no to an Armagnac,' he said. 'But tonight I think I will.'

So I asked for the bill, and Claude – to my relief – insisted on paying for the wine. We got up to leave (with me edging sideways around the table to avoid confronting the sight of the sheer drop through the glass panel that was all that stood between me and a screaming plummet down to certain death) then, stuffed and tipsy, we made our way back to the lift and gently descended to street level.

'Kate.' He placed both his hands on my shoulders and

looked at me, his dark eyes serious. 'I'd like to invite you back to my place for a drink – or a coffee. But there's no pressure.'

Like I'd need any pressure. The wine had gone to my head – I felt pleasantly mellow and dizzy not only with wine but also with relief at feeling my feet firmly on the ground. If I went home with Claude, and stayed there, I'd not only be escaping whatever next-door's DJ had in store for the night but also taking our relationship to the next level.

Plus, I had my usual date-night ammo with me in my handbag, so there'd be none of the sickening next-morning regret I'd experienced with Daniel.

'Let me get the cab, then,' I said, smiling up into his impossibly handsome face.

'If you insist.'

For the first time since we'd arrived at the restaurant, I took my phone out of my bag. I'd been on too many dates where my companion had been constantly distracted by his screen – or, worse, actually glued to it throughout – and I'd resolved not to be that person. Claude, too, had politely confined checking his phone to the few minutes I'd spent finding my way to the plushy, fragrant ladies' loo.

But now, I regretted my good manners instantly. Before I could even tap through to the Uber app, my notifications were clamouring for my attention. There were thirty-eight new messages on the Girlfriends' Club WhatsApp, and I had five missed calls.

And there was a text message from Daniel.

Where the hell are you? Andy's gone AWOL.

TWENTY-SIX

When I arrived at Daniel's house twenty-five minutes later, there was already quite the party going on. If you count Abbie, Patch and Daniel all sitting around the dining table drinking coffee and tapping anxiously at their phones as a party, that is. To be honest, it didn't feel much like one. Not only were Matt, who was away with work; Naomi, who was looking after her and Patch's twins; and Rowan and Alex, who were visiting Alex's sister, not present, but the atmosphere felt distinctly sombre.

'Any news?' I asked as soon as Daniel had opened the door and gestured to a seat and the cafetière, from which I helped myself eagerly. Sleep wasn't going to be on the cards tonight anyway, and if search parties were going to be mounted, I'd better sober up as fast as I could.

'Nothing.' Daniel sat down next to me, his legs outstretched. I could see lines of dust on his faded black T-shirt, as if he'd leaned over his workbench to reach out for tools, and the edge of the surface had imprinted itself on his clothing. He returned my sidelong glance at him with one of his own, taking in my full face of make-up, swishy skirt and freshly manicured nails. 'Where've you been, anyway, Kate? Out partying?'

'Just out,' I replied evasively.

'On a *date*?' Abbie asked. 'Come on, share the deets.'

'Look, it doesn't matter where I've been,' I said. 'I'll tell you later. Where's Andy? When did you see him last?'

'He went out at seven – said he needed saffron for the risotto he was making. And he never came back,' Daniel explained.

'And it doesn't take that long to find a shop that sells saffron, even in Peckham, does it?' Abbie joked half-heartedly.

'Peckham's a cultural melting pot, I'll have you know,' Daniel said. 'There's every ingredient known to man within about ten minutes' walk of here. Why do you think I'm worried?'

'It's half past ten now,' I said. 'If something had happened to him, you'd have heard, surely?'

'Depends on what happened.' Grimly, Daniel picked up his phone and flicked it to life, staring at the screen but clearly seeing nothing that hadn't been there last time he'd checked.

'We can't exactly call the rozzers, can we?' Patch said. 'He's a grown man; he's only been gone a few hours. They'd laugh us out of town.'

'Did he take his phone with him?' I asked.

Daniel nodded. 'But it's going straight to voicemail. His passport's here, at least, so we know he hasn't done a runner abroad again.'

'If his phone's off then he can't be using it to get around,' I mused. 'Or to – you know. Contact people to buy anything.'

To buy drugs. My unspoken words hung in the air.

'It's not necessarily off, though,' Abbie pointed out. 'He could just have his calls diverted to voicemail. How the hell do you even buy drugs these days, anyway?'

'Instagram, apparently,' Daniel said.

'Seriously?' Suddenly, I felt very old, clueless and out of touch.

'Although to be fair,' Daniel went on, 'this is Peckham. It's not just obscure spices you can get within ten minutes' walk of here. He could just as easily have done it the old-fashioned way, from a guy on a street corner.'

'But you don't know that's what he's doing,' I said, trying to convince myself as much as my friends. 'He could have bumped into an acquaintance. He could have met someone and hooked up. He could have gone for a walk and got lost.'

'If he'd got lost, he'd have used the map on his phone,' Patch said. 'Same if he'd run into someone and was having a drink or whatever. He'd have messaged Daniel.'

'Not if his battery was dead,' Abbie pointed out.

'And hook-ups don't take three hours,' I said. 'Not last time I had one, anyway.'

Daniel glanced sideways at me again and I felt my face flame.

'Sounds like you've been hooking up with the wrong people,' he said.

'I thought we all knew that,' I retorted, and it was his turn to look embarrassed.

I noticed Abbie looking curiously from me to Daniel and back. The last thing I needed right now was her putting two and two together and getting – well, four. I knew that if my friends found out what had happened, they'd all fly straight into matchmaking mode, trying to convince me that what had happened hadn't been so bad – that it actually had the potential to be *really good*, and why didn't I have a proper talk with Daniel and see if we could make a go of things? After all, they'd say, the two of you have always been so—

'We should go out and look for him,' I said. 'There's absolutely no point us all sitting around here speculating about what might have happened.'

'Yeah,' Daniel said. 'Because when we go and look for Andy, it always ends well.'

'Well, it did, didn't it?' I snapped back. 'I mean, we found him. And he was in one piece. And we brought him back.'

And everything changed between you and me, and there's no way I can see of changing it back, even if I wanted to, which I'm not sure I do.

'Abbie and I will go,' Patch said. 'You two stay here, and you can let us know if he comes back.'

'Why do we need to stay?' I argued. 'He's got keys, hasn't he, Daniel?'

'He does, but I've got to say I'm not one hundred per cent confident he won't have lost them. Especially if he...'

Again, the words he meant went unsaid. We all knew what Andy had been like when his drug use had been at its peak. He'd almost burned Abbie and Matt's flat down once by making a cheese toastie with the iron and then leaving it switched on. He'd lost more mobile phones than I could count, or possibly pawned them and claimed to have lost them. One time he'd turned up at my place with a cat he said was lost, even though it was in perfect health, had a collar on and was complaining vocally about being kidnapped, and I'd had to get him to retrace his steps so we could return it home.

The man was a total liability. The thought of him slipping back into his old ways was too awful to contemplate, and I could understand why Daniel couldn't bear to voice the prospect of Andy returning to that life, dragging us all into the chaos with him even though he hadn't meant to.

'That settles it, then,' Abbie said. 'We'll go; you stay here. We'll keep in contact.'

She took her phone out of her bag and tapped through to the map, Patch leaning over her shoulder and peering at the screen.

'Which is the dodgiest of your local pubs?' he asked. 'The Duke's Head?'

'Nah, that's gone all upmarket,' Daniel said. 'Seitan burgers and craft ale. Try the Coach and Horses first.'

'Gotcha.'

'Actually, I quite fancy a seitan burger and a craft ale right now,' I heard Patch say to Abbie.

She laughed and said something in response, but I couldn't make it out because the door was closing behind them.

The flat was suddenly very quiet. I could hear the hum of Daniel's fridge, the distant rattle of a passing train, a breeze rustling the leaves of a plane tree outside the window. It felt like a silence that could last a long time.

Then Daniel said, 'So where were you tonight?'

'Does it matter? I came as soon as I saw your message.'

'Maybe I was just making conversation.'

'Fair enough. I was out with someone.'

'Someone like... a boyfriend?'

I nodded, trying to look casual but feeling suddenly tense and weird inside – guilty, almost.

'First date?' he asked. 'One of your Tinder dudes?'

'Actually, no. Second. And I met him through work. I mentioned him to you when we were... Before.'

I didn't want to remind myself – or him – of that evening by the sea in Alsaya, which already felt like about a hundred years ago.

'Second? That's going some, by your standards.'

'Daniel, I don't know if I've missed a memo or something, but I don't have to justify my love life to you.'

'I wasn't asking you to. Just making conversation, like I said. What's the guy's name?'

I considered refusing to tell him, saying he needed to butt out. But what would be the point? I'd only give him the satisfaction of feeling like he'd embarrassed me – and then that silence would descend over us again, and if I had to endure that for more than about ten seconds I might scream.

'He's called Claude.' *Like I told you when we were in Turkey. And like I'd bet my almost-full bottle of Le Labo perfume you remember.*

'And it's going well, is it?'

'Seems to be. We were actually on our way back to his place when I found out about...' I gestured vaguely with my hands. 'All this.'

'Poor old Claude,' Daniel said, with a grin that didn't look entirely sincere. 'Thought he was in like Flynn and got packed off home with blue balls. Let me know his address – I'll send flowers.'

Now I couldn't help rising to his provocation. 'Don't be so bloody ridiculous. And what the hell were you thinking, anyway, letting Andy go off on his own? Anything could have happened to him, and *you'll* be responsible if it has.'

'Oh, I will, will I? What did you expect me to do, put one of those backpacks on him with reins like toddlers have and not let him out of my sight?'

'You should have gone with him. He's on crutches, for Christ's sake.'

'And a grown-ass man, and a guest in my home, as opposed to a prisoner. And under strict instructions from his physio to stay as active as possible. He'd already started frying onion for a bloody risotto, Kate. I wasn't to know he'd do a disappearing act in between that and chopping the garlic.'

'I still think—'

'You still think *what?* That between us, we can somehow control Andy's life and dictate what he does? Because that worked just great before, didn't it?'

'Jesus, Daniel. You know perfectly well I never tried to control anyth—'

Then I stopped. We both stopped, because there was the

unmistakeable sound of a key scraping at the door, fumblingly, trying and failing to find the lock.

I sprang to my feet.

'Leave it, Kate,' Daniel said. 'He's perfectly capable of letting himself in. Probably.'

I sank back onto the sofa, weak with relief but shaking with pent-up anger that had nowhere to go, feeling like the hard chair I'd been sitting on before wasn't equal to holding me up. Moments later, Andy walked into the room.

I say walked. He was on his crutches, for one thing, so it was more a sort of three-point swing. He'd got much better at using them, I'd noticed, but it was still awkward. Especially as he couldn't quite manage to move in a straight line. He executed a sort of parabola from the front door to the kitchen, where he deposited his keys and a small brown paper bag. Then he manoeuvred to another door and opened it. Inside, I could see a washing machine and tumble drier stacked one on top of the other, a hoover and ironing board, and shelves holding cleaning products.

'Ooops,' Andy said, almost as if he didn't know we were there. 'Mustn't piss in the futility room.'

He veered off again, found the right door, and we heard the sound of copious urination. Then he reappeared, clocked us, and broke into his familiar megawatt smile.

'You're still up!' he cried. 'I thought I'd only been gone five minutes and then I saw the time. Flies when you're having fun, doesn't it? But now we can all have fun together, because look what I brought.'

He snatched the brown bag off the table and tossed it over to Daniel, who caught it effortlessly, one-handed. He upended it onto his outstretched palm and I saw a small ziplock bag tip out.

'Daniel,' I said, 'for God's sake don't! Not now.'

'Calm down, Kate.' Daniel waved the bag in front of my

eyes. 'It's only saffron. Where've you been anyway, mate? We sent out a search party.'

'You did? Oh blimey. I suppose that's the naughty step for me, then. You didn't ring the peelers, did you?'

'We reckoned there was no point, on account of you being big enough and ugly enough to look after yourself. In theory, at least.'

'We were really worried, Andy.' My voice came out all thin and high-pitched with indignation and anxiety. 'Abbie and Patch are out looking for you right now.'

'They are?' Andy's eyes widened. 'Maybe I should go out and look for them, and then you two can come out and look for me. It'll be like that Agatha Christie novel where they all go missing, one after another.'

He collapsed on the sofa next to me, giggling.

'I'll text them,' Daniel said. 'Tell them they can stand down and go home.'

'But what about my risotto? Tell them to come over. We can have a party, just like old times.'

'It's almost midnight, mate. I'll make you a cup of tea.'

'Fanta?' Andy suggested, hopeful as a child. 'Please tell me there's Fanta in the fridge. My mouth feels like I've been sucking virgin Tampax. Not that I've ever seen a Tampax, virgin or otherwise. I've led a sheltered life, you know, Katie babe.'

He looked at me, his pupils tiny, his eyes clearly struggling to focus on my face.

'Not sheltered enough,' I managed to reply, but Andy had already moved on.

'Tunes! We need tunes! Come on, fire up the old Spotify.'

Daniel obliged, sitting down on the armchair opposite us. He played the music at a low volume, so as not to piss off his neighbours, and let Andy talk, agreeing with him, contributing occasionally to his rambling reminiscences, bringing him more Fanta and a pack of Doritos when he said he was hungry.

It was a practised ritual we'd enacted countless times before. I sat in silence, listening to them, feeling the last of my anxiety dissolve – not because I wasn't worried any more, but because I simply couldn't endure being worried any longer.

At some point, their voices and the music drifting over and past me, I fell asleep.

TWENTY-SEVEN

THEN

2009–2010

Two days after Abbie and Matt's discovery of Andy's theft and him turning up at my flat, he checked into a residential rehab centre. It was significantly less plushy than either of us would have liked – but, as I said to him, he had to cut his coat to suit my cloth.

He wasn't allowed to contact me while he was there, and I spent the whole time fretting about what I'd done. What if Andy never forgave me for the ultimatum I'd issued? What if he came out changed, diminished, not the friend whose jokes made me laugh until I cried or the lover whose body I'd look at in my bed, unable to believe my luck that he was there? What if it didn't work, and he immediately went back to his old ways, leaving me thousands of pounds poorer and fresh out of ideas?

Two weeks into his stay there, I had a call from Daniel. Since my housewarming party a year or so previously, I'd barely seen him on my own, and only occasionally when Andy and I were out with the group and he turned up to join us. He and

Andy often went out together, I knew, but I didn't share their fondness for nightclubs so never asked to go along.

So his suggestion that we meet up for a coffee took me by surprise. I didn't have the chance to think of a reason not to go, and besides, I knew how close he was to Andy, and seeing him would be a substitute – albeit a poor one – for seeing Andy, who I was missing desperately.

But almost as soon as I laid eyes on Daniel, lounging almost horizontally on the comfortable banquette seat, leaving the hard chair opposite for me, I regretted my decision. It wasn't that looking at him was any hardship; he was as handsome as ever. Andy, I'd learned, liked to surround himself with people he considered beautiful, and it was easy to see how Daniel, with his tawny hair, silver-grey eyes and jaw you could use to crack walnuts, had made the cut.

But he looked at me with undisguised coldness, and I realised at once that this wasn't going to be a friendly catch-up.

'So,' he said, 'how's Warden Norton?'

Confused, I put down my cappuccino and sat across from him. 'How's who?'

'You haven't seen *The Shawshank Redemption*, then. He's the prison guard.'

'Look,' I bristled, 'I didn't arrange for Andy to attend drug rehabilitation out of spite, you know. And it's not exactly hard labour – he's perfectly comfortable. He's receiving medical care he desperately needs. I have no idea why people who claim to be his friends didn't think to do this years ago.'

'I see. So in spite of the fact I've been Andy's friend since university and you've known him all of five minutes—'

'Two years, actually.'

'All of *two years*' – he placed mocking emphasis on the words – 'you know what's best for him, and the rest of us don't.'

'Matt and Abbie agreed with me. And Matt's known Andy years longer than you have, if length of tenure as his friend is how we're judging whether people are qualified to know what's best for him.'

Daniel shrugged. 'Just strikes me as a bit dramatic, that's all. The bloke likes a bit of ching – it's hardly the crime of the century.'

'I never said it was. But stealing money from friends who trusted you strikes me as pretty high up there.'

His eyes widened, and I realised he hadn't been privy to this part of the story.

Sensing victory, I pressed on, forcing myself to adopt as reasonable a tone as I could. 'Look, like I said, I didn't do this out of spite. I want Andy to be happy and well and not destroying his life and losing the people closest to him. Surely that's what you want too?'

'Hear me out, Kate. I get that you think Sinclair's on a bit of a self-destruct mission. But what you don't seem to see is, he can't. He's bulletproof.'

Part of me was horrified by this idea – I'd seen Andy at his most vulnerable, his most fragile. When I held him in my arms, his body sweating and shaking, I felt like I was cradling a child, or a precious possession I needed to protect at all costs, with invading robbers banging on my door. But also, I felt a flicker of understanding.

'How do you mean?' I asked warily.

'Where did you grow up, Kate?'

Surprised, I said, 'Somerset. Why?'

'So tell me about that. What was it like?'

'My uncle's a farmer. He was the eldest son, so he got to inherit the land and all that. My dad's a solicitor, Mum works in a school – she's head of year now. I'm an only child and I guess they wanted the best for me. So I went to uni in London and now I'm here. No apple-growing for yours truly.'

Daniel grinned at my half-hearted attempt at humour, but his smile lacked any real warmth. 'Tough gig, huh?'

'Of course not. Not at all.'

'Exactly. Not at all. If you'd fallen through the cracks – if there'd even been cracks for you to fall through – what do you think would have happened?'

'I don't know what you mean.'

'Come on, Kate. You're a smart woman. Take where I grew up. Small town on the south coast. Massive deprivation. Huge unemployment. Substance abuse off the scale. I look at the kids I did GCSEs with, and half the girls didn't get to twenty without having babies, and at least half a dozen of the boys have done time. I got lucky – my stepdad was a carpenter, and I was passionate enough about learning from him to go to college and study design. And then I met Andy.'

I knew from Abbie that Andy's parents' Oxbridge ambitions for him had been thwarted when he tanked his A levels and he'd ended up at what Andy himself had described as a 'no-hopers' former polytechnic'. So I just nodded.

'He swanned around there like he was some kind of god come to earth,' Daniel went on. 'Don't get me wrong, I love the guy. But the difference between him and the rest of us was – well. You know.'

'Of course, I know Andy's parents were wealthy,' I said. 'But they aren't any more, right? They got totally rinsed in the financial crisis. Abbie said.'

'Totally rinsed in the sense that they had to flog their four-mil house in Hampstead and the investment property Andy was living in rent-free, sure. But Andy's godfather, who owns that art gallery, will always have a job for him when he gets desperate. Andy's rich grandmother would have paid for him to go to rehab if you hadn't.'

'If Andy's rich grandmother could have persuaded him to go to rehab,' I pointed out.

'Fair point. Your powers of persuasion must be quite something. But that's not the point. You know – and I know, and

Matt and Abs would know if they weren't so busy being fucking kind to everyone all the time – that nothing truly bad will ever happen to Andy Sinclair. He'll always have a safety net.'

'He needs us,' I insisted. 'We're his friends. He's fallen out with his family. He needs people who love him. He needs help. That's why I helped him.'

Daniel shrugged again, pushing his too-long fringe back from his eyes. 'Well, I guess we'll just have to see if it works. I'd hate to see you throwing good money after bad.'

It did work. Andy checked out a month later, tanned and relaxed, and moved back in with me, just until he could get back on his feet. It wasn't an arrangement either of us would have chosen – I liked my privacy and Andy liked his freedom. But it was what it was, and we did our best to make it work. He slept on the sofa in the living room, only sometimes coming into my bed. If he was seeing other people, he did it elsewhere, and I turned a blind eye.

But it meant seeing a lot of Daniel. With Matt sticking to his decision to cut Andy out of his life, a vacancy for Andy's best friend had been created, and Daniel stepped in to fill it. Daniel never voiced it to me, but I sensed he felt relieved at how happy Andy appeared, and gradually his manner to me warmed. And I could see how close the two of them were and felt myself gradually warming to Daniel in return.

And we had fun, in those first weeks and months. Mindful that we didn't want to put temptation in Andy's way, we devised a programme of entertainment that would have gone down well in a swanky old-people's home. We cooked our way through Anna Del Conte's *Gastronomy of Italy*. We played endless games of Scrabble. We went to the opera and the ballet and to the beach for fish and chips.

Each day, Andy seemed more serene, more content. Gradually, the wariness with which I'd been watching him eased. I grew more comfortable with Daniel, too – spending a couple of nights a week and most weekends in his company made me realise he could be engaging, irreverent and funny.

I let my guard down. Foolishly, perhaps – but I was happy. I believed everything would be all right. I thought I'd saved the day – saved Andy from himself, even.

Then, one Friday night, I went out after work. It wasn't meant to be a massive night, but one pub turned into three and then someone suggested going to Brick Lane for a curry. I didn't want to say no – these were my colleagues, and I'd been missing out on socialising. Daniel was at my flat keeping Andy company (or babysitting, as he'd ironically said in his text message). I had no reason to believe everything wouldn't be okay.

It was midnight when I got home. Expecting Daniel to have left and Andy to be asleep (he'd developed an almost unnerving appetite for sleep), I let myself into the flat as silently as I could.

But they were both there in the living room, awake. Cocktail glasses stood on the coffee table, next to a shaker and a full ashtray.

And when Andy turned to greet me, there was white powder on his top lip and panic in his eyes.

TWENTY-EIGHT

NOW

I dreamed I was back in Alsaya.

I was in bed, and Daniel was next to me – I could smell him and hear the rhythm of his breathing. But I couldn't touch him – when I reached out a hand, there was only emptiness there, as if the bed had been cut in half and the side where he was sleeping moved away. I tried to reach further, but I couldn't – sleep held me firmly still.

I could hear the rush of waves breaking on the shore, far louder than it had been in my actual room, where the hum of the air conditioning had dulled the sound of the sea. And I could hear gulls, too, their shrieking calls so loud overhead I feared they'd flown in through the open balcony door and were wheeling above me, their bright eyes watching me, their cruel beaks opening to—

With a muffled scream and a gasp, I sat up. I was on the sofa in Daniel's front room. Someone had covered me with a blanket during the night and slipped a pillow under my head – that must have been what smelled of the lemony shampoo Daniel used. It was a flock of green parakeets I could hear outside, not gulls at all. And the sound I'd thought was waves, or breathing, was coming from Daniel's workshop, presumably a saw or sander.

I was still in the clothes I'd worn for my date with Claude. My tiered maxi skirt was bunched up around my thighs and the underwire of my bra was digging painfully into my armpit. I stood, easing the knots out of my shoulders and spine. Amazingly, in spite of my less than comfortable night, I felt refreshed and calm. Whatever challenges the day had in store for me – and there were likely to be plenty – I was ready to face them.

Or I would be, once I'd had a wee and a coffee, and hopefully borrowed a toothbrush.

The bathroom door opened, and Andy emerged in a T-shirt and underpants, leaning on one crutch. His hair was damp from the shower and his face very pale, dark shadows ringing his eyes.

'Morning,' I said cautiously. I knew from experience that Andy's mood after a heavy night was never sunny – he'd be morose at best, bitter and quarrelsome at worst.

But he smiled, although it was a sickly shadow of his normal radiant beam. 'Morning, Kate. Coffee?'

'Yes please. I just need to...' I gestured to the bathroom.

'There's spare stuff in the cupboard under the sink. Our Daniel runs quite the luxury lodging house here.'

I wondered whether the stock of spare toothbrushes and the like had been placed there for the benefit of guests who'd stayed over in Daniel's bed, rather than crashing on his sofa. The idea brought a stab of jealousy that was startlingly intense.

I cleaned my teeth, borrowed Daniel's hairbrush (so there were at least some advantages to the wanky hair) and removed last night's make-up as best I could with shower gel, then rejoined Andy in the kitchen.

He pressed the button of the coffee machine and it roared to life, sending a stream of almost-black liquid into the espresso cup waiting below.

'Thanks,' I said. 'You're a lifesaver. How are you feeling this morning?'

Andy passed me my coffee and we went to sit on the sofa together. Up close, he looked even worse than I'd thought at first – exhausted and haunted, flakes of dry skin coming away from his lips, his eyes bloodshot. For the first time, I noticed that the hair around his temples was thinning.

'I'm so frightened, Kate. I'm sorry for last night, but mostly I'm scared shitless.'

'You don't have to apologise to me. It's not your fault.'

'Yes, it fucking is. I went out to the shops and I passed a pub and thought, "You know what, I'll just grab a quick drink." Not in the nice pub, mind you, in the sketchy AF one. The vodka practically took the skin off my tongue.'

'You always were a picky bastard,' I joked.

He coughed out a half-laugh. 'I knew, Kate. I knew what I was doing there. I didn't admit it to myself, but I did. As soon as I saw a group of guys going into the toilet, I tagged along and got their dealer's number. And – well, you can imagine what happened next.'

I could. The lost hours, doing a line then having another drink and doing another line, until the coke was finished and he came home, pissed and buzzing like he'd had the best fun ever.

'I could have not gone into the pub. I could have not tagged along with Dodgy McDodgyface and his dodgy mates. I could have not rung their dealer. I could've flushed the stuff down the bog or even sold it on. I could've stopped so, so many times, and I didn't.'

'Is that what you're scared of?' I asked. 'That next time, you won't be able to stop again?'

He nodded wanly. 'I was doing so well. Almost two years clean. I didn't even get fucked up to celebrate my anniversary, which I thought was pretty good going. But in hospital, being on morphine, it was like my whole body went, "Well hello! I've been missing this." And I had the perfect excuse, didn't I? It was pain relief. It was all legit. They said I needed it.'

'You did need it.'

'I needed it like a hole in the head. But I have to carry on taking it, otherwise it's just too sore and I can't do my physio, and they said that if I don't, I'll end up with a permanent limp.'

He gestured down to his lap, and the crutches that were propped up against the arm of the sofa. I reached over and covered his hand with mine.

'Hey, Andy. Don't be scared. Remember the first time you went to an NA meeting, how scared you were then?'

'Properly shitting it.' He gave a little shudder at the memory.

'Exactly. But you got through it. You kept saying how scary recovery was, how waking up every day and getting through it clean was huge, but you did it anyway. You've got this.'

'Am I Mummy's brave soldier?'

I laughed and moved my hand to punch him lightly on the shoulder. 'You can call me whatever the hell you like. But pick up the phone, ring your sponsor or whatever they're called and get yourself off to a meeting. Now. This morning. Before you stop having the Fear and tell yourself you don't need to go.'

'All right. Only if you bring me my phone, though. I'm aching like crazy.'

It was an unwelcome echo of the old Andy – the Andy who'd said, *Just fifty quid, come on, Katie babe. You know I'll pay it back*, or *Come on, let's open another bottle – it's only midnight. Don't be so bloody boring*, or *I promise I'll stop, I just need you to be here for me*.

But now wasn't the time to remind him of that. I fetched his phone and discreetly looked out of the window while he made his call.

'I'm in luck,' he said. 'Laura's going to a meeting in town at midday. She's going to drive me there. I'm meeting her for breakfast first.'

'Great! Want me to walk with you to wherever you're meeting her?'

'No, I'll get the bus.'

'Let me walk you to the bus stop, then.' I knew full well that between Daniel's house and the bus stop were two pubs – the chichi, gentrified one with the seitan burgers and the dodgy one where Andy had ended up last night. Plus God knew how many street corners. And never mind the dealer's number, which I felt sure was still saved on his phone.

'I don't need a minder, Katie babe. Not just yet, anyway.'

'I don't want to be your minder. I just want to make sure you—'

'You know what they say, Kate?'

'What?'

'If you love something, set it free.'

His walls were coming back up. There was nothing to do but let him go and hope that he was meeting who he said he was meeting, going where he said he was going. He was still sufficiently raw and fragile to be on the level with me, I reckoned, and to need the comfort he knew he'd get from people who'd been through the same stuff as him.

He was also raw and fragile enough that it could quite easily go the other way, and the dark paranoia that inevitably accompanied a come-down could send him straight back to the dodgy pub or the dealer.

But that was just a risk I had to take – or let Andy take himself.

I waved him off a few minutes later and went to find Daniel in his workshop.

The sun hadn't yet reached the windows that lined the room, but the morning light was bright and clear. The hum of machinery had stilled and Daniel wasn't wearing a mask. He was working with a soft cloth, rubbing what I guessed was some sort of wax into the bevelled curves of a mirror frame. He had headphones in his ears and was singing along, off-key, to what I recognised as The Smiths.

When he saw me, he stopped, pulled out the headphones and set down the cloth.

'Don't mind me,' I said. 'I was enjoying the recital.'

He grinned. 'No one, but no one, has ever enjoyed my singing. Fact.'

'Okay. I was enjoying listening to you making a twat of yourself when you thought no one could hear.'

'That's more like it. How's…?' He gestured towards the door to the flat.

'Gone to a meeting. At least that's where he said he was going.'

'Best place for him right now, I reckon. Did you sleep okay?'

'Yeah. Thanks for the pillow and stuff.'

'You were totally sparko. Didn't even move when I took your shoes off. Looks like Pierre didn't stint on the booze.'

'His name's Claude.'

'Whatever.' He picked up the mirror, carefully angling it towards the light and inspecting the patina on its frame. Although he'd covered its glass with clingfilm to protect it, I could see the reflection of his face clearly, my own behind it, shiny and make-up free after my rudimentary morning cleanse. 'You going to see him again?'

An automatic, snarky reply sprang to my lips – *What's it to you?* But I didn't say that. 'I don't know.'

'Really? Last night you were all set to go home with him, now you don't know if you can be arsed with a – what is it – third date? Don't you fancy the guy?'

'Sure, I fancy him.'

I thought back to the previous night – the daydream I'd indulged in of Claude and me together, a power couple in our fancy house with our privately educated children. It felt a world away from this cavernous, dusty space where Daniel made old things new again. A world away from how I'd felt holding Andy's hand on the sofa, my feelings torn between tenderness that was almost maternal, concern born out of years of friendship, and a fierce rage that came from a different place entirely.

'But?' Daniel put down the mirror, picked up his cloth and started stroking at the wood again, working his fingers carefully into every cranny.

'It feels – I don't know. Not real, somehow. I think we're quite different people.'

'Really? With your high-powered careers and your Net-a-Porter clothes? You seem pretty well matched to me.'

'What? For all you know he could work in the mailroom.'

'You don't date guys who work in the mailroom, and they couldn't afford to take you for dinner in fancy restaurants.'

'As it happens, I paid for our dinner.' Not the wine, but Daniel didn't need to know that.

'And anyway, I—' He stopped, bending down over his work again but not so low that I couldn't see the flush of red creeping up his tanned neck.

'You *what*?'

'Looked him up on LinkedIn.'

'Daniel!' I burst out laughing. As clearly as if it was in front of me, I could see Claude's online profile: his handsome face, professionally shot by a photographer who knew how to light black skin; his Salvatore Ferragamo tie; his CV listing the Sorbonne, Yale and Cambridge followed by a string of jobs at blue-chip companies in London and abroad.

'What's so funny?'

'You. You are. Who the fuck put you in charge of vetting my boyfriends?'

'I was just curious,' he muttered.

'Curious enough to remember he's called Claude, not

Pierre, and find him online without knowing his last name. Of course you were.'

'What is his last name, anyway?'

'I'm not fucking telling you. Find it on LinkedIn if you can't remember.'

We were both laughing now, awkwardly but without animosity. It felt good to have this moment with him – like we were friends again, sharing the sort of banter we used to have before everything turned sour. I wanted it to last, but I knew that it wouldn't be long before the shades of the past – distant and so, so recent – descended again.

I said, 'I should get home. See how things are with the Airbnb guests.'

'Suit yourself.'

'Thanks for letting me stay. And message me when Andy gets back safely, okay?'

Daniel nodded, turning back to his work as if I'd already left.

So I did leave. I walked the length of the workshop, breathing in the smells of wood and varnish and wax. I pulled open the door to Daniel's flat and smelled coffee and the staleness of the cigarettes Andy must have smoked last night, and the lemon sharpness of Daniel's shampoo.

Then I let myself out and walked slowly to catch the bus home.

TWENTY-NINE

I barely bothered to attempt sleep that night, even though Daniel's message saying Andy was safely home had put my mind at rest on that score. As soon as the karaoke machine next door started up at half past nine, I climbed wearily out of bed and headed for the kitchen. I baked a coffee and walnut cake and put it on a wire rack to cool while I made a batch of tahini and halva brownies. Then I made a buttercream for the cake and iced it. I made cheese scones and lemon iced buns.

At three in the morning, I was contemplating starting a Sachertorte but realised that the elderly people who attended Mona's drop-in coffee mornings would only be able to cope with so many baked goods, and I didn't want to be the one responsible for the whole lot of them developing type II diabetes. So I cleaned the kitchen and went to bed, bone tired, the music stopping just as I put my earplugs in and the first dawn light began to brighten the sky outside my window.

Mona tutted when she saw me. 'Oh my days! Another bad night? You look like a ghost, my dear. And I haven't seen you for the longest time – I've been having to buy cakes at the Tesco

Express and the guests haven't been best pleased. They say there's no substitute for home baking.'

'It's feast or famine for them, I'm afraid,' I said. 'I was away for a couple of weeks, but now I'm back and it looks like my neighbour's flat is being used as an Airbnb and it's hen party central, so your guests are going to be doing well out of me.'

Mona prised the lids off the tins and Tupperwares and inspected the contents. 'Delicious – but there's enough here for a Macmillan coffee morning. You're not planning to keep this up, are you?'

'It's not really sustainable,' I admitted. 'And I'm starting a new job next week, so something's going to have to give. I can't turn up on my first day after two hours' sleep, smelling of chocolate.'

'Is there nowhere else you can stay while it gets sorted out? You need to look after your health, you know, Kate.'

'I know. I'm hoping eventually I'll get so tired I'll just sleep through whatever they get up to, but there's no sign of it happening yet. I could book myself into a hotel or something, I suppose.'

I thought longingly of an air-conditioned, soundproofed Premier Inn room, with sheets that had been washed by someone else and all the bacon and eggs I could eat in the morning. And then I remembered my sadly depleted bank balance and realised that wasn't exactly sustainable either.

I could throw myself on the mercy of my friends. But Rowan was in the process of moving out of the two-bedroom flat she shared with her daughter and into the house she'd found with her boyfriend, and was surrounded by the stressful chaos of packing boxes and bubble wrap. Abbie and Matt were heading off on holiday, and Naomi's three-year-old twins slept even worse at night than I did.

And then I thought longingly of Daniel's wide, comfortable sofa, where I'd slept so blissfully the night before last. I remembered the firm pillow under my head, smelling of his shampoo; the duvet that had been tenderly placed over me during the night; the delicious fragrance of coffee the next morning. Admittedly, I'd had a fair bit to drink, but it had been a magnificent sleep – the sleep of the gods.

And I really ought to see how Andy was doing, anyway.

I took my leave of Mona and got on a bus, making the now familiar journey south-east to Peckham. I should really have called or texted before heading over there, but my mind was too foggy with tiredness to compose any words. If he wasn't in, I'd just go home, I promised myself.

But Daniel was in. He opened the door a few seconds after my knock, the mask he wore for his woodworking hanging off one ear, his hair mussed as if he'd been running his fingers through it, the sleeves of his overall apparently hastily pulled over his shoulders, because the front was open to expose his tanned, muscly torso.

The sight of him made a jolt of desire pulse through me, and I wished I'd bothered to put on some make-up before leaving home, or at least worn something more attractive than the faded denim shirt dress and trainers I had on.

His face broke into a smile when he saw me, and I felt a weird melting sensation inside me, like buttercream frosting when you spread it on a too-warm cake.

'Kate. This is unexpected.'

'I just popped round to see how you and Andy were doing.'

'I'm all good. He's out – gone to see a movie, apparently.'

Our eyes met and I knew we were thinking the same thing. 'Going to see a movie' could mean just that – or it could mean something completely different.

'Really? Why didn't you go with him?'

'Why didn't you go with him to his meeting?'

'I tried. I offered to go and meet his sponsor with him, or at least go with him as far as the bus, but—'

'Same.' Daniel shrugged and carried on in a near-perfect imitation of Andy's voice, '*Don't expect me to believe you want to sit through* Sonic the Hedgehog 2. *And besides, you'd nick all my popcorn.*'

'But couldn't you—'

'I'm not his keeper, Kate. And neither are you. In a couple of weeks, he'll be going home. I won't be able to control what he does then, so there's no point me trying now.'

He was right, and I knew it.

His expression softened again. 'Coffee?'

'That would be great.' I followed him into the sunny living room, hearing the welcome hum of the espresso machine as he flicked its switch. 'I'm not sure there's enough coffee in the world right now to make me feel awake, to be honest.'

He glanced sharply at me. 'Another date with monsieur last night?'

'Actually, no. I might be seeing Claude next week. But last night was all about the party animals next door. Look.'

I swiped my phone and showed him the Airbnb listing: 'Spacious flat on the River Thames, perfect for hen and stag weekends.'

'Blimey.' He handed me a coffee, and I sat on the sofa. 'That's a bit out of order. Can't you get the listing taken down?'

'It's my neighbour's tenants. He's raised the issue with Airbnb, but – you know – processes. It won't go on forever – at least I bloody hope not – but it'll take a while to resolve, apparently.'

Daniel took a seat next to me, crossing one lean calf over the other thigh. 'It's not like you to take stuff lying down like that.'

I could think of at least one thing I wouldn't mind taking lying down, but I wasn't going to say that to him. 'To be honest, I'm too bloody shattered to do anything about it. And anyway, what could I do?'

'Knock on their door and ask them nicely to turn the volume down?'

'I tried that. It lasted five minutes and then they turned it up again. And even if I got one lot of guests who were decent and considerate, that's not to say the next lot would be.'

'Hmmm, yes, I can see how you might not want to knock on the door of a massive stag party at midnight in your pyjamas.'

'They'd probably think I was the stripper they'd ordered and ask me in.'

Daniel gave me a look that made me feel like all the poppers on my dress were about to ping open. 'That doesn't bear thinking about. Actually, scratch that. It *totally* does.'

'Never mind that,' I said primly. 'The point is, they're there and there's nothing I can do about it for the time being.'

'What you need to do,' he said, holding out his hand for my phone, 'is affect the ratings of the place. Look at them now – loads of reviews saying how great it is, how clean, the view, central location, all of that. No wonder your hens and stags are queueing up to book it.'

'Yeah, but I can't leave reviews slagging it off. You have to have had a verified booking.'

'You could book it for a weekend and say it's shit?'

'I already thought of that. But it's booked solid all summer.'

'So what you need to do is something that's going to impact the guest experience. Could you organise a rat infestation or something?'

'Jesus, no. What if they infested my place too?'

'Fair point. Play your own music even louder?'

'That wouldn't exactly help me sleep, would it?'

'Guess not.' He frowned, and I admired the way his long eyelashes swept down over his grey eyes as he thought. 'You could haunt it?'

'I could what?'

'Bang pan lids. Move things around mysteriously. Dress up in a white Victorian nightie and appear from behind doors.'

'It's a converted 1920s warehouse, not Victorian. And besides, I don't have the keys.'

'Hold on, I think I might have a plan. You've got a decent sound system, haven't you?'

'Sure. I mean, it's nothing special but it's okay.'

'Right. So you don't play music – you play something else. Come with me.'

Bewildered, I followed him into his workshop. The space was cavernous and silent, all the machinery switched off. On the bench, I could see a part-assembled table, its legs thrusting upwards. The familiar smell of turpentine and varnish and linseed oil and whatever else he rubbed lovingly into those sleek, glossy pieces – like a man grooming racehorses, I thought fleetingly, or massaging every curve of a lover's body – hung in the still air.

'The acoustics in here are *fantastic*,' Daniel said. 'I discovered it when I started making videos for TikTok. I've got quite into the whole sound-editing malarkey – I'm just learning, but I make a decent fist of it. We can cut out any dud bits and I'll chop it around and repeat bits to give you a good three hours of quality audio.'

'Sorry if I'm being dense.' I hesitated in the doorway. 'But what, exactly, are we doing here?'

'Making a sex tape, obviously.'

'Making a *what*?'

'Sex tape. Not a real one, doofus. Unless you particularly want to – although, no disrespect, I don't recall you being much of a screamer.'

My face flamed, remembering that night with Daniel in Alsaya. I couldn't possibly say if I'd screamed or not – it had felt more as if every inch of me had been silently singing, like the women in the operas Daniel and I had watched with Andy. Only apparently quieter. Thank God.

But he remembered it too. And he was suggesting – what, exactly? That we did it again? But he'd said, *Not a real one.* So he didn't mean that. My face must have given away my utter confusion, because Daniel said, 'Kate, you really are a bit slow sometimes. Have you not seen *When Harry Met Sally?*'

'Oh!' Relief, tinged with disappointment, flooded me. 'I get it. Like when Meg Ryan faked an orgasm in Katz's Deli. I've been there. The salt-beef sandwiches are—'

'Kate. Focus, please. Think Pornhub, not Tripadvisor.'

'Sorry.'

'Good. Now, come over and pull up a stool.'

Seconds later, we were perched on opposite sides of Daniel's workbench, his phone propped up between us against one of the table legs. He opened an app and pressed a red button.

'You go first,' I said, overcome with shyness.

'I think not. What kind of man do you want your neighbours to take me for?'

'Okay, fine. If you insist.' I took a deep breath and exhaled it on a long, 'Oooooh.'

'You like that?' Daniel said, his voice low and guttural.

'Yes!' I squeaked in surprise at the way his words had made me feel.

'You want more?'

'Yes! Give me more! Lower. No, higher!' I felt myself entering into the spirit of things, and Daniel nodded approvingly.

'Ah,' he gasped. 'Baby, that feels so good!'

'Do me!' I said. 'Do me hard!'

'You want it hard? Do you, you dirty, dirty bitch?'

'Oh God, yes! I want to feel you hard and deep!'

'Then suck my dick and call me Master.'

'What the—'

'And don't talk with your mouth full.'

Meeting each other's eyes, we dissolved into giggles.

'It's okay, I can cut the laughter,' Daniel said. 'Come on, you're doing great.'

I cleared my throat. 'I need your hard cock! Fuck me, baby.'

'Ride me like a cowgirl. Ah, yes! Your pussy is so wet.'

'You're so big.' Which, I recalled with a frisson, was true. 'Harder! Harder! More!'

'Take it!' Daniel bellowed. 'I know you can take it! That's my girl!'

'Give it to me!' I yelled. 'Give me all your hot spunk!'

Daniel moaned at top volume, and I followed suit. We *oohed* and *aahed* and gasped and exclaimed. And all the time, we didn't break eye contact. Part of me wanted to collapse into laughter again at our hammy performance – but a bigger part was intensely, powerfully aroused by the fantasy we were creating and the real memories it evoked. I could almost feel his body pressed against mine, his hair on my face, his sweat mingling with mine.

'Yes!' I screamed. 'YES YES YES!'

'YES!' Daniel echoed. 'Oh fuck YES!'

We kept it going until I felt like my vocal cords would give out – until, at last, we both subsided into gasps that were genuine, spent not just in our charade but in reality.

'That'll do.' Daniel stopped the recording.

I reached across the bench and we high-fived. And then we turned back towards the doorway. Silhouetted against the light from the flat, Andy was watching us. I had no idea how long he'd been there.

He broke into applause. 'Bravo! I have absolutely no idea what that was about, but if practice makes perfect, you two are clearly nailing it.'

THIRTY

THEN

2010–2015

After the night I returned home to find Andy and Daniel in my flat, things eventually returned to some sort of stability.

At least, after the initial fallout, which was nothing short of nuclear. I prided myself on being quite an even-tempered person, but that night I went absolutely ballistic at the two of them.

I remember freezing in the doorway, taking in the scene, and saying, 'What the fuck is going on here?'

'We're just having a chilled night in, Katie babe,' Andy said, apparently having decided his best defence was just to front it out. 'Why don't you join us? Our Daniel makes a mean manhattan.'

'I don't want a bloody cocktail. What do you think you're doing? You've been clean for months and now you're—'

'Chill out,' Andy said. 'It's Friday. We're just letting off some steam after a busy week. Looks like you've had a few yourself.'

Which was true, of course. 'So what if I have? I'm not the one with a substance abuse problem.'

'And who decides that?' Andy snapped. 'Just who are you to say that it's fine for you to go out and get shitfaced with your mates, but we can't hang out here and have a few drinks?'

'It's more than a few drinks. Don't try and tell me you haven't been using, because I know you have. I'm not stupid. And as for you' – I rounded furiously on Daniel – 'what the hell are you playing at? Why did you let this happen?'

'Kate, calm down.' Daniel stood up, swayed slightly, and came over and took my arm, steering me into my bedroom. I was suddenly conscious of his height, his strength, the fact that even with the adrenaline of rage and shock coursing through me, there was no way I could resist him physically.

He sat us both down on the bed. 'Deep breaths, Kate. Come on. Flying off the handle isn't going to achieve anything.'

'Don't tell me to calm down, and don't play the responsible adult with me. Do you understand what you've done here?'

'Nothing. I've done nothing. I came over to see Andy and he said he wanted a drink, so I made one. When he rang his dealer, what did you expect me to do?'

'Stop him! God, don't you *get* it? This is a *massive* relapse. He's worked so hard to get clean, and you've chucked it all away.'

'Not me, Kate. You don't seem to realise it, but Andy's an adult. He gets to make his own decisions and his own mistakes.'

'Mistakes? This isn't accidentally replying to all on an email chain, Daniel. This is literally life and death.'

'Kate, it *literally* isn't. You're not Andy's mother, you know. You need to stop trying to control him, because it won't work.'

'I'm not trying to control him! I'm trying to *help* him.'

'It looks a whole lot like control from where I'm sitting.'

'Does it? In that case, I suggest you go and sit somewhere else. I thought you were my friend – and more bloody importantly, I thought you were Andy's friend. But I see what you are now. You're a traitor, an enabler – a *pusher*. You might as well have shoved that coke up his nose yourself. I want you out – now.'

I freed myself from his grasp and marched to the door, flinging it open. Of course, Andy was hovering on the opposite side.

'There's literally nothing more thrilling than people fighting over you,' he said.

His refusal to take the situation seriously – admittedly only because he was as high as a kite – enraged me further.

'You heard me, Daniel. Get the hell out of my flat.'

'Fine.' Daniel got to his feet. 'I'll go. Hopefully you'll see sense in the morning.'

'How about me?' Andy gave a nervous giggle. 'Should I stay or go, as the song says?'

All at once, my anger drained away, replaced with a deep weariness. 'Suit yourself. I literally don't care what either of you do any more.'

Andy stayed. And I'd lied about not caring any more – probably to myself as much as to him. The next morning, I woke up with a mild hangover and a crashing sense of doom, which hovered over me as I lay in half-sleep before remembering what had happened the previous night. I got up, half expecting Andy to be out – or gone.

But he was in the living room, where he'd neatly folded the spare duvet on the sofa, tidied away all the detritus from the previous night and made coffee. When he saw me, he snapped shut the copy of *GQ* magazine he'd been reading and jumped to his feet.

'Kate. Are you okay?'

I nodded, tight-lipped.

'I'm so sorry. Seriously, I can't apologise enough. For Daniel as well as for myself – although I doubt you'll get an apology out of him. He's as stubborn as an ox – typical Leo. Anyway, will you forgive me?'

'It's not about whether I forgive you,' I said. 'It's about whether this happens again.'

I remembered the almost smug confidence with which I'd assured myself that I wouldn't let Andy do to me what he'd done to Abbie and Matt. So far, he hadn't – he hadn't taken anything from me, not money or valuables, so there was that. But, with Daniel's encouragement, he was already riding roughshod over the agreement we'd had, the trust I'd placed in him.

'It won't happen again.' He took my hands, his eyes wide and pleading. 'It won't, I promise. I'm firmly on the straight and narrow, as of now. I'll make us shakshuka for brunch. I'll do the hoovering, now you're awake. I'll even iron your stuff for next week. Just don't be cross with me, because I can't bear it.'

In the face of his smile, I felt my anger thawing. Andy must have sensed it, because he leaped into pampering mode, pouring me coffee, cooking food for us, suggesting we watch *Saturday Kitchen* together while he painted my toenails.

His charm offensive worked, and he spent that night in my bed.

THIRTY-ONE

NOW

'What do you mean, you don't have a stepladder?' Daniel looked at me in astonishment, like I'd just told him I didn't have a fridge.

We were in my bedroom, a few days after our recording session, and he was holding the sound bar from my television, which he'd said needed to be fixed to the wall above my bed in order to ensure maximum penetration (so to speak) of our sex-noise recording into the neighbouring apartment.

'I just don't. I told you, I'm scared of heights. What would I want a bit of kit that plays right into that in my flat at all times for?'

'For when you need to carry out advanced DIY projects such as – you know – changing a lightbulb.'

'My lightbulbs are LED. They last ages.'

'But not forever. So what do you do when you need to replace one?'

'I...' Now I thought about it, it was slightly ridiculous. 'It depends. Sometimes I've asked Jintao next door to come over and give me a hand. He's got a stepladder. Or I wait until I'm getting a handyman in to do other things and ask them to do that too.'

'For an independent woman, Kate, you certainly need men to help you out with a load of basic stuff.'

'As it happens,' I bristled, 'the last time I paid someone to change my lightbulb, it was a woman electrician. So there.'

'Doesn't alter the fact that you'd rather sit in the dark than stand on a step two feet above ground level.'

'Look, are you going to do this thing with the speaker or are you just going to pick a fight?'

'I'm going to put up the speaker just as soon as I've finished picking a fight with you.' He grinned, and I couldn't help smiling back.

'God, you really are the most annoying person I have ever met.'

'I could say the same about you.'

'Just as well there's a level playing field. If there was disparity in our annoyingness, that wouldn't be fair.'

A favourite saying of Andy's sprang into my head: *All's fair in love and war*. It looked as if it wasn't war between Daniel and me any longer – but could I dare to hope for love?

Resolutely, I pushed the thought from my mind. 'So are you going to drill a hole in my wall or what?'

'No, I'm going to have the speaker hold itself up through sheer force of will. Of course I'm going to drill a hole.'

'But what about—' I looked at my pristine bedroom, the walls painted an even pale grey, and at my neatly made bed, on which – in the absence of a stepladder – Daniel was presumably going to have to stand. But I bit back my protests – he was helping me out, after all. He'd spent over an hour editing the audio we'd recorded (with headphones, thank God – if I'd had to listen to it I'd have cringed myself inside out) and now he'd given up a morning to come and install the speaker in a position that would cause maximum annoyance to the residents next door, and get it set up on a timer to start playing at five in the morning.

It would be churlish to complain about him drilling holes in my walls or his feet on my duvet. Especially as, in other circumstances, I would have been delighted to have them there.

But he said, 'Grab me a chair from the other room and I'll stand on that. You don't want my great trotters on your bed.'

When I returned with the chair, he'd slid the bed to one side, revealing the embarrassing jumble of suitcases, shoeboxes and other crap that I kept under there (doesn't everyone?). But he ignored it, moved the chair into position, got out his drill and spirit level and set to work. A few minutes later, the speaker was in place.

'Job's a good 'un.' Daniel stepped down, but without looking, and his left foot descended on one of the shoeboxes that had been under the bed. He stumbled, righting himself quickly but kicking the box to one side, spilling its contents over the floor. 'Shit. Sorry, Kate.'

'That's okay.' Hastily, I dropped to my knees and gathered up the contents of the box – mostly old letters, photographs, birthday and Christmas cards I hadn't looked at in ages. Maybe, I thought, once the Airbnb situation was resolved and my flat felt like a safe haven again, I'd spend an evening going through them all, drinking wine and indulging in a bit of maudlin sentimentality.

'You missed one,' Daniel said, joining me on the floor. 'Here you— What the hell?'

In his hand was a birthday card Andy had given me when I turned twenty-nine. He'd had it printed by one of those places where you upload a photo online and they post you a card – or a mouse mat, or a coffee mug or whatever – with your chosen image and text on it.

Andy's chosen text was: 'Happy birthday to the world's best fuck buddy.' And the picture was a selfie he'd taken of us in bed together, covered up to our chests by my duvet but still clearly naked.

I could remember what he'd written inside: 'I checked in all the card shops but they didn't have one that was right, so I made it myself. Love you to bits, Katie babe. Stay as beautiful as you are.'

I'd treasured it at the time, reading the greeting over and over, but I'd never found the words to ask him whether he meant it – whether he did actually love me – or whether it was just something he'd written there, in his flamboyant fountain-pen scrawl, because he had to put something and he wanted to make me happy on my birthday.

'It's just a card.' I tried to take it from Daniel, but he held on to it, staring down at the photograph and the words with an expression of dawning comprehension on his face. 'Daniel. That's mine.'

Finally, he let go, and I shoved the card back in the box, cramming the lid down on the overflowing contents.

But there was no lid that could cover what Daniel now knew. The secret Andy and I had kept for so long wasn't a secret any more.

He stood, dusting his hands on his jeans, and said, 'Okay. Now I get it.'

'Get what?' I scrambled to my feet.

'All of it. Why you weren't surprised about Ash. Why you always acted like you owned him. Why he—' He stopped.

'You were saying?' My voice came out steady, but I didn't feel steady – not one bit. I felt ashamed – frightened, almost, as if I'd been caught out in a crime and now I was going to have to pay the price.

But there'd been no crime. Andy and I were consenting adults. If Daniel felt somehow excluded, or deceived, or even lied to, surely that was between him and Andy, and nothing to do with me? No one had been cheated on here; no one had been hurt.

Except me. And I would deal with that on my own, just like I always did.

Silently, Daniel pulled my bed back into position, covering the jumble of my belongings. He picked up the chair and carried it back to the living room, and I followed in his wake, my heart pounding. He didn't sit down; he walked out onto the balcony and stood leaning against the railing, looking down at the river as I so often did.

There was no sound from next door – if the drilling had woken the hen party guests, they weren't ready to kick off the day's festivities just yet.

'Daniel? What's wrong? Why are you being so off? I get that it's a shock, I get that it's weird you didn't know. But it was a private thing between Andy and me. It wasn't anyone else's business.'

'Did you not listen to him when he preached the gospel according to Narcotics Anonymous to us? Did it all go straight over your head because you didn't want to hear what he was saying?' Daniel demanded.

'What the hell has that got to do with anything?'

'"We're only as sick as our secrets." Does that mean anything to you? Anything at all?'

'What, you're saying I should have outed him to everyone? Because I don't think—'

'How long did this go on for?'

I considered saying again that it was none of anyone else's business; that it was private; that if Andy had wanted Daniel to know, he'd had ample opportunity to tell him. But then he turned and looked at me. His cold grey gaze made me feel like a prisoner in an interrogation chamber, or a supplicant in a confessional.

I heard myself telling the truth – the truth I'd never told

anyone before. 'Five years. Something like that.' More like six. Seven even. Longer than I wanted to admit to anyone, certainly not to Daniel – and certainly not now.

'Right. So the whole time Andy's habit was escalating and escalating, you helped him keep that secret? You let him hide that massive thing about himself, while he got deeper and deeper into it. No wonder he was so fucked up. No wonder he still is.'

'Hold on. You're not seriously saying Andy using was *my* fault? My fault, because we had sex a few times a month?'

Shit. I hadn't meant to reveal any more detail than I had to, and now here I was doing just that.

Abruptly, I switched from defence mode into attack. 'You're the one who enabled him, anyway, not me. When I'd paid for him to go to rehab, you sat right in the front room of my flat while he did lines on my coffee table, and *you* didn't stop him. And you say his addiction is *my* fault?'

'What the hell did you want me to do?' Daniel demanded. 'Grab the stuff out of his hands and flush it down the toilet? You know he'd just have bought more.'

'Maybe you could have tried not letting him buy it in the first bloody place. I did my best. He never used when he was alone with me. I was helping his recovery. As far as I could tell, you were helping him to use.'

'So you said at the time.'

He was right – I had said it at the time. That and a whole lot more, before finally throwing him out of my flat.

It was only now that I was beginning to suspect my anger had been misdirected. My feelings for Andy – which I'd never admitted to anyone, certainly not to him – had been so powerful I'd been willing to blame anyone and anything for his problems, except Andy himself.

'Maybe you should have listened to me at the time,' I said, suddenly weary.

'Maybe you should have used your brain and admitted what was right in front of your nose,' Daniel snapped. 'You were enabling him, just as much as I was. Giving him a place to stay, cooking for him, dancing to his tune like he was one of those fucking Tamagotchi things. All because you wanted him to love you.'

'He *did* love me. He does love me. Just not in that way any more.' But my voice didn't come out as certain as I meant it to.

'Addicts don't love anyone, Kate. At least, not as much as they love their drug. He used you. You just don't want to see it. I'm leaving now. Hope the thing with the speaker works.'

He pushed past me, gathered up his things and left. But even after he'd gone, his words seemed to hang in the air of my apartment, almost visible, like the motes of dust in his workshop.

Only, when the sun went down, I'd still be able to see the truth of what he'd said.

THIRTY-TWO

Three days later, at four in the morning, I found myself in my kitchen alone, grimly rubbing butter into flour to make the base of a raspberry crumble traybake, listening to the muffled sound of Daniel and me simulating sex through my earplugs.

Perhaps the sensible thing would have been to deactivate the timer, but then everything – the hilarious, bizarrely erotic recording session in his workshop, the drilling into my bedroom wall, even the shattering row – would have been for nothing. The Airbnb guests, a new hen party who'd arrived the previous afternoon, had got back from whatever bar or club they'd spent the evening in at about two, and the music had started immediately, putting paid to any chance I had of sleeping.

Not that I'd managed to sleep much anyway – I'd spent the earlier part of the night the same way I'd spent the previous nights: lying in bed, my mind roiling with memories of what Daniel had said to me, about how Andy had behaved towards me, about my own mixed-up emotions – about who was right and what on earth I would do next.

Occasionally, my brain had given me a break from all that and allowed me to worry about my new work contract, beginning in just two days, and how hopelessly unprepared I was to put my professional A game on and do my job properly.

So it had been with a kind of perverse pleasure, once the last clash of bottles, blare of music and shriek of laughter from next door had died away, to get up, come into the kitchen and let the staged, pre-recorded shagathon commence.

The only problem was, I couldn't have anticipated how it would make me feel. Each moan, gasp and exclamation of put-on desire reminded me of the real thing. Not just sitting opposite Daniel in his workshop fighting back giggles as our eyes locked, but the real thing – that night (how could it only have been one night?) in Alsaya, when sex with him had felt so inevitable, so natural, so fricking amazing.

There was no hope now of it ever happening again. I'd burned my bridges. If things had been different, perhaps I could have told him about Andy and me in a way that would have been easier for him to accept. It only happened a few times. He wanted to know what it was like being with a woman. It was just one of those things that friends do.

But it hadn't been. At the time, it had meant so much more to me. I'd colluded in the deception, the dishonesty, rather than telling our friends, because that was what Andy had wanted.

I recalled Daniel's words – not his, obviously; presumably they'd been quoted to him by Andy on one of his evangelical post-NA-meeting highs – 'We're only as sick as our secrets.' I didn't know the context of the saying, but I understood instinctively what it meant.

I'd allowed the secret Andy and I had kept to influence so much of my life. I hadn't had a real relationship in years because of the not-real one I'd had with him. I'd lied to my friends – not just by omission but properly, when I'd cancelled plans at the last minute because Andy wanted to see me. And now, I'd scuppered whatever tiny chance there might have been of salvaging something with Daniel – a friendship, or the something-more I realised I'd been dreaming of – from the mess we'd found ourselves in.

I pressed biscuit dough into the base of a baking tin, added raspberry jam and a layer of almond topping, then sprinkled crumble over it all and slid the tin into the oven. It was Saturday; Mona's group didn't meet on weekends and there was no way I was going to sit in my flat alone, listening to myself have fake orgasms and stuffing my face with Bakewell slices.

I needed my friends.

I opened the Girlfriends' Club WhatsApp group on my phone, hoping that my recollection of Abbie's holiday plans was correct.

Kate: Morning all. Anyone up? How's everyone's Saturday looking?

Naomi: Groundhog Day here. Toby and Meredith were tag-teaming all night, with one bellowing at me while the other slept. Patch has gone to the gym but when he gets back I'm handing over the kids and going the fuck to bed.

There was no response from Rowan – I didn't expect there to be. I imagined her curled up against Alex's back, sleeping the blissful sleep of the loved-up, probably weighed down by Alex's giant black cat. Thinking of Balthazar reminded me painfully of Daniel, and how he'd fed treats and most of our dinner to the cats in Alsaya.

Abbie: We just landed at Gatwick. It was a flying visit but Italy was incredible. I've eaten my body weight in pasta and gelato and I feel so relaxed I'm practically horizontal. Healthy eating plan starts today.

Kate: Any chance you're free later, Abs? I've made Bakewell slices.

Abbie: Scratch that, healthy eating plan starts tomorrow. Want to come over at about ten? We should be unpacked by then, and Matt's going to pick Shrimp up from the cattery.

Kate: See you then. You're a lifesaver.

While I waited for the oven timer to beep, the sex recording came to an end at last. I flicked through to the Airbnb app, where I had next-door's listing waiting on screen, and was gratified to see a new review.

Great place, shame about the porn stars next door.

I allowed myself a small, triumphant fist-pump. It was early days, but Daniel's plan seemed to be working.

Just after ten, I arrived at Abbie's. The sun had come out, and I walked from the Tube station carrying my Tupperware box of cake and a bottle of wine (because, after all, it was after midday somewhere in the world) feeling more light-hearted than I had all morning, although with a slightly dreamlike feeling brought on by lack of sleep, as if the whole world had gone kind of blurry and shimmery around the edges.

Abbie opened the door seconds after my knock and ushered me in. The house was chaos – a load of washing hanging damply on the airer, open suitcases on the floor, the washing machine going full blast and a dirty pan in the stove that looked like it had been used for bacon and eggs. But I couldn't have cared less and nor could she – over the years, we'd been exposed to so much messiness in each other's lives that a messy, post-holiday house was neither here nor there.

'You brought wine, you angel!' she exclaimed. 'I was just

wondering if it was too early for a sneaky G&T. I got used to having Aperol Spritz with breakfast on holiday.'

So we settled ourselves on the sofa, the open bottle and box of cake in front of us, and Abbie filled me in on the details of their trip abroad – the food, the weather, the handsome waiters.

'So what did I miss while we were away?' she asked at last.

'Oh God.' I buried my head in my hands. 'I've had a falling-out with Daniel. Another one.'

'Oh, mate. The two of you – you're the on-again off-again of friends. What happened?'

'It's kind of a long story.' I'd longed to confide in her, but now that I was, I wasn't sure where to begin – with the night in Turkey after the party on the yacht? With the long-held secret that my relationship with Andy had been more than a friend-ship for so many years? With the new feelings I'd begun to develop for Daniel?

'Let me guess,' she said. 'He found out about you and Andy?'

'What?' I gawped at her in astonishment. 'You mean you...?'

'Kate. We *all* knew. It was obvious that something was going on between the two of you, and it was just as obvious that Daniel was jealous.'

'Why didn't you ever say anything to me?'

'Why would we? If you or Andy wanted us to know, you'd have told us. And I can see why he didn't. Being out as bi is tough. It's not rational, but it makes dating harder – people find it hard to understand that if you're going to cheat, you're going to cheat, and the pool of potential people to cheat with being double the size doesn't actually make a difference. So I get why he wanted to keep it between the two of you.'

I remembered what Ash had told us about her insecurity around Andy and realised Abbie was right.

'What do you mean about Daniel being jealous? Of me and Andy being friends? Come on, Abs, we're not six years old.'

'Well, he's always been a bit of a closed book. But think about it, all this time, he's never had a long relationship. Girl-friends, sure, but no one serious. I always thought it was because he was hoping that one day you'd come to your senses and realise he was right for you. But you never did.'

'He'd be right for anyone,' I admitted. 'Even if he does have wanky hair.'

'So what's the problem then? I mean, assuming it's over between you and Andy?'

'It was over years ago.' I sighed. 'I couldn't do it any more – not feeling the way I did about him, and him being the way he was – is. I got to the point where I was just done. And Daniel helped me realise that he wasn't going to change.'

'There you go, see? He's always had your back.'

'Except now he hates me.'

'Don't be daft. How could anyone hate you? You're fab. Of course he doesn't.'

'Well, he's got a funny way of showing it.'

Before she could respond, the door opened and Matt came in with Shrimp, their highly disgruntled cat, in a carrier, and demanded to know whether there was any cake left. Although I knew he wouldn't have minded me carrying on pouring out my heart to his wife – and would probably have had words of wisdom of his own to contribute – I felt suddenly all talked out. So shortly after that, I said goodbye and headed home, leaving them to their backlog of laundry and their cosy home, wondering if I would ever share such a life with anyone.

THIRTY-THREE

On Sunday night, I bowed to the inevitable and deactivated the timer on the speaker. There was taking a consistent approach to my campaign against the noisy Airbnb guests, and then there was starting my new job with at least some semblance of competence, which I certainly wouldn't achieve if I'd been kept awake all night by my own recorded sex noises.

In any event, there was silence from next door. Either the guests had checked out early, or they'd gone out for the evening – either of which was okay with me. If they did return drunk and rowdy in the small hours, I'd be prepared, because I fully intended to be in bed by eight, just as soon as I'd ironed a shirt for the next day.

But the night passed uneventfully. I slept surprisingly well and woke at seven feeling refreshed and raring to go – although churning with first-day nerves. Carefully, I pulled together my 'polished and professional' look, putting on tights, a suit and heeled court shoes for the first time in weeks. Looking at my reflection in the mirror was like looking at a stranger – I'd almost forgotten what Senior Risk Management Executive Kate Miller looked like.

I only hoped that she hadn't forgotten how to manage risk.

I was in the office by nine, following a brief panic when I hadn't been able to locate the glass tower in which the company was based, hidden as it was amid the forest of near-identical glass towers in the heart of the City of London. I signed in and collected a temporary pass and then, taking a deep breath, joined the crowd of other suited, shiny-shoed executives in the lift.

The first couple of hours of the day passed as they always did on the first day of a contract: filling in forms in the HR department, being shown where to find the coffee machine and the ladies' loo, adjusting my desk chair to the correct height and moving the mouse from the right to the left side of my keyboard, signing into my new email account and sifting through several dozen messages that might as well have been written in Turkish for all the sense they made to me.

Only today, I was trying my hardest not to think about Daniel – a problem I'd never had to deal with on my first day in any job before. Images of his grey eyes, cold with pure anger, kept appearing in my mind. The echo of his voice played constantly in my mind, like he'd installed a speaker in my head not just in my bedroom. When an email appeared in my inbox from someone called Daniel Something, my heart leaped with absurd hope.

At midday, just as I was wondering whether anyone would ever give me any actual work to do, Sasha, my line manager, appeared next to my desk.

'We have a face-to-face with the wider team on the first Monday of the month,' she said. 'Downstairs in the main boardroom.'

I followed her and a stream of my new colleagues, whose names I'd been told but instantly forgotten, down a flight of stairs and into a glass-walled meeting room. The people might have been unfamiliar, but the setting was just like every other

City boardroom I'd entered over the years. There was a polished wooden table with slots for wiring cut out of its top. There were chrome-framed chairs upholstered in inoffensive grey-blue fabric. There were people clutching notebooks looking eager and people staring at their phones looking bored. There was a wall-mounted screen and a paper flip chart in the corner.

So far, so normal.

Only seated at the end of the table, deep in conversation with the woman next to him, was Claude.

I literally froze in the doorway, then some sort of survival instinct – or more likely autopilot – took over, and I followed Sasha to a seat at the far end of the table. Claude caught my eye, smiled and actually winked. I felt my features compose into a polite smile.

What the *hell* was he doing here? We'd been in touch inter-mittently since our last date, and he'd suggested meeting up again, but a date hadn't been confirmed, and the truth was I had been too occupied with my other problems to give much thought to him and where our relationship was going – if indeed we even had one.

And besides, I realised, when it came to romance, there had been very little space in my mind for anyone who wasn't Daniel.

'Good afternoon, team,' Sasha interrupted my jumbled thoughts. 'We're excited to welcome two new joiners today. Kate Miller will be with us for the next six months, working with the Compliance team on derisking our European opera-tions. And Claude Anjambé, who'll be leading on Governance. If we could all just go round the table and introduce ourselves. We'll start with you, Lisa.'

One after the other, twenty-five or so people recited their names and job titles. I tried my best to focus on them – these were my colleagues now; if I got a Teams notification from someone called Melanie asking me to pop past her desk for a catch-up about something, it would be useful to remember whether she was the blue-eyed blonde woman or the heavily pregnant one with the pixie cut.

But my thoughts refused to be tethered, and my eyes kept straying back to Claude. There was no doubt I'd been right to fancy him. Even in a room full of people, even when he wasn't speaking, he seemed to command attention. His presence was magnetic: the way he held his pen in his long, elegant fingers; the husky timbre of his voice when he said his name; the bright flash of his smile.

There was just one problem. He wasn't wearing an overall with the arms tied round his waist. His smile didn't make my insides go funny. He didn't have wanky hair.

Okay, that was more than one problem. But it all boiled down to one thing – he wasn't *Daniel*. And, I was beginning to realise with a stab of longing so intense it felt like pain, if I couldn't have Daniel, I didn't want anyone else, no matter how desirable.

Somehow, I got through the meeting, my pen flashing over my notepad as I wrote down as much information as I could, knowing that without notes, my brain had as much chance of retaining anything other than the potent memory of Daniel's kisses as the battered wire sieve I used for my midnight bakes.

At last, the hour drew to a close. Chairs scraped on the polished wooden floor, chatter broke out as people shuffled towards the exit, and phones buzzed and trilled as they were taken off silent mode.

Including my own, with a message from Claude.

Fancy a spot of lunch?

I looked up from the screen. He was hovering by his place at the end of the table, looking at me expectantly. I nodded. He held up a hand, five fingers outstretched, and gestured towards the elevator. I nodded again.

Five minutes later, having retrieved my bag from my desk and dashed to the bathroom to comb my hair and top up my lipstick, I met him by the lift. A few other people stepped in with us, so we all made our way to ground level in silence, gazing up as if fascinated at the slowly descending floor numbers.

Outside, the sun was shining. Crowds of City workers were emerging from the surrounding office blocks like bees from hives, going in search of pollen – or more likely Pret a Manger.

'What do you fancy?' Claude asked. 'Salad? Sandwich? Sushi?'

'A sandwich would be great,' I said. Sushi would have felt too fancy somehow – too much like a date.

'I guess I took you by surprise back there.' Claude smiled at me, lowering his sunglasses over his eyes. 'They wanted to keep the offer under wraps for as long as possible. Fortunately, I had a load of holiday saved at the old place, so I barely had to work any notice. And here we are, colleagues once again.'

'Only for six months,' I reminded him. 'I'm a hired assassin, remember? I do my thing and then move on.'

'Not from everything, I hope.' He gestured to the door of a sandwich shop – not one of the basic ones selling tuna baguettes and egg mayo on squashy white bread, but a high-end place advertising Reubens and salt beef on rye. 'This do you?'

'Looks great.' Normally, I'd have been salivating at the prospect of hunks of warm, juicy salt beef squirted liberally with mustard and sharp with pickle. But now, I realised, the prospect of food was distinctly unappealing.

'Fancy eating outside?' he asked. 'It's such a glorious day.'

'Let's do it,' I agreed, and we took our brown paper bags of food and drink and made our way to a bench in a garden square.

The sun was warm on my face. Eager pigeons strutted

around our feet hoping for crumbs. Claude chatted about our new colleagues and the challenges he would face in his new, even more senior role. My sandwich was even better than I could have hoped.

But I felt a sense of sadness and inevitability, because I knew what I was going to have to do.

I tried to respond animatedly to Claude's news of how our former colleagues were getting on (Lauren had been promoted, Lucia sacked, Gareth and Stephen were awaiting a disciplinary hearing after shattering a meeting-room table having sex on it after the annual away day). I gave him an edited update on how Andy was doing, without touching on the potential seriousness of his relapse and without mentioning Daniel. I heard about his forthcoming trip to Paris to see his old university friends. And then, once we'd finished our lunch and it was time to head back to the office, the moment I'd been waiting for arrived.

'So, Kate,' he said, standing up and carefully folding the used napkins, empty sandwich wrappers and soft-drink cans into the bag they'd come in, 'I was wondering when you're free to meet up again? Outside of work, I mean.'

I hesitated, hunting for the right words to use, and Claude seemed to take my silence as acceptance.

'There's a new place that's opened in North London,' he went on. 'A climbing wall. Six storeys and twenty-one routes up, with a vertical drop slide. I'm keen to give it a try – would you like to join me?'

I picked up my bag and slung it over my shoulder. There was no good way to do this, so I might as well do it quickly.

'Claude,' I said, 'here's the thing. I'm not great at stuff like that. I hate taking risks. I'm scared of heights. When we went on that amazing date in the hot-air balloon I was so frightened I almost passed out.'

He stopped, turned to face me and put his hands on my shoulders. 'Oh no. I had no idea, Kate. You should have said. I'd have never expected you to do something that made you uncomfortable.'

'I know. I should have told you at the time. But I didn't. I didn't want you to think I was as much of a wuss as I am.'

The megawatt smile flared out again. 'You're no wuss. I've seen you in action at work. You're a *lioness*. But lionesses don't climb, right? So we'll do something else. What would you like? Theatre? Dinner?'

I looked up at him. All the future I'd imagined for us – the luxury, the companionability, the kudos of being with a man who was such a prize by any measure – was promised to me in his handsome face.

'No,' I said. 'You deserve someone who'll go up in a hot-air balloon with you or climb six storeys and love it. You deserve a girl you can skydive and bungee jump with. You want to have adventures with someone as adventurous as you. And that's not me. I'm sorry, Claude. But I'd cramp your style, and I don't want to do that.'

And besides, I'm in love with someone else. But I didn't say that, not yet. I would if I needed to, but I suspected I wouldn't.

'I see,' he said, and I suspected he understood not only what I had said but also what I hadn't. He turned away from me and we fell into step, making our way back to the office together. 'I appreciate your honesty. But we'll still be friends, yes?'

'Friends. Of course.'

I knew – at least, I hoped – we would be. At least until he met some ballsy, daredevil woman who'd challenge him as much as he challenged her, and I'd fade into a distant memory – just someone he knew from work and briefly dated before realising it wasn't going to work out.

And I realised that I, in those few minutes between eating sandwiches and returning to my desk, had taken a leap into the unknown, setting aside a future I thought was mine for the taking in favour of one that could hold anything at all.

THIRTY-FOUR

As is always the way when starting a new job, I didn't want to look like a shirker and be the first to leave, even though I still had very little actual work to do. So I lingered in the office until six thirty, perusing the HR manual and brand guidelines and reading emails I'd been copied into for no discernible reason other than that cc'ing multiple people apparently made the sender and their message feel more important.

At last, enough of my colleagues had logged out, gathered up their things and headed for the lift for me to feel able to do the same. I emerged into the warm summer evening and walked home, feeling the familiar tension across my shoulders from sitting at a desk all day, yawning from the unaccustomed fatigue of concentrating on important things and pretending to concentrate on unimportant ones.

A nice, quiet evening at home was what I needed, I told myself. A healthy, solitary dinner and an early night. It was what the rest of my life held, so I might as well get used to it again.

But, just as I was slipping the key into my front door, a woman emerged from the next-door flat. She was wearing jeans and trainers, and her hair was scraped back off her face. She was carrying an overflowing bag rattling with cans and bottles in one hand and a mop and bucket in the other.

Next-door's cleaner, I thought. Poor woman must have had quite a job on her hands.

'Evening,' I said, with a friendly smile.

But I was met with a stony glare. 'You.'

I raised my eyebrows in surprise. 'Can I help you?'

'It's you that needs help,' she snapped. 'Sex addiction is a real thing, you know.'

Light dawned. Not the cleaner, then, but Jintao's tenant, who'd broken the terms of their contract by subletting the apartment. When I'd checked the Airbnb listing earlier, I'd discovered that it had been removed – either Daniel's and my cunning plan or Jintao's strongly worked email had done the job.

There was no point getting into an argument with her – whatever fight there'd been between us, I'd clearly already won.

So I smiled confidingly. 'You know how it is. Sometimes passion just gets the better of you.'

'Three hours,' she said. 'Night after night. I'm amazed you can walk.'

'I am a bit stiff, now you mention it. Although not as stiff as my partner's going to be when he comes round later, haha.'

'Jesus,' she muttered. 'Inflicting your sex life on other people. It's just disgusting.'

'Pure filth,' I said brightly. 'Speaking of which, this corridor could do with a going-over, while you're about it. Have a lovely evening – I certainly intend to.'

And, with a cheery smile, I swung open the door and stepped into the blissful silence of my flat. But my quiet evening in didn't go quite according to plan.

I poured myself a glass of wine and ate some cheese and crackers while I drank it, then turned on the taps and sloshed scented oil into the bath, planning on a long, luxurious soak while catching up on the Girlfriends' Club WhatsApp (bracing myself for the reaction to my decision not to take things further with Claude – *You did WHAT? Are you CRAZY?*). But before the bath was half full, I heard the melodious ring of my doorbell.

The trouble with having a video doorbell, I reflected, was that there was no opportunity to enjoy – or endure – those heart-stopping moments between knowing someone is out there and finding out who it is. Normally, I'd have had a few seconds of delicious or apprehensive anticipation – could it be a delivery of something fabulous I'd ordered and forgotten about? Could it be flowers from Claude, with a note begging to be given another chance? Could it be Jintao's tenant squaring up for a proper fight? Could it – chance would be a fine thing – be Daniel?

But, thanks to the power of technology, one glance at my phone told me my visitor was Andy.

I switched off the taps and hurried to the door, flinging it and my arms open.

'Surprise!' he said, hugging me. 'Look – only the one crutch. I walked up the stairs under my own steam, too, instead of using the lift.'

'Strong work. Come in and sit down –you must be knackered after all that. Cup of tea? I'm afraid I'm out of Fanta.'

It had taken a long time to break the habit of offering Andy alcohol when he turned up unexpectedly, but I'd got used to it during the time he'd been sober, and laid in a supply of posh tea from Fortnum's. According to him, it was not the next best thing – not even close to the best thing – but it was worth it for the satisfaction of rinsing me out of a quid per teabag if he couldn't have booze.

But he said, 'Come on, Katie babe. I can see you've got a bottle open. Don't be a spoilsport.'

'But aren't you—?'

'I haven't touched anything stronger than my painkillers in

days. Scout's honour. And as soon as I finish taking them, I'm going to kick the booze into touch too. I'm just having a wee holiday from total sobriety. Doctor's orders, innit?'

The pain-relief medication certainly was, but I was willing to bet no medic had said anything to Andy about a glass of Chablis being a necessary aid to his recovery.

'Andy, you know that's a terrible idea. Come on – I'll make tea for us both. I've got a violet one you've never tried before – apparently it's limited edition.'

'You know what they say. "Grant me the serenity to accept the things I cannot change, the courage to change the things I can, and the wisdom to know the difference." You're a wise woman, Katie babe.'

'Wise enough to lay money on the fact that no one ever quoted the AA serenity prayer as an excuse to have a drink.'

'You'd lose your stake, because I just did. Come on. You don't even have to pour it – I'll do it myself. You're an innocent bystander.'

He walked past me to the fridge, barely needing to use his crutch at all, opened it and took the bottle of wine from the rack in the door, pouring some into my empty glass and some into a clean one. My mouth opened to protest, but what could I do? Pour it down the sink? Chuck him out? Insist he ring his sponsor right fucking now?

Of course, I could do any or all of those things. But ultimately, they'd make no difference. Andy would make his own choices. I'd tried and failed in the past to influence him. All I could do was deal with the fallout when it happened – or choose not to deal with it.

The courage to change the things I can. The one thing I could change was my reaction to his behaviour. Quite how to change it, I wasn't sure – but change I must, for the sake of my own sanity. I picked up both our glasses and carried them over to the coffee table.

Andy sat down with an audible grunt. 'Those stairs took it out of me. The physio's going great – although I have to say the girl I've been seeing is no Mistress Whiplash. But I still feel the old war wound when there's damp in the air.'

'Get you, Granddad. So to what do I owe the pleasure of your visit? You didn't come here just to show off about how you can hobble on one crutch instead of two, and annoy me by drinking my wine.'

'I came to say goodbye. Or rather, *au revoir*. I'm heading home tomorrow. I've officially been discharged from our Daniel's infirmary.'

'Really? Are you sure you'll be all right on your own?'

'Give over, Katie babe. I've lived alone for donkey's years. I'll be fine. They've offered me one of those alarm things in case I fall down the stairs and get stuck like a beetle on its back. And work want me back – I'm to be put on light duties, apparently, just phoning clients and doing admin until I can drive again.'

'Well, that's great news,' I said. 'You like your job. You're ace at selling advertising, even if you have to do it over the phone for a bit, rather than swanning around to fancy offices in your Merc.'

'Yeah.' Andy sighed, gazing down into his wine glass, which was already almost empty. 'I've been thinking about it. I mean, you know I'm all for late-stage capitalism. Love it to pieces. But when I was in Turkey, seeing how Ash lived, I kind of got to realise that maybe there's more to life than making money. Other stuff that's more important, like, you know, friends. Community. Saving the planet. Love.'

'All those things are massively important. But you can still have them while raking in shedloads of cash.'

'Like you do.'

Like I did – except I did far less than I should for the environment, my contribution to the community consisted of dropping off Tupperwares full of cake with Mona once or twice a week, and when it came to love – well. The less said about that the better.

'Right now, if I were you, I'd be cutting myself some slack,' I said. Andy had got up, shuffled over to the fridge and fetched the wine bottle, splashing more into both our glasses. I winced, but said nothing. 'You need to focus on your health for a bit, maybe. On getting better. You're two years off forty, Sinclair. You're got all the time in the world to save the planet.'

'Save myself, and let the rainforests look after themselves?'

'Basically. What are you going to do about the rainforests, anyway? You could go vegan, I suppose, if you wanted to make a difference.'

Andy shuddered. 'Life without steak tartare wouldn't be worth living. I sometimes think life without drugs isn't, either.'

'Don't say that. You don't really mean it – you were so happy when you were first on the programme. So kind of... I don't know. Serene.'

'Yeah, serene. Fab, isn't it?' He grimaced. 'You know what? I'd trade you all the serenity in the world for a night on the lash, frying my sinuses with blow and fucking anyone who'd stay still long enough to let me.'

'That's not true, though. You were miserable.'

'Only when I was coming down. The rest of the time was great. And even the come-downs weren't so bad, when I was with you.'

I remembered those days, holding Andy while he cried and shivered, fetching him Fanta from the corner shop, frying cheap sausages to try and tempt him to eat, staying up late talking to him even when I had important work stuff the next day in case he went out and got loaded again. Picking up the pieces of him, and the crumbs of love he gave me in return. Maybe they hadn't been so bad for him, but they had for me.

I said, 'It was dreadful for me. I'm not going to lie, it was. For Abbie and Matt as well. And for Daniel, I expect.'

Daniel, I realised, had never really said. He loved Andy, too. Andy's descent into chaos must have been as hard for him to witness as it had been for the rest of us.

'I've changed,' Andy said. 'I'm not like that any more. You know I'm not.'

I looked at him. His eyes were the same sparkling blue above the grey collar of his sweatshirt. The lock of hair combed carefully over his brow was the same bright gold, now I couldn't see the place where it was thinning at the temples. The winsome smile he gave me was as familiar as my own face when I looked in the mirror.

'Actually,' I said, 'I think you're just the same.'

'Oh, Kate.' He reached for me, suddenly enveloping me in his familiar, violet-scented embrace. 'You're such a fucking bitch. My bitch. I love you so much. Please let me stay with you tonight.'

THIRTY-FIVE

THEN

2015

With the inevitability of night following day, or an avalanche taking out the side of a mountain, Andy broke his promise to me. He broke it over and over again, over the next few years. Every time, I vowed that this would be the last time – that I couldn't allow myself to be hurt that way again. And every time, I broke my own promise to myself, which I guess made me just as much to blame for the situation as Andy was.

After the initial seismic falling-out with Daniel, our cosy outings as a threesome didn't resume, but Andy stayed in my flat – after all, he had nowhere else to go. But, over the next few weeks, there were nights when he didn't return home, days he spent on the sofa, morose and self-pitying, flicking through the channels on the TV with the curtains closed, complaining that the sunlight was giving him a headache.

He wasn't working – I had no idea where the money to buy drugs was coming from, or the money to buy the expensive bottles of champagne he often bought for us to share, even though I'd said I didn't want them. He just sat, went out, slept and then sat some more.

Then, one night, he went out and didn't come home the next morning, or the morning after that. At first I was accepting, then annoyed, then increasingly worried. I rang the police, but they didn't seem particularly interested in an adult man choosing to leave the place where he'd been staying. I rang round local hospitals, but to my relief he wasn't there. I asked my friends if they'd heard from him, but they hadn't – not until a week or so later, when Rowan rang to tell me she'd had a drink with Daniel, who had told her that Andy had moved into 'some dodgy bedsit in Dalston with a guy he met out clubbing'.

And that, I told myself, was that. Of course, I was devastated – hurt and confused and blindsided by the idea that Andy would simply up and leave without saying a word to me. But, I told myself, it was a symptom of his addiction, of the chaotic life-style he seemed increasingly drawn to. And as the weeks turned to months, my hurt receded, and my devastation turned to relief.

Then, on my birthday, Andy knocked on my door with a huge bunch of red roses. He was sober, he seemed happy, he said he'd missed me terribly and he was sorry for the way he'd behaved. I'd just been dumped by a guy I'd been seeing for a few weeks, and although I'd known deep down the relationship wasn't going to go anywhere (when did my relationships, ever?), I was feeling bruised and vulnerable.

And Andy was at his charming best. Sensing my sadness (or was it weakness he sensed?) he ran me a bath, and while I soaked in the scented water, he baked me a birthday cake. In funds for once, he took me out to a little Lebanese restaurant for dinner, during which he drank only peppermint tea while insisting I work my way through a bottle of cheap red wine.

He moved back in for a few months after that, until he disappeared again. And there we were – the pattern repeating itself again and again. There were long periods when I didn't see or hear from Andy, and shorter ones when he burst back into my life, adoring and adorable, sometimes sober, sometimes not. Every time, I found it impossible to turn him away.

Of course, life carried on. I sold my first, tiny flat and moved to a bigger one in a nicer area. I got promoted at work and then was offered a better, higher-paid role at a different company. I saw my friends and dated and splashed out on a Mulberry handbag.

But, always, Andy and his problems were there in my life. He moved into a flatshare with a friend, but then when that didn't work out, he moved back in with me for a few months. He met a guy from Seattle and stayed out there for a bit, and his social media was peppered with pictures of mountains and city skylines and cups of coffee, until he came home again because he had no green card and no money. Then he went back to live with his parents, but his rows with them were so awful he turned up on my doorstep in tears, begging to be allowed to stay.

That was in April, when I'd known Andy for eight years. And he was in as dark a place as I'd ever seen him. His jokes came less frequently, he was worryingly thin and, no matter how much time I spent cooking his favourite food, he never seemed to want to eat. Mostly he slept on the sofa, but when he woke from a nightmare, he'd come into my bed, shivering and frightened, and I'd hold him in my arms until he slept again.

He didn't take cocaine in my flat – not when I was there anyway. But he was taking it somewhere – and I was increasingly sure that it wasn't just cocaine.

All that summer, it seemed, I spent being batted around like a pinball by Andy's moods – giddy and fun-filled one day, bitter and silent the next, overflowing with self-recrimination and apology the next. My work suffered. I struggled to sleep at night. I gained a stone from comfort-eating at home and main-lining chocolate at work to keep myself awake.

And almost the worst thing about it was that I felt I couldn't confide in Abbie or my other friends about what was happening. I was being taken for a mug – deep down, I knew it and I knew they'd know it. But admitting it would mean admitting I'd been wrong about Andy – about the possibility that I could change him. And it would mean admitting what our relationship had become and revealing the secret about Andy I'd promised to keep.

Then, one Thursday in August, I got a call from Daniel. It was right in the middle of what the newspapers call the silly season – everyone was on holiday, work was quiet, the City was almost deserted apart from a few bewildered-looking tourists wandering through the streets looking for St Paul's Cathedral. So the pub where Daniel suggested we meet – which I guessed he'd chosen because it was near to my work, and I wouldn't be able to use inconvenience as an excuse not to come – was quiet.

He was already there when I arrived, sitting at a corner table with a pint of Guinness and a glass of white wine in front of him. He stood up to greet me, but we didn't hug each other as we might once have done.

'Kate,' he said. 'How are you?'

'Not too bad. You know, busy. You look well.' It was true – he was tanned and smiling, blonder streaks bleached in his hair, which didn't appear to have seen a barber's shop for several weeks.

'I wish I could say the same about you,' he told me bluntly, sitting back down and pushing the wine across the table to me.

'I've not been sleeping well,' I said defensively. 'And I don't want a drink.'

'Have it or don't,' he said. 'Suit yourself.'

'Oh, for God's sake.' I took a sip of the wine. 'What do you want, anyway?'

'I wanted to see you. Because no one else has, not for ages. Abs and Matt say you keep making excuses, because you're "snowed under with work".' His fingers sketched ironic quotes around the words. 'In August.'

'Well, I am. Half my team's off on holiday and I'm having to pick up the slack.'

'Instead of going on holiday yourself. Patch said he and Naomi invited you to go to Ibiza with them, but you're "too busy".'

'So what if I'm busy? What's it to you?'

'Except it's *not* because you're too busy. It's because you're too scared to leave Andy alone. Isn't it?'

I shook my head, taking another gulp of wine. All at once, I felt overcome with exhaustion. I wanted to have a massive, cathartic cry. I wanted to sleep for a week. I wanted to wake up alone in my apartment and not worry about anything or anyone except myself.

'You look like shit, Kate. I'm sorry, but you do. You say you haven't been sleeping and man, it shows. When was the last time you got out for a walk, or went to the gym?'

'I walk to work every day.' I felt a lump forming in my throat and my eyes stinging with the threat of tears. *I must not cry.*

'Look,' Daniel said, more gently, 'I know you're trying to do your best by Andy. But it isn't working, is it?'

'Andy's fine. Isn't it you that keeps saying he's a grown man and he can make his own decisions?'

'Sure, and he can. But that doesn't mean he gets to make them on your dime, at the expense of your health. I'm worried about you, Kate. I know you think I'm public enemy number one right now, but I do actually care about you.'

'And Andy?'

'I care about him too. But I can't help him.'

'And you think you're helping me?'

He picked up his glass and drained it. 'I'm just giving you a bit of friendly advice. Get him to move out, before he breaks you.'

And that night, before the resolve Daniel's words had given me could fade away, I did just that. It was awful. Andy cried and pleaded, but I stood firm. I said we would always be friends, but not lovers ever again. I said I'd always care about him, but he couldn't stay with me any longer. I gave him until the end of the weekend to find somewhere else to stay, and evidently he did, because on Sunday he packed his things, said goodbye and left.

I expected to feel bereft, weighed down with guilt. But I felt only overwhelming relief.

THIRTY-SIX

NOW

I'd been to Andy's flat in Manchester once before, about five years ago. Then, like today, I'd turned up unannounced – Andy wasn't the only one who could choose to just rock up, rather than calling or texting like a normal person. Then, I'd had a pretty good idea what I was going to find, and my suspicions had been confirmed as soon as he opened the door. He'd been in as bad a state as I'd ever seen him: pale, gaunt, trembling, the smell of unwashed clothes and unwashed body hitting me like a blow to the face.

When he'd seen me, his face had broken into a delighted smile, then fallen again as he'd taken in my look of horror at what I could see – not just him but the flat beyond, dusty and almost empty, only a bare mattress on the mezzanine level where he slept. He'd invited me in and offered me coffee, but there was no coffee, and the fridge was empty apart from a bottle of vodka with only an inch or so in the bottom.

I'd stayed for a few days, doing what I could to clean and stock the kitchen and trying to get Andy to eat. But I'd known, even while I was lugging a bundle of his clothes to the laundromat or pushing a trolley round Tesco or scraping mould off the grouting in the shower, that I was wasting my time.

As soon as my back was turned, I realised with a sense of grim futility, things would return to how they'd been before. It might take a while, but within a few weeks, Andy would be back where he was before my visit, unwashed, unfed, existing only from one increasingly fleeting high to the next.

I'd never visited him again – at least not until today. And today, I was equally uncertain what I'd find when he opened the door – if he opened it.

'It's only been a week, Kate,' I told myself firmly. 'At least he won't have had time to flog all his belongings. Look on the bright side.'

But the bright side, on this cloudy Manchester morning, was proving elusive. Although it was officially summer now, the city didn't appear to have got the memo. The sky was heavy with rain, the heavens threatening to open and soak me through at any moment. I hadn't brought an umbrella – I'd left my flat that morning on an impulse, the urge to see him suddenly so strong that not even the extortionate price of a last-minute train ticket could put me off. A blustery wind cut through my thin jacket, and I could feel goosebumps rising on the skin of my thighs under my light cotton skirt.

'Way to go, Kate,' I muttered. 'You might at least have thought to check the weather forecast before you left.'

But I hadn't – I hadn't thought of anything, really. When it came to Andy, acting rationally had never been my strong point, and why change the habit of a lifetime?

I fumbled my phone out of my handbag and flicked open the map app. Because I'd only been here once before, the route was unfamiliar, and the converted warehouses and modern glass towers lining the canal all looked much the same. But I remembered it being under fifteen minutes' walk from the station, and I was pretty sure I'd been about that far already.

The map confirmed I was correct – it was just here, just around this corner to my right.

I paused now, feeling the need to compose myself and collect my thoughts. But what was the point? Why bother planning what I was going to say when I didn't know who I'd be addressing my words to – buzzing Andy or sober Andy, Andy riding the wave or Andy coming down, flippant Andy who'd meet any attempt at seriousness with yet another joke, or tearful Andy full of self-hate and remorse.

I'd just have to deal with what I found, when I found it. And for all I knew, he might not even be in. He could be with a friend or a lover. He could be out doing some perfectly normal Saturday activity like shopping for food or seeing a movie. He could be in some sketchy pub scoring coke or he could be at a meeting. Absolutely anything was possible.

The street I'd turned into was beginning to look familiar now, the way a place does when your memory of it is so vague and distant you might as well have seen it in a dream. But I recognised the restaurant on the corner – it had been a Mexican place last time, I recalled. I'd taken Andy there for food but he hadn't wanted anything except frozen margaritas and I'd been powerless to stop him ordering one after another while I picked without enthusiasm at my tacos. Now it was an artisan pizza place. If we went there today, I thought glumly, it might be negronis Andy drank while I forced down a quattro stagioni.

There was a florist next door to it, and on impulse I went in and bought a bunch of roses, a successor to the flowers Andy had presented to me on my birthday all those years ago as a peace offering or a bribe or just a simple gift – I couldn't be sure now what he had meant it to be, and I suspected he hadn't really known himself.

And here was the building where he lived: Wood Quay. I stood for a moment before the serried ranks of buzzers, my hand not obeying my brain's command to lift and press one. But then a couple with a baby in a buggy appeared in the lobby and the man politely held the door open for me, so I had no option but to enter.

I hitched the strap of my handbag more securely onto my shoulder, took a deep breath and headed for the stairs. Andy's apartment was on the second floor and it didn't seem worth taking the lift, but my legs felt disconcertingly weak as I climbed – just nerves, I told myself. There was no way some mysterious wasting illness had attacked my quadriceps between London and here.

And here was Andy's front door – again distantly familiar from my previous visit. Last time, I remembered, I'd been able to detect the smell of smoke and long-accumulated grease before Andy had even opened the door. Today, I couldn't smell anything at all.

I lifted my hand to knock, but before I could, the door flew open, making me jump backwards in fright.

Andy jumped backwards too, and then we both burst out laughing.

He was wearing the leopard-print apron and rubber gloves with neon-pink faux fur around the cuffs that I'd given him years ago as a joke Christmas gift. He had a feather duster in one hand and a microfibre cloth in the other, and a strong smell of bleach emanated from inside the flat.

'Katie babe,' he said, a delighted smile spreading over his face. 'This is a surprise. And you've caught me mid-spring clean. Isn't it extraordinary how grubby a place gets when you're away, even though you're not there to dirty it? It's like the dust had a massive fucking party while I was away, and I've been too busy at work to get to grips with it until today. Come in and I'll put the kettle on, since I'm in full 1950s-housewife mode.'

Giddy with relief, I followed him into the flat. It was clean and orderly – there was nothing untoward to see at all. The cushions on the sofa were plumped, the bed on the mezzanine level neatly made. Andy's crutches stood propped in a corner, but he was walking easily without them.

He stripped off the gloves and flicked on the kettle, and I leaned my hip against the kitchen counter, feeling like my legs might no longer be able to support me.

Andy dropped teabags into two mugs – rose and fennel flavour, I noticed; he was clearly keeping up the posh tea habit I'd got him started on – and then turned to me, counting on his fingers with exaggerated concentration.

'One, two... Yes, I make it three.'

'Three what?' I asked.

'Three unscheduled appearances from my friends since I moved here. One from you back in – what was it, 2018? One from our Daniel a couple of years later, and now this. I don't have much recollection of your last visit, if I'm honest. I'd been hitting the old marching powder hard, and I was a bit out of it.'

'You drank margaritas.'

'So I did! And very delicious they were too. But I'm guessing you're not here to sample the delights of the local hostelries this time.'

'I'm not,' I agreed. 'I wanted to talk to you about— Hold on. You say Daniel came and visited you here too?'

'He sure did. About a year or so after you came up. Only he didn't treat me to tasty salty cocktails.'

'No? That doesn't sound like him. What did he do?'

Andy poured boiling water over the teabags. 'He frog-marched me off to my first NA meeting.'

I felt my eyes widen in surprise. 'Seriously?'

'Seriously. He said enough was enough, and he wasn't going to stand around waiting for me to kill myself, and it was time to get a grip. And a grip's exactly what he got – on my right elbow, if I remember correctly. He took me down to the local community centre where the meeting was happening – he'd researched it all, the sneaky bugger – and left me there. And the rest, as they say, is—'

'But is it? Is it really? I mean, when you were in London, you were...'

'A blip.' He stirred the tea and fished the teabags out with a teaspoon, then turned to face me. 'Seriously, Kate. I'm not going to lie – I can't promise that I'll be clean forever. But I'm clean now, and that's the best I can do. I've finished the good drugs they gave me in Turkey – I'm on plain old ibuprofen now, so I don't have that excuse any longer. So I'm just doing my best.'

'One day at a time?'

'That's the badger. Now, come and sit down and tell me what the hell you're doing here.'

I followed him through to the living room, my mind whirring. It had been Daniel who'd spurred Andy into attending Narcotics Anonymous, which had led to his longest sober and drug-free spell ever? Daniel? I'd had no idea – I'd assumed it had been some kind of epiphany Andy himself had that had led him there. But it had been Daniel, whose attitude towards Andy's drug use I'd always assumed to be entirely laissez-faire.

I'd been wrong. It was yet another thing to add to the growing list of Shit Kate Was Wrong About.

'It was Daniel I came to talk to you about, actually,' I said.

'I figured. Come on then, share it with the group.'

'I... Andy, do you think he hates me?'

Andy guffawed – a proper belly laugh that was so unlike his normal laughter I suspected it wasn't entirely sincere. 'He doesn't hate you. Quite the opposite, in fact.'

'Really? What makes you think that?'

'I don't think. I know.'

'Have you spoken to him?'

'Not recently, no. Not about you, anyway. He's been ringing up and checking up on me every day, like a proper mother hen.

But your name hasn't come up. It's rather pointedly *not* come up.'

'Then why...?'

'Katie babe, I'd like to invite you to join me on a journey back in time, to the distant days of – oh, when was it? Ten years ago? Twelve? After my sojourn in that ghastly rehab place where the dining room smelled of cabbage all the time and the only thing to do when they weren't raking over your relationship with your mother in therapy sessions was stand outside in the rain and smoke and smoke until your fingers turned sepia.'

'It wasn't that bad, was it?'

'It was diabolical. It did the job though, I'll say that for it.'

'Until it didn't,' I reminded him.

'Until it didn't. But that's precisely the point I wanted to draw your attention to. Remember, after you so kindly packed me off there like you were sending a load of old clothes to the Cancer Research shop—'

'I did not!'

'That's how it felt at the time. Anyway, when they eventually let me out, you, me and our Daniel were quite the threesome. Remember?'

I nodded.

'And...' Andy took a long, audible breath. I sensed that he was about to drop the glibness and be honest, the way he sometimes did. 'And the two of you – I could tell. You were getting on. You were *vibing*.'

'I guess we were, a bit. But only because we were hanging out with you.'

'You poor little innocent flower. You couldn't even see it yourself. Well, I could. And let me tell you, I didn't like it one bit.'

'But nothing would've ever—'

'It would. It one hundred per cent would. I could see it coming a mile away. And even if I hadn't, Daniel told me.'

I felt my heart give a little lurch of excitement and colour spring into my cheeks. 'He did?'

'Yep. That night when you were off on your Friday-night-out-with-work shenanigans.'

'So why—'

'Why didn't he tell you himself? Because I took evasive action, obviously.'

My heart stopped skipping like a lamb in springtime and plummeted, like a cake sinking when you open the oven door too early.

Before I could say anything, Andy went on, 'I mean, don't get me wrong. I was an addict, Kate. I'm still an addict. Any excuse would do. But I knew that if I did what I did that night, all hell would break loose. There'd be no more cosy trips out to the opera for us. The Scrabble board would be seen no more. I'd have you to myself again.'

'But I could have chucked you out. I could have blamed you, not him.'

I should have done, I realised.

'That was a gamble I had to take,' Andy said. 'But I backed the right horse. And even if I hadn't, at least I'd have got my hands on that bloody lovely nose candy.'

'Andy.' I looked at his familiar, wryly smiling face and it was like looking at a stranger. 'My God. I can't believe you did that.'

'Addicts do some wild shit. And hey – it worked. Didn't it?'

'Until it didn't,' I said again. 'Until we were in Alsaya, and it was just the same between us.'

'Oh, Kate. I've fucked your life up good and proper, haven't I?'

I felt a brief surge of pure, white-hot anger. *Yes, you have, Andy*. And then I realised that wasn't true. There was only one person who'd let this happen, and that person was me. I could have laid down boundaries with Andy way earlier. I could have realised the consequences his addiction and our relationship would have on me, and I hadn't. Or if I had, I'd been wilfully blind to it. I'd let my love for him – a love which, I realised now, had changed over the years into something entirely different – sweep away every shred of judgement I ought to have had.

'Nah,' I said. 'I reckon that's on me. I should probably be getting home.'

'So you should,' Andy said with a grin. 'If you get a hustle on, you'll make the five thirty-seven and be back in London by half eight. You could be throwing yourself into our Daniel's arms before yonder sun has set.'

THIRTY-SEVEN

I didn't do as Andy had suggested and race straight to Daniel's. I had a long train journey to spend alone with my thoughts, and I wanted to make sure I had things straight in my head.

Of course, my mind turned, with the inevitability of a plant leaning towards the sun, to Daniel. I remembered Abbie telling me he'd always had my back and realised it was true – that the anger and resentment I'd allowed myself to build up over the years towards him had been horribly misdirected.

I'd been angry with him, when I should have been angry with Andy.

Not that it was entirely Andy's fault. He'd been – and still essentially was – in the grip of a sickness that was bigger than him, stronger than his friends, more powerful than his desire to do the right thing or our urge to protect him. I hadn't been able to see that, but Daniel had. He'd seen how I was allowing myself to be sucked in, taken advantage of, used by Andy for sex and comfort and a place to stay.

I hadn't said any of that to Andy – not today and not last week, when he'd flung himself into my arms begging me to love him. I'd disentangled myself gently, told him that the decision

I'd made before had been the right decision and I'd always be his friend, but I couldn't allow myself to get drawn back into a cycle of chaos and lies and mistrust. I told him, with all the kindness I could muster, that he would have to leave – that he would have to turn to the support he got from the programme and his sponsor and his own desire to stay clean, because I couldn't play that role in his life any more.

I was done putting him first – I had to put myself first.

He wasn't on his own and he never would be – I, Daniel, all his other family and friends would always be there for him, picking up the pieces when they needed picking up. But I no longer believed that by giving and giving until I had nothing left to give, I could somehow save him from himself.

The realisation left me full of relief, but also strangely empty. As empty as I knew my flat would feel when I arrived home – silence filling the space where Andy's and my voices had been, where the recording of Daniel and me pretending to have sex had been, where next-door's music had been.

And my heart felt silent too, empty and still.

I remembered going to see Mona the previous morning, after a sleepless night which I'd spent baking cherry cake and gingerbread and flapjacks, standing on my balcony and looking out at the dark, slow-moving river while I waited for them to cook and then to cool. She'd tutted consolingly when she saw me and said, 'When our guests complain about the jammy dodgers, I tell them that at least it means Kate's getting a decent night's rest.'

'And when I can't sleep, at least it means I get to bake for them,' I said. 'Swings and roundabouts, right? And there's something about baking – it always makes me feel a bit more cheerful.'

'Of course it does.' She nodded sagely. 'Cake makes everything better. Thank you, Kate, and have a good day.'

Cake makes everything better.

It didn't, of course. It was just flour and eggs and butter and sugar. But it was also time, expertise and love. It was a way of saying thank you to Mona for the work she did, providing a sanctuary for lonely people. It was a way of bonding with my friends. A way of soothing my own soul in the small hours of the morning.

It could even be an offering of peace, I thought.

So when the train inched into the station at last, I didn't go to see Daniel. I didn't go straight home either. I went to the supermarket and stocked up on ingredients. I dug out the heart-shaped tins I'd bought to make a cake for Abbie and Matt's ten-year anniversary. From memory, using the recipe my mum always made when I was little, I baked a chocolate cake. Not just any chocolate cake – the ultimate, perfect one, sinfully rich and feather-light, sprinkled with brandy, sandwiched with raspberry cream and topped with glossy ganache.

And the next morning, I placed it carefully in my nicest tin and got on the bus that led to Daniel's home.

But once I was seated on the top deck, my cake cradled carefully in my lap, doubts assailed me. What a bloody stupid thing to do. What the hell would he make of a woman he couldn't stand rocking up to see him on a Sunday morning bringing – of all things – a cake, like he was my ageing aunt or something? What if he had someone there with him – one of those women who stayed overnight before availing themselves of his extensive collection of spare toothbrushes? What if he told me to fuck off?

What if he laughed at me?

At least you'll have tried, I told myself firmly. *As risks go, baking a cake and getting a bus isn't exactly up there with sinking your savings into bitcoin or abseiling off a cliff.*

Still, despite my internal pep talk, I had to fight the urge at every stop to get off, go back home again and stuff several slices of the cake into my gob, washed down with gin, before having a good old cry and seeing if there was anyone on Tinder who looked nice.

But I didn't get off. I stayed put, my stomach churning with nerves and my heart beating harder with every stop.

At last, the bus began to inch along Daniel's local high street, the smells of the greengrocers, butchers and fishmongers lining it wafting in through the open window. There was the shopping arcade where we'd met for coffee what felt like a year ago, although it was actually only a few weeks. There was the dodgy pub and the less dodgy one.

And here was the familiar stop at the end of Daniel's road.

Clutching my cake tin as protectively as a new mother with her baby in a sling, I alighted and walked slowly down the tree-lined street. The leaves of the chestnut trees were fully out now, creating a canopy of green over my head and rustling in the gentle breeze. I could hear music coming from an open window. A black-and-white cat lay on a wall, sunning itself, and I wondered if Daniel stopped to fuss it when he walked past.

Lucky cat, I thought, then smiled at my own silliness. If my plan paid off, within just a few minutes I might be submitting to his caresses myself. But I wasn't going to get ahead of myself.

I stopped in front of his door, noticing for the first time how different it was from his neighbours' – a smooth slab of hardwood, varnished but unpainted, the grain of the wood as bright in the sunshine as the lighter streaks in Daniel's hair. The knocker looked like it was made of pewter, a glossy deep silvery-grey.

I reached out my hand, raised it and let it fall. Then I waited.

And waited.

There was no answer – he must be out.

The fact that I felt crushing disappointment rather than relief told me all I needed to know.

You can try again tomorrow, I told myself. *The cake will keep. You can text him, like a normal person, instead of turning up on his doorstep like a nutter.*

And then I thought, *Or you could try round the back. If he's in his workshop, maybe he didn't hear the knock?*

So, fresh hope and nerves jangling inside me, I walked down the narrow alleyway that led to the back of the building. I'd never been there before – I only knew from seeing the metal roll-up door at the back of Daniel's workshop that there must be some kind of yard out there, presumably where he loaded pieces of furniture into his van. Clearly in my mind, I could picture the muscles moving in his arms as he carefully lifted a heavy item, his brow furrowed in focus, his strong back braced to take the weight.

I turned the corner at the end of the alleyway and froze – because there in front of me was Daniel, doing exactly what I'd imagined him doing. The rear doors of his van were open, backed close up to the open shutter leading to the workshop. He was carefully manoeuvring a heavy object wrapped in sacking up into the vehicle, his arms below the sleeves of his faded black T-shirt moving just as I'd imagined, his hair falling over his eyes, his jawline taut with concentration. I could hear the scrape of his work boots on the concrete and smell sawdust and turpentine.

He placed the package in the van and stepped back, wiping his palms on his jeans. Then he turned and saw me.

'Hello,' I said faintly, stepping towards him, clutching my cake, sweat springing out on my palms and my breath coming fast, as if I'd been running rather than sitting on a bus.

'Kate. This is a surprise.'

'Yes. It was meant to be.'

'Actually' – his face broke into a guarded smile – 'I was just on my way to see you.'

'To see me? Why?'

'To bring you something.' He gestured to the back of the van.

'Oh. Wow. That's random, because I brought you something, too.'

'Right.' He was smiling properly now, almost laughing at the absurdity of it. 'What is it?'

'I'll show you mine if you show me yours,' I countered.

'Ladies first.'

'I'm no lady, Daniel. You ought to know that by now.'

'But a gentleman never tells,' he argued.

'And you're no gentleman.'

'You've got me bang to rights.' Grinning, he closed the van doors. 'Anyway, it's a peace offering.'

'Funny, that. Mine is too,' I said, adding humbly, 'It's a cake. I made it for you.'

'A cake?'

'Yes. It's like, you cream butter and sugar together, add cocoa powder, flour and eggs, a teaspoonful of vanilla extract, stick it in the—'

'I know what a cake is, you crazy woman.'

'I thought you might, if I jogged your memory. So I brought you one. Here.'

He took the tin from my outstretched arms. 'Thank you, Kate.'

'Don't mention it. Can I ask – were you on your way to bring me your' – I gestured to the van – 'thing? What is it?'

'It's a stepladder,' he muttered.

'A stepladder?' I parroted.

'You know, they're pieces of furniture you need to use when you want to reach high things.'

I burst out laughing. 'I know what a stepladder is, you crazy man.'

'It's antique Italian walnut,' he said. 'And library steps, strictly speaking. So wider than normal, and the treads have got leather on them so they're not slippy. It folds up so you can put stuff on it when you're not using it.'

'It sounds like the kind of stepladder I'd want, if I wanted a stepladder.'

'I think you'll find you do. Tell me about the cake.'

'It's chocolate with raspberry filling. It's in the shape of a' – I felt myself blushing – 'a heart.'

'That sounds like the kind of cake I'd want, if I wanted a cake.'

'Come on, Daniel. Everyone always wants cake.'

'This is true. But there's something else I want more. Come inside for a second.'

I followed him into the spacious, echoey workshop. The familiar beams of dust-filled light slanted from the windows, spilling in their regular squares on the floor. The air was cool and still. I could see the back of Daniel's T-shirt darkened with sweat from his work and smell the clean fragrance of his hair.

He put the cake tin down on the workbench and turned to me, his arms outstretched. 'Come here.'

Easily, as naturally as if I was coming home, I stepped into his arms. He pulled me close, so I could feel the whole, hard length of his body against mine, his back moving beneath my hands as he breathed.

'I'm sorry,' I said. 'I misjudged you. I never knew it was you who got Andy to go to NA. I thought I was the only one doing right by him, when actually you were, too. And I didn't realise...'

'Didn't realise what?'

I lowered my eyes, feeling my face flame. 'I didn't realise, back in the day, that you... Well, that you kind of liked me.'

'Probably wouldn't have been any use if you had,' he said. 'Given you were kind of otherwise occupied.'

'Yeah. I was. I thought I was in love with Andy. I guess I was in love, but in a totally screwed-up way.'

'Quite the Messiah complex you had going on, back in the day.'

'I just thought I could make him better. I thought if I loved him enough, everything would be all right.'

'Kate,' he said gently, 'we both love him. And hopefully everything will be all right. But if it's not, it's not down to us to fix him.'

'I know. I realise that now. Actually, I realised it a few years back, thanks to you. But I could never actually say thanks, because I was too busy hating you. And I'm sorry about that, too.'

'I'm sorry, too. When I realised what had been going on between you and Andy, it all kind of made sense. And I'm not going to lie, I was jealous. I thought if you still felt that way about him, there still wasn't any hope for me. I behaved like a total plonker.'

Any hope for me? Excitement rose inside me, like the flame that had lifted me and Claude into the sky in that hot-air balloon, back in the spring.

But I hid my elation with sarcasm. 'Yeah, you did, actually. You always were a bit of a plonker.'

I felt his ribs move as he chuckled. 'If you're being shitty to me again, I take it we're friends?'

I pressed my face against his chest, breathing in the warmth and strength of him. We could be friends again now. We could put everything behind us and move forward, closer and happier. But it wouldn't be enough.

'Daniel,' I said, 'I don't want to be your friend.'

'No?' He moved away and looked down at me, his grey eyes serious.

'No. I want to kiss you and rip all your clothes off.'

His eyes glittered. 'That sounds pretty amicable to me, if I'm honest.'

'So you'd be amenable to that?'

'I would. So long as we get to eat that cake afterwards.'

'And after that, do it all again?'

'Kate,' he said, 'we can do it as many times as you like. We've got all the time in the world.'

He took my hand, and we walked the length of the workshop, through one patch of light and then another, until we reached the door to his flat, and then we walked together to his bedroom. I didn't have to wonder what it would be like, because I already knew. I didn't have to worry about his feelings, because I knew they matched mine.

All we had to do was make up for lost time – and I was confident we'd be able to.

After all, as he'd said, we had all the time in the world.

A LETTER FROM SOPHIE

Dear reader,

I want to say a huge thank you for choosing to read *Not in a Million Years*. If you did enjoy it, and want to keep up to date with all my latest releases, just sign up at the following link. Your email address will never be shared and you can unsubscribe at any time.

www.bookouture.com/sophie-ranald

Shortly after I started writing *Not in a Million Years*, my sister Vicky embarked on an epic holiday to Europe from her home in New Zealand, planning to spend time in Italy and London with her two adult sons and their father. Because it had been four years since I last saw her, I was delighted at the prospect of spending time together and excitedly started making plans for long chats, cooking meals together, showing her my home and introducing her to our cats for the first time.

But it was not to be. On a walk in Perugia, my brother-in-law had a fall and fractured his hip, landing him in hospital, where he needed extensive surgery and a lengthy recovery time before he was fit to fly home. It was a random and unfortunate example of life imitating art – I'd already set out the plot of this novel, with Daniel and Kate flying to Andy's rescue and finding him in hospital with a strikingly similar injury, although not in Italy but in Turkey. Although I'm not a superstitious person, I couldn't help but feel that my novel had somehow tempted fate and caused the accident and its aftermath.

My brother-in-law is now recovering well and everyone is safely home; the book is finished and I've been able to set aside any niggling ideas that this was in any way My Fault. But *Not in a Million Years* will always be associated in my mind with that strange coincidence.

All that said, I really hope you've enjoyed reading this novel and reconnecting with Kate and her friends, who you may have met before in the pages of *PS I Hate You* and *Santa, Please Bring Me a Boyfriend*. Please do take a few moments to leave an online review, or get in touch on social media and let me know what you think.

With love from Sophie

facebook.com/SophieRanald

twitter.com/SophieRanald

instagram.com/sophieranald

ACKNOWLEDGEMENTS

If it takes a village to raise a child, it takes a crack team worthy of a Steven Soderbergh movie to produce a novel. I'm fortunate to work with an incredible group of people, all of whom contribute their talent, hard graft and unstinting support to my books and to me.

Huge thanks are due to the wonderful Alice Saunders of The Soho Agency, which has represented me since I wrote my first novel ten years ago. I'm so grateful for her wisdom, humour, kindness and encyclopaedic knowledge of the industry (not to mention her ability to pick the best lunch spots!).

Not in a Million Years is my tenth novel to be published by Bookouture, but my first to have been edited by the lovely Jess Whitlum-Cooper. Embarking on a relationship with a new editor could have been disruptive and daunting, but Jess is a joy to work with and has ensured that the publication process went seamlessly from start to finish – thank you!

Huge thanks also to the rest of the team at Bookouture: Noelle Holten, Kim Nash, Peta Nightingale, Mandy Kullar, Imogen Allport and Jess Readett, who work tirelessly behind the scenes on publicity, production and promotion; as well as my brilliant cover designer Lisa Horton, cracking copy-editor Rhian McKay and eagle-eyed proofreader Laura Kincaid.

And finally, to my wonderful friends, darling partner Hopi and precious cats – you're the best and I love you all.